NEWS FROM ABROAD

NEWS FROM ABROAD

DONALD R. SHANOR

COLUMBIA UNIVERSITY PRESS ■ NEW YORK

Columbia University Press

Publishers Since 1893

New York   Chichester, West Sussex

Library of Congress Cataloging-in-Publication Data

Shanor, Donald R.

p. cm.

Includes bibliographical references and index.

ISBN 0-231-12240-3 (cloth : alk. paper)

1. Foreign news — United States. I. Title

PN4888.F69S53 2003

070.4'332—dc21

2002041602

Columbia University Press books are printed on permanent
and durable acid-free paper.

Printed in the United States of America

c 10 9 8 7 6 5 4 3 2 1

For Constance, Elizabeth, Rebecca, and Zoë

CONTENTS

PREFACE

The American media are caught between profit and performance. Protected by the Constitution, anointed with the role of a Fourth Estate that monitors the other three branches of government, the nation's newspapers and broadcast outlets are also beholden to their shareholders and other owners in an era when 20 percent profits are considered only as a bar to be raised.

These dual duties were difficult enough to perform in the ordinary conditions of the nation's life. But since the terrorist attacks of September 11, 2001, and the mobilization of the nation to respond to them, the media have had to accept an additional burden.

It centers on news from abroad. Most of the media neglected the issues and affairs outside America's borders in the decade between the celebrations at the end of the cold war and the frightful beginning of the war on terror. Most made up for the neglect in the days and months that followed by abandoning some of their less pressing pursuits like Hollywood and courtroom dramas to deal with the ideas, causes, and tactics of the terror movements threatening the United States.

This book is about the media's response to the challenges of reporting on the United States and the world, both before and after the attacks on New York and Washington thrust journalists into the role of national informant, explainer, and consoler. It is also about the conflicts inherent in the media's other role as money earner.

With many thousands of centers of news, producing papers, magazines, radio, television, and Internet information, no single judgment can be applied to the media's performance before or after September 11. Many journalists and organizations have won praise and prizes; others have been criticized for their shortcomings. ABC, one of the leaders of American journalism, managed to take both positions on the issue of what kinds of programs the public would get to watch, expressing pride in its news division and then undermining it by trying to replace *Nightline*, its best program, in the hope of earning more money from comedy.

Financial considerations also have left most newspapers less able to serve their readers' needs of comprehensive coverage and analysis of the new situation in the world. Automation has saved newspapers as much as 25 percent of their salary costs, but in most cases, the money hasn't been spent on hiring extra editors or reporters or expanding the scope of coverage and inquiry. Instead, editorial staff has had to undertake production duties, leaving less time to work on stories, develop sources, and do the job of backgrounding and explaining.

Local television has done far less, although its profits, particularly in larger markets, are generally higher, with 50 percent returns not unusual. Most stations rely on the reduced staffs of the local newspapers to get leads for their coverage, and most ignore subjects of any complexity. Although a range of outside services are available, foreign news is a rarity. Many of the nation's radio stations are run virtually on automatic pilot, with little or no news of any kind to interrupt the flow of music and commercials.

Not everyone in the executive suites of the media groups agrees that profits should come before all else. The nation is fortunate that most of its leading newspapers have managed both financial and journalistic success. It's in the thousands of newsrooms in smaller cities, whether local radio and television or hometown newspaper, that cost cutting over the years has limited broader coverage of public affairs news, including foreign news.

Three powerful forces—technology, immigration, and globalization—are beginning to make their presence felt in the media world, complicating the issue of whether quality or earnings should prevail. In only a decade, the World Wide Web has become the main source of information for millions of Americans, particularly younger people and particularly about international affairs. The surge of Latino and Asian immigration is changing the focus of many media toward more coverage of the regions from which the new Americans come. Global businesses putting down roots across America, along with the arrival of immigrant doctors, refugees, scholars, and manual workers, has made news from abroad local news in Houston; Miami; Anniston, Alabama; and many other cities.

A fourth force, more powerful than the others, is the people who provide the news. All these efforts to serve the public better—and to continue earning money—are based on the ideas, innovation, and energy of individuals—from the executive producers and editors who put together the hourly patterns of the world's news, to the correspondents who supply their ingredients, to the managers who figure out how to pay the bills.

ACKNOWLEDGMENTS

In addition to the many working journalists in newsrooms across the nation and abroad who chose not to have their comments, critical and uncritical, attached to their names, I'm grateful to the following people and institutions for their help with the book. None can be held responsible for its imperfections, content, or findings, which remain solely my responsibility. They are Elie Abel, Jonnet Abeles, Jim and Carlotta Anderson, Maribel Bahia, Al and Phyllis Balk, Kate and Jerry Baum, Frances Chastain, Charles and Sarah East, Bill Eaton, Susan Eaton, Lisa Eckelbecker, Osborne Elliott, Jan Ellis, Milt Freudenheim, Marshall Ganz, Norman and Barbara Gelb, Robert Greenberger, James Halbe, Stephen Hess, James Hoge, Ben and Sarah Hyatt, Tara Joseph, Katy Katama, Joan Komner, Robert and Christine Korengold, Alice and Bill Marsh, James McCartney, Robert and Muriel McCord, Phyllis Meras, Robert Merry, Charles and Laurana Mitchelmore, Joan Mowrer, Dagmar Mussey, David Newsom, Charles Novitz, Ralph and Jan Otwell, Sy Pearlman, Deborah Potter, S. C. Quiddick, Larry Radway, Ethel Leith Ross, Steve Ross, John Schidlovsky, and Xu Chengshi. The support of the Cabot Foundation and the U.S. Institute of Peace helped in the initial research for the book; Columbia University's Graduate School of Journalism and School of International and Public Affairs provided resources and advice. The libraries at Columbia University, Brown University; and Edgartown, Oak Bluffs, and Vineyard Haven, Massachusetts, as well as the Library of Congress and the Boston Public Library, were valuable sources of research materials. Thanks also are due to these institutions: the American Press Institute, the American Society of Newspaper Editors, the Associated Press Managing Editors, the Freedom Forum, the International Center for Journalists, the Medill School of Journalism of Northwestern University, Motel 6, The Nieman Foundation, the Pew

Foundation, the Poynter Institute, the Project for Excellence in Journalism, the Radio and Television News Directors Foundation, the Shelter-Kit of Tilton, N.H. Special thanks go to W. Phillips Davison, Frederick T. C. Yu, and Wallace Irwin, my coauthors and editor for the first News from Abroad, published in 1980 by the Foreign Policy Association. Extra special thanks go to my wife, Constance C. Shanor, for her support, ideas, criticism, and editing.

PART I

DOES FOREIGN NEWS MATTER?

CBS basically no longer has bureaus overseas. —*A CBS News executive*

The notion that Americans don't care about foreign news is a canard that's put out by the accountants. —*Tom Bettag, executive producer of ABC's Nightline*

1

INTRODUCTION: THE TEST OF WAR

The attacks on the World Trade Center and the Pentagon thrust Americans into the middle of the vicious conflicts of nationalist, religious, and ethnic extremists that had always been fought in other parts of the world.

The terrorists were able to succeed mainly because the United States had neglected its intelligence gathering and airport security. But it was also left unprotected by the failure of its networks and most of its newspapers to provide the regular news and analysis of trends abroad that might have been able to provide a warning of the level of hatred against it, the resources available to channel that hatred into acts of destruction, and the number of martyrs willing to sacrifice their lives to carry them out.

It took two wars at the turn of the twenty-first century to call Americans' attention to the dangers of ignoring the rest of the world in their daily concerns and to the shortcomings of most of their media in covering international events. The first lesson, in 1999, was Kosovo, but it made little impact. The second was the attacks on the World Trade Center and the Pentagon and the Afghan war that followed. Their impact is yet to be fully measured, but there were discouraging signs only a few months after the attacks that international news was again being seen by managers as an expensive luxury. ABC's attempt to replace *Nightline*, a program noted for its thoughtful international coverage, with the comedian David Letterman was the clearest expression of corporate priorities that put profits before public service.

September 2001 was a time when both the strengths and weaknesses of the American media were quickly displayed on television and computer screens, radios, the front pages of newspapers, and the covers of newsmagazines. It was also a time of concern about some of the fundamental tenets of journalism:

access to information versus censorship and aiding the enemy versus informing the public.

The three venerable network anchors showed their professionalism and earned their multimillion-dollar salaries in marathon performances that played to the largest audiences since the dramatic events of the cold war. More than a hundred newspapers sent out extra editions on the streets, and hundreds more moved streams of electronic bulletins on their Web sites. But all media, old and new, were hampered by the lack of reporting from their own foreign bureaus to provide some of the missing pieces of the attacks: a crime with only victims and little information about the perpetrators.

Only 12 of the 120 newspaper front pages chosen for the Poynter Institute's best-selling book on coverage of the attack carried stories on who might have staged the attacks. Of these, only two, the *Boston Globe* and *Christian Science Monitor*, filed the story from abroad, drawing on their experienced correspondents from the region, the *Globe's* Charles Sennott and the *Monitor's* Scott Peterson. Most of the rest used an Associated Press Washington story based on U.S. government sources.

Within minutes of the attack, the Cable News Network's long-standing and costly commitment to international news proved its worth. The men and women it had deployed around the world began to file the reaction, background, and context of the story, drawing on its technological head starts like videophones and the journalistic advantages of knowing officials and sources on all sides of the conflict. With veteran reporters like Nic Robertson and Christine Amanpour serving as in-the-field anchors, CNN gave its viewers the closest possible experience of being there. It was hard to imagine that only a few weeks before the attack, the cable network's new management had announced plans to replace some of its international coverage with more profitable entertainment news. At least for a period, seriousness won unprecedented ratings for CNN, with 3.3 million viewers—ten times its normal audience—over a twenty-four-hour time period for the week that included September 11.

Despite CNN's performance, most Americans reacted to the tragedy by seeking out the familiar. On the night of the attack, eighty million viewers—four times the usual audience—turned to the three main networks for news. The anchors were on from that morning until late evening—Peter Jennings alone logged nineteen hours, and in the next four days, ABC News broadcast for ninety-one hours, the longest continuous report in its history.

The wire services were in action minutes after the first plane hit in New York. The Associated Press and Reuters began moving a string of short bulletins, mobilizing newsrooms across the nation. New York's *Daily News* more than doubled its 700,000 circulation in the days after the attack, which it covered with more than a hundred reporters and thirty-four photographers. The *New York Times* sold as many copies—more than 1.2 million—across the country as it did in the city. The *Wall Street Journal*, so close to the attacks that its office had to be evacuated, managed to publish all but a few thousand copies of its normal 1.8 million national circulation, using an emergency newsroom in a New Jersey production plant and its printing sites across the country.

Twenty-eight of the thirty-two papers in the Knight Ridder chain, which had been heavily criticized for cutting costs at the expense of adequately reporting national and foreign news, put out extra editions after the attacks. Knight Ridder sent eleven correspondents to the Afghanistan region and formed a reporting team in Washington of sixty journalists from its newspapers and its bureau there.

The news of the attacks and the U.S. and world response pushed out all other prime-time broadcasting on the commercial networks for the next several days. Public broadcasting's *NewsHour* and *Washington Week in Review* were on for four hours the first evening and replaced other scheduled programs for the next several days. Bill Moyers returned to the air in a series called *America Responds*. PBS's modest ratings numbers rose by 23 percent, from 1.1 before the crisis to 1.4. *Frontline*, a PBS documentary series, pulled a two-year-old investigation of Osama bin Laden from the shelves, brought it up to date, and had it on the air in two days.

National Public Radio began twenty-four-hour coverage minutes after the first attack on the Trade Center, with news, discussions, and complete audio of news conferences. Most listeners praised its coverage, but some complained that the network was being "too objective" when it broadcast perspectives from the Arab world that were critical of the United States. Unlike the commercial networks, NPR was as strong abroad as it was at home, able to broadcast immediately from the Middle East, Europe, and the borders of Afghanistan at a time when listeners were eager for reaction and explanation. In the days that followed, it shifted a number of correspondents to add depth to its original foreign lineup. Foreign editor Loren Jenkins had thirteen reporters in the area of Afghanistan and the Middle East at the height of the crisis, many of them in the thick of the fighting. Correspondent Ivan Watson went into Kabul with the victorious Northern Alliance troops, reporting the joyous welcome they received from the people of the capital but also the troops' atrocities committed on Taliban soldiers as they fought their way to the city.

Radio coverage was dominated by NPR, the radio networks of CNN and the Associated Press, and the few remaining all-news stations still maintained in big cities. Public Radio International's *The World* stayed on the air for six hours instead of its usual one, bringing in reports from its own correspondents and the worldwide British Broadcasting Corporation network. NPR's Web site, which usually gets 70,000 visitors a day, got 400,000 on September 11.

All-news radio outlets like WCBS and KCBS in New York and Los Angeles were hampered by their lack of a foreign infrastructure. In the decade before the attacks, the corps of radio correspondents abroad had been cut, as it had for the television networks. But all-news radio did far better than the vast majority of stations. Most stations of the giant radio conglomerates, Infinity and Clear Channel, had all but eliminated news from their formats. Their millions of listeners in small cities and towns had to turn elsewhere for not only the international aspects of the attack but also the local reaction.

Web sites were the victims of overload and infrastructure damage at the World Trade Center, and their main service to users, once they were up and running with stripped-down services, was simply as another way to receive what the newspapers, wire services, and broadcasters were reporting. But many more people found the Internet valuable as a quick source of information. After those first dramatic days of overload, usage was up 15 percent.

Newspapers that had been printing little about the nation and world suddenly found a need for explanation and background, and they rushed to sign contracts with supplemental services they had long ignored. Knight Ridder reported a 30 percent increase in Web site purchases and added sixteen college newspapers to its campus news service. The Los Angeles Times–Washington Post news service picked up at least fifteen new clients, and Scripps-Howard and the *Christian Science Monitor* also added a number of new outlets.

From the start, however, there were doubts that such an interest in foreign news could be sustained. "When the war ends, will the budgeteers of the newsroom meet their new obligations and provide the resources to cover an increasingly complex world?" former CBS correspondent Marvin Kalb asked in an op-ed article. "Unfortunately, all the evidence suggests that most networks and newspapers will return to the good old days of Monica, Diana and O.J."[1]

But Chris Peck, former editor of the *Spokane Spokesman Review* and president of the Associated Press Managing Editors (APME), promised at the APME convention shortly after the attacks that it would indeed be different in the future. "Just one month ago we understood in an instant the fundamental role that newspapers play in the modern world," he said. "We must remember in thirty days and in six months from now that news is far more than Chandra Levy and Britney Spears. It is up to us to make the connection between world events and our communities."[2]

Much ground had been lost in the previous decade. Despite a vague awareness in the United States that ethnic conflicts were at danger levels around the world, when powerful economic ties across borders meant that jobs in the

American Midwest depended on events in the Arab Middle East, and when the United States had emerged from the cold war as the uncontested leader of the free world, the American public was being less well served than it had been for decades earlier by its newspaper and broadcast reporting from abroad.

Across the country, the good local newspapers that once devoted 10 percent of their columns to international news were providing about 2 percent. The evening news programs of the television networks had reduced their international coverage from 40 percent to as low as 8 percent, and similar reductions had taken place in the newsmagazines. The solution to shrinking TV network audiences had been to make news more entertaining or simply to replace it with entertainment. The newspapers became accomplices to this trend. Although few daily newspapers in the United States have foreign editors, many have television and entertainment reviewers.

The United States had about 350 newspaper and broadcast correspondents working abroad, fewer than a third of the number of correspondents that foreign nations send to cover the United States. Only the *New York Times* and CNN had journalists in Afghanistan at the time of the attacks. Within hours, the networks, wire services, major newspapers, and the magazines rushed teams to the Pakistani border to try to recover.

But no one could recover, in days or weeks, the loss of the worldwide listening and observation posts that once had been maintained by the American media on every continent but since had been dismantled to save them money. These bureaus, staffed mostly by local journalists and specialists, were as important for informing the people of the United States as was its government's network of embassies, consulates, and Central Intelligence Agency stations. Not only were they as important, but in many cases in the past, they also were far more effective, as the contrast between the on-the-ground reporting and the official claims of victories showed in the Vietnam War. At their best, these bureaus combined the efforts of the local staff and resident American correspondents familiar with the region. But they could also be pressed into service to supply the background and current information that a visiting correspondent needed to cover a story on short notice.

The remaining bureaus had been crippled by the many dismissals. The cost was immediately apparent, as a telephone conversation from the Middle East with a veteran American network producer revealed a few days after the outbreak of the Afghan war. "They cut some of our best crews," he complained, including a "fabulous cameraman and people I'd worked with for ten years who knew what they were doing" in covering crises from the Middle East to Yugoslavia. Now, he said, "there are no grown-ups" in the network's main European bureau, no one with the contacts to plan international coverage or the experience to grapple with the logistics, government restrictions, and languages needed to carry it out successfully.[3]

Most of the television networks' overseas bureaus—and those of many of the newspapers and newsmagazines—had been simply shut down. ABC, which advertises itself as America's leading source of news, slashed its foreign bureaus from seventeen to six in cost cutting that began in the 1980s. CBS's overseas presence was reduced to four bureaus, and NBC's, to five. Two of ABC's casualties, Damascus and Frankfurt, had served the network well as observation posts for terrorist movements.

Although the Big Four newspapers providing comprehensive coverage of foreign affairs—the *New York Times, Washington Post, Los Angeles Times,*and *Wall Street Journal*—maintained their standing during this fallow period, many others with good reputations but smaller budgets did not. Detroit's two papers once competed for readers by stressing their foreign reporting. Now one, the *News*, has all but abandoned the field to the *Free Press*. Chicago's *Tribune* and *Daily News* and Dallas's *Morning News* and *Times-Herald* had the same kind of competition until the stronger papers, the *Tribune* and *Morning News*, forced the weaker ones out of business.

No one is able to say that if the old corps of correspondents and the original number of bureaus had been in the field in the months before the terrorist attack, warnings of what was being planned would have been sounded. Certainly the terrorists' preparation eluded far larger and technologically better equipped intelligence operations in the United States and many other countries. What can be safely said, however, is that the chances of digging out such information would have been far better had there been long-established newspaper and television news bureaus in the region, with correspondents able to piece together elements of the terrorist puzzle over time.

But even if a warning had been beyond the reach of the best of the bureaus abroad, there were many functions that a solid corps of foreign correspondents could have performed for the American public. The first would have been to make Americans aware of the danger after the attacks on the USS *Cole* and the U.S. embassies in Tanzania and Kenya through a thorough exploration of terror groups' identities, ideologies, and capabilities. Just as important would have been the kind of depth reporting showing that the poverty, hopelessness, and misrule of such a large part of the world spawn and encourage such desperate acts.

Only two television programs, CBS's 60 *Minutes*, and PBS's *Frontline*, produced such reports in the crucial period between the 1998 attacks on the American embassies in Africa and those on the World Trade Center and the Pentagon. The only newspaper to offer a major investigative piece on the embassy bombings and the security failings they demonstrated was the *New York Times*.

Would more such coverage have deterred the attackers? Not at all. Might it have called attention to the need for better airport security and led to the thwarting of the terrorists before they could strike? No one will ever know, but the many past cases of the press's successfully prodding government on safety, the environment, and civil rights point to the likelihood that it would have.

As with Kosovo two years earlier, the war was magnificently and courageously covered after the shooting began. But both conflicts showed the costs of the apathy during the long periods building up to the final crises, when more attention could and should have been paid to the many hostile forces and factors that ended up with American air and ground forces engaged in battle.

The end of the cold war and the diminution of the direct threat from Russia are the reasons most often given for this media neglect of foreign news. Others argue that a more prosperous America has a natural wish for more distraction from the world's problems: entertainment, not information, and if information at all, then the entertaining kind.

Even before September 11, voices were also being heard in the journalism profession, the public, and the international community that post–cold war explanations were poor excuses for saving money on the expensive business of international coverage. Russian threat or not, prosperity or not, it was argued, it is now more important than ever that the public be kept informed of the world outside the United States. At the same time, demographic and technological changes were beginning to influence the state of international coverage. Unprecedented increases in immigration in the 1990s expanded the audiences for news from the homelands of these readers, listeners, and viewers. The surge in Internet usage created an entire new branch of the information industry as well as providing millions of additional readers for traditional media using the Net.

Criticism and ideas for better coverage have proliferated since September 11. According to a study by the Project for Excellence in Journalism, a Washington think tank, before the attacks, the three evening news broadcasts carried "more than a third lifestyle, celebrity and crime." On the morning shows, celebrity and lifestyle stories made up more than 75 percent of the news. Although September 11 brought a complete change in emphasis, with eight in ten evening news stories devoted to national or international affairs, the study's authors suggested that whether the change would last depended on how much the mood of the country had also changed.[4]

In coverage from abroad, only the *New York Times* and a few other organizations were in a position to begin filing stories from the scene of the new war that America found itself fighting. When the planes struck, the *Times* had Barry Bearak in Afghanistan for the Taliban trial of American missionaries and John F. Burns, a Pulitzer Prize winner and an expert on the region, in Pakistan.

Bearak's war reporting also won a Pulitzer, with another *Times* reporter in Afghanistan, Dexter Filkins, a finalist. CNN had thirty reporters and support workers in Afghanistan at the time of the attack and, for some time, provided the only television reporting from inside the country.

The other networks were far less well prepared. CBS had eight correspondents stationed abroad, three of them in London, and ABC and NBC were similarly thinly staffed. To cut costs, they used contractors for many of the basic functions of translating, video editing, and finding locals to help with interviews and security. But such ad hoc arrangements are woefully inadequate compared with those of a fully staffed bureau able to keep close track of political currents and sometimes to anticipate the big story rather than merely rushing in to cover it or to voice-over someone else's footage of it.

As Americans turned to their familiar network news programs to learn about the terrible events and why and how they had happened, the network anchors were hindered by an acute shortage of reliable coverage from overseas. When they were able to scrape up news from abroad at all, it was frequently a patchwork of local footage narrated from studios far from the scene.

Not all the criticism came after the fact. Months and years before the events of September 11 in my interviews for this book, many in the news business were warning of the effects of neglecting serious coverage of international issues.

"CBS basically no longer has bureaus overseas," an executive of the network told me. Its London bureau processes news gathered by other organizations, most of them European, and has it read by an American who is usually hundreds of miles from the scene of the event. A former CBS producer with long experience abroad agreed. "We react to coverage by others; we don't originate it," he said.[5]

Tom Bettag, executive producer of ABC's *Nightline*, stated half a year before the Trade Center attack that "the notion that Americans don't care about foreign news is a canard that's put out by the accountants" to justify corporations' cost cutting for news gathering abroad.[6]

As the attacks showed, small and distant conflicts can lead to bigger and closer ones. Remote wars can spawn human disasters like famine and massacres. Young American men and women in uniform can be quickly and dangerously involved in either kind of crisis, and either kind can suddenly create a need for American aid or relief. A reliable network of journalists might be able to deliver the early warnings that could head off these disasters.

A nation whose prosperity is based on a global economy needs constant information about the prospects of threats to that economy. Cultural isolation from the trends of European, Asian, and African art, literature, and music is not as dangerous as political or economic ignorance, but it comes at some eventual cost to the American public.

Not enough of the nation's editors, producers, and managers listened to these arguments before the terrible day of tragedy at the World Trade Center and Pentagon. Soon afterward, however, old attitudes began to change, mostly the result of the September attacks, although not entirely. For years, polls of newspaper and broadcast audiences have contradicted media management claims that no one wants to see, hear, or read foreign news. Six in ten newspaper readers are "highly interested" in international news, according to research by the Knight Ridder newspaper chain. A poll conducted for the Radio-Television News Directors Foundation (RTNDF) found that 88 percent of Americans were interested in having their local TV news cover more events from around the world. A Freedom Forum poll determined that 55 percent of Americans were concerned that "there is too little coverage of international news" in their media. All these opinions were recorded before September 11.[7]

Foreign coverage waned despite a surge in technological progress that now makes it possible to have instant-action pictures, reportage, and commentary from almost anywhere in the world. But this same technology has hugely broadened the media field, and both newspapers and the traditional networks are worried about losing audiences to cable and the growing Internet. The response of the networks and many newspapers has been two-faceted: to cut costs and lighten up. Each facet has been detrimental, if not disastrous, to their coverage of foreign news.

One after another, continent by continent, the networks closed their bureaus, until they now have no permanent network offices in Latin America or Africa and only a handful in Europe and Asia. The networks cover the world with seven or eight correspondents apiece, fewer than a quarter of those the *New York Times* has sent abroad and a small fraction of the Associated Press's foreign staff. Network executives argue that the many millions of dollars saved from news budgets keep the still-expensive evening news programs afloat, and they further justify the closings abroad by saying they can fly in correspondents and crews on short notice to cover the really important stories. But small stories play as important a role in the public's understanding of a country or region, since they provide context, flavor, and, above all, continuity. Without functioning news offices abroad, the networks have lost their capacity to track the trends and daily politics that often indicate when conflict is coming, and their reporting can no longer be used to help to head it off by alerting the public.

"As long as the networks consider it legitimate to close bureaus and reduce staffs abroad, American audiences are going to get less than the best the professionals have to offer them," the former evening news producer quoted earlier pointed out. "Without someone there, you are never going to be able to be the first to report events abroad." Without strong bureaus to anticipate crises, "you are going to get there after the story."[8]

And it's not only crises that they can predict. Correspondents who know their territory can contribute both early warnings of trouble to come and reports of success in fields like literacy, democracy, and public health. They know about the rivalries between fundamentalists and modernizers, the tension among ethnic groups, and whether environmental or food supply disasters are looming. These kinds of stories are the most difficult to get past the scrutiny of editors and producers looking for the hard or dramatic lead, like the arrival of U.S. troops or food supplies. But if journalists' early warnings are broadcast and printed widely enough, they might make it possible to prevent ethnic arguments exploding into civil strife, pollution damaging health and resources, or crop and population policies leading to famine.

The connection of this kind of reporting to U.S. interests, both political and pocketbook, is clear. If sources of tension or misery can be identified far enough in advance to alert the international community to try to help solve the problem, those shipments of midwestern grain or camouflaged paratroopers may never need to take place.

Kofi Annan, secretary-general of the United Nations, has called for new efforts "to enhance our preventive capabilities—including early warning, preventive diplomacy, preventive deployment, and preventive disarmament."[9] The media should be central to the first aspect of this strategy of prevention—providing the early warning—but almost every trend in the past decade makes them less and less capable of the task.

The loss of space and airtime for the thorough and consistent coverage of sources of crisis has left the public without the knowledge it needs of potential conflict areas. This in turn lessens its ability to pressure officials to do something about the conflicts before they grow into larger wars. The media's greatest contribution to preventing conflict was achieved in the 1980s, when South Africa began its largely peaceful transition from apartheid repression to multiracial rule. Since then, there have been failures to act, for which media must bear part of the responsibility, in Rwanda, Sudan, Somalia, East Timor, Bosnia, Kosovo, and, finally, Afghanistan.

COVERING THE AFGHAN WAR

The drain on foreign-reporting resources in the decade before the Kosovo and Afghan wars affected not only coverage in the field but also the decisions of many news executives who had no experience in getting journalists and camera teams into place and fighting on their behalf with governments trying to restrict what they reported. Instead of going to court, as editors did to defend their right to publish the Pentagon Papers, television news executives went to the White House and agreed with officials to limit their coverage.

The same technology that allowed battlefield reports to be made by video-phone also put foreign and perhaps hostile sources of news into the living rooms of Americans. Editors and producers found themselves at odds with the government as well as some of their audience in their decisions on what news to carry and what to suppress, and the government was often the victor. In the middle was the al-Jazeera satellite television network, praised by Washington after its founding in 1996 as the prime source of objective information in the Arab world but suddenly condemned after the attacks for its broadcasts from the camp of Osama bin Laden. First, Secretary of State Colin Powell put pressure on the emir of Qatar, the country that owns the network, to "tone down" the coverage that Powell contended was giving the terrorists a propaganda advantage among al-Jazeera's 35 million Arabic-speaking viewers around the world and the English-language networks that pick up its feeds. Al-Jazeera, Powell said, was providing too much broadcast time to "vitriolic, irresponsible kinds of statements."[10]

The network responded as it had in the past to complaints by Arab governments. Its chairman, Hamid ibn Thamer al-Thani, said the network was beholden to no government and followed only journalistic standards: "All these accusations are proof that we are trying to be professionals." The network's chief editor, Ibrahim Hilal, told the *Washington Post*,

> We are in the business of news. Our policy is to air all shades of opinion. The attention of the world is riveted on Afghanistan. If we don't show it, who will? We put every word, every move of President Bush on the air. Arabs accuse us of being pro-American, even pro-Israeli. The Americans say we're pro-Taliban. We must be doing something right.[11]

Next, National Security Adviser Condoleezza Rice told the U.S. networks that bin Laden might be broadcasting coded messages to his operatives over al-Jazeera. The White House spokesman, Ari Fleischer, conceded that there was no immediate evidence that the bin Laden tapes contained secret signals, but the White House appeared to be just as concerned about their propaganda value. At best, he said, the statements that were broadcast were "propaganda of a most insidious nature; at worst, it could be actually signaling to his operatives" and "inciting people to kill Americans."[12]

The networks responded by promising to screen tapes carefully and broadcast excerpts, not full texts, of the statements of bin Laden and his lieutenants. "Nobody took umbrage at this," CBS News president Andrew Heyward recalled. "We are all giving the government the benefit of the doubt; the propaganda issue is a legitimate issue." CNN said it would not broadcast any live statements from al-Qaeda: "CNN's policy is to avoid airing any material that we believe would directly facilitate any terrorists' acts."[13]

In so doing, the networks lost their chance for some real news. Bin Laden and his aides were striking out at everyone, Kofi Annan as well as moderate Muslims, and warning of nuclear or biological attacks. Such remarks were better propaganda against al-Qaeda than anyone in the United States could have devised. But under pressure from the White House, the networks broadcast only brief excerpts of their tirades.

CNN's apparent caution might be traced to its role during the Gulf War, when it was the only foreign broadcaster allowed to operate from inside Iraq. Its position gained it many exclusive reports of the U.S. bombing of Baghdad and its effects but also the enmity of politicians in the United States, which accused it of being a propaganda conduit for Saddam Hussein.

Condoleezza Rice implicitly acknowledged the power of al-Jazeera as a way to reach the Arab world with the American message when she gave the station an interview only a few days after she had warned about its potential to harm the U.S. war effort. She was soon followed by the secretary of defense, Donald Rumsfeld. Al-Jazeera handed her the classic soft question when its interviewer asked what message she would like to deliver. "This is a war against the evil of terrorism," she said. "The president understands Islam to be a faith of peace."[14]

Representatives of twenty media organizations, including the Associated Press Managing Editors and the Radio-Television News Directors Association, groups that include most editors and broadcast news directors, criticized the government's restrictions on news gathering, stating that despite the critical situation after the attacks, "we believe these restrictions pose dangers to American democracy."[15]

In some cases, however, media outlets were practicing and approving self-censorship. CNN, the main conduit for al-Jazeera, announced that it would "consider guidance from appropriate authorities" before deciding what to broadcast in the case of stories that might endanger the U.S. war effort.

Later, Walter Isaacson, the chairman of CNN, told his foreign correspondents to balance news of the destruction and casualties in Afghanistan with reminders of what the terrorists had done in the United States. "We must redouble our efforts to make sure we do not seem to be simply reporting from their vantage or perspective," he wrote in a memo that was leaked to the *Washington Post*. "We must talk about how the Taliban are using civilian shields and have harbored the terrorists responsible for killing close to 5,000 innocent people."[16]

An NPR report on the laxity of security for biological weapons stored in the former Soviet Union brought listener responses like these: "Why are you advertising ways they can hit us again?" and "Why don't you censor yourselves?" Correspondent Daniel Zwerdling, who had broadcast a similar report on the lack of preparedness against bioterrorism in the United States, said he avoided details that could help terrorists. "Did I self-censor? Absolutely."[17]

But in an expanded media universe, there were many ways for Americans to get around restrictions, whether government or journalistic, and gain access to other points of view. The many Americans who can understand Arabic could hear directly from al-Jazeera; about 150,000 have direct access through their satellite dishes. To many viewers, it's not a question of propaganda but of the distinctive Arab point of view, something they can't get from the American cable or network news.

Gita Fakhry, who headed al-Jazeera's United Nations bureau at the time of the attacks, says that although the station became closely identified with bin Laden, its handling of the crisis was rooted in BBC standards of objectivity. The station was founded in 1996 after the BBC closed its Arabic-language service, and much of its staff was recruited from BBC ranks. She conceded that al-Jazeera was much more cautious than Western stations in its use of labels. Instead of "the war on terrorism," she said, al-Jazeera used the circumlocution "the war that is perceived to be on terrorism." But its main emphasis was trying to give both sides. One result was more reporting of the civilian toll of the American bombing in Afghanistan, and in this, al-Jazeera was not alone. "Many more images of civilian casualties were broadcast on other networks than on United States networks," Fakhry observed. "The consequences of the air campaign were not apparent to U.S. viewers."[18] Those U.S. viewers who wanted other perspectives on the war and terrorism could find them on PBS and C-SPAN. More than 250 public stations carry the BBC or Britain's Independent Television Network (ITN), an increase of 10 percent after September 11. C-SPAN carries the news and analysis of the Canadian Broadcasting Corporation and Germany's Deutsche Welle.

The BBC, ITN, and Sky, the third British international network, made it clear that whatever might be happening in the United States, they would refuse to censor bin Laden's statements before broadcasting them. The three networks told the British government that their own editorial discretion would be the only guide of what to broadcast. ITN and Sky are commercial entities, but the BBC is dependent on government license fees and Foreign Office support for its World Service.

Al-Jazeera found itself so much in demand that it decided to start an English-language Web site that would greatly expand its reach outside the Arab world. The number of the Arabic site's visitors jumped from about 700,000 a day to three million after the terror attacks, and the network said that requests from English-speaking viewers poured in from all over the world for a site that would serve them.

Professor Sreenath Sreenivasan of the Columbia School of Journalism, an expert on navigating the international sites on the Internet, uses a site entitled *Ajeeb.com* to get a free, instant translation of Arabic services. "Ajeeb gives you what is known as a 'gist' translation," he said, "basically allowing you to get the flavor of the wording, if not an exact translation."[19]

Fahad al-Sharekh, who runs *Ajeeb.com,* is a Kuwaiti citizen educated in the United States. He uses machine translation to provide his free Internet service, but for stories beyond the headlines, he has a staff of human translators to deal with the complexities of Arabic and English. Most of his customers are Arabic-speaking people who want to know what's going on in the English-speaking world, but more than a million English speakers logged on in the first month after the attacks to read what al-Jazeera and the Arabic-language newspapers were reporting. The Americans, too, decided to go bilingual. MSNBC started an Arabic-language version of its online service to provide an objective news channel to the Arab world, to be offered in partnership with Good News 4 me, an Arab-language site. CNN also added Arabic to the many languages of its Internet presence, choosing a site for its translation services in the Dubai Media City, a zone generally free of the restrictions on media content prevalent in most of the Arab world.

With CNN and MSNBC in Arabic and al-Jazeera in English, it's clear that some important language barriers are being bent a little for Internet users. But even if the languages are understood, there is plenty of international dissonance over the conduct of the campaign against terror.

Journalists and editors played an important a role in appealing for tolerance toward Muslims and others in the United States who might be branded as terrorists. Editorials and news stories across the country stressed this theme, with outlets like New California Media (NCM), which surveys and translates the foreign-language media in that state, among the leaders. NCM posted a variety of appeals from Chinese, African, and Muslim papers and broadcasters on the Web. The Japanese American newspaper *Nichi Bei* warned that just as in the days after Pearl Harbor, "innocent citizens of this country are scapegoated." Afghan American media provided details on the infighting in the region, some of it, in the Afghan tradition, accompanied by heavy editorializing. These accounts were translated, picked up by mainstream newspapers, and passed along to a wider audience. A weekly radio show broadcasting in an Afghan language in California provided an English-language Web site. Some sites drew attention to the human rights violations of the Taliban; others criticized the U.S. bombing.

THE KOSOVO WARNING

The Kosovo war was a minor event compared with the terror attacks that drew much of the West into conflict with al-Qaeda and the Taliban. But it provided the valuable lesson that neglect of foreign coverage weakens public understanding of the issues at stake abroad and leaves the field open for governments to act without too much regard for public opinion.

The war was the worst fighting in Europe since World War II, with about ten thousand Kosovar Albanians killed by Serbian forces in savage ethnic cleansing and up to one thousand Serbs, both civilian and military, killed by NATO bombing. The war left a desolate landscape of burned-out homes and farms and bombed bridges, factories, and refineries, with a loss of property estimated by Yugoslav officials at $100 billion.

As tragic as the toll was the fact that the war might have been avoided if a number of factors—not the least the neglect of the issue by the American media—had been different. In the critical months of January and February 1999, before the first bombs fell and the biggest Serbian offensive against the ethnic Albanians in Kosovo began, the American television networks and most of the nation's newspapers left the public woefully ill informed about the issues and the possible alternative courses of action. They devoted relatively little coverage to the crucial January talks in London, at which the West and Russia decided to force Serbs and Albanians to negotiate under the threat of bombing, or to the unsuccessful Serbian-Albanian negotiations in Rambouillet, France, the next month. Since the United States was by far the strongest element in the North Atlantic Treaty Organization's military pressure against Yugoslavia, a better-informed American public opinion might have been important to deciding whether to prolong the negotiations or begin the bombing. But the dearth of media coverage, in great contrast to that during the Vietnam era, left the diplomats free to go ahead with the war.

President Bill Clinton's impeachment and acquittal, not the Kosovo talks, dominated the evening news, talk shows, headlines, front-page stories, political columns, and opinion pieces during that January-February period. Few would quarrel with the collective news judgment of the nation's editors and producers in giving precedence to a once-in-a-century event over negotiations about a distant foreign province. The White House's preoccupation with the impeachment defense, in fact, was another reason that diplomacy failed to solve the Kosovo crisis without war.

But even without the drama of a White House scandal as competition, foreign news coverage in American media had been faring badly for years. The three main networks had made their statement about foreign coverage nine months before the Kosovo conflict, when Dan Rather, Peter Jennings, and Tom Brokaw went to Cuba for on-the-scene anchoring of the historic visit of Pope John Paul II and his confrontations with Fidel Castro. Back in Washington, however, there was a sensational development in the Monica Lewinsky scandal that brought them speedily home. Networks willing to skimp on historic confrontations could not reasonably be expected to cover obscure diplomatic meetings, even if American lives might be at stake. And so it turned out to be with the Kosovo peace negotiations.

Recalling the Kosovo bombing and refugee footage that dominated the evening news and newspaper front pages during the 1999 fighting, American audiences might have difficulty with the idea that foreign coverage in general and coverage of Kosovo in particular had been neglected. Rather, the point of my analysis is that the story was largely ignored *before* it burst into warfare. More than six thousand journalists covered the Kosovo fighting, with spectacular images of bomb strikes and poignant interviews with refugees. But only a few dozen reporters were on hand at the peace talks. One of them, who headed an American network crew in London, remembered that despite repeated attempts he could not sell his headquarters on the story. "New York saw it as one of the many conferences that never decide anything and never have an end, and wasn't interested."[20]

There was little exciting in London or Rambouillet to report or photograph, only the usual slow process of a diplomatic negotiation: leak, concession, claim and counterclaim, and finally breakthrough or breakdown. But this unspectacular talking stage is the very point at which public opinion can assert itself before lives are lost. Those media that covered the talks closely and thoroughly made it clear that there was little chance of Yugoslav President Slobodan Milosevic's agreeing to all the Western demands and every likelihood that if the bombing began, he would retaliate by accelerating his campaign of ethnic cleansing. If public opinion in the West had been alerted to the likely prospect of failure by the end of the Rambouillet talks and their brief continuation in Paris the next month, the easiest of all expedients, extending the deadline until there was progress, might have been attempted, with the possible result of saving lives and property.

The peace negotiations, however, were stories without celebrities and not even too many Americans, which are two of the criteria that seem to matter when foreign news is reported at all. That the negotiations would affect Americans greatly, as well as Kosovars, Serbs, and many other Europeans, was the job of the networks and newspapers to explain, and in this, they fell short. "News is something people don't know they're interested in until they hear about it," Reuven Frank, former president of NBC News, told the *Columbia Journalism Review*. "The job of the journalist is to take what's important and make it interesting."[21]

The most important opportunity that the media missed to inform the American public about what was at stake in Kosovo was the last week in January 1999, when Secretary of State Madeleine Albright flew to Moscow to gain Russia's agreement on a plan being proposed by Western European leaders and the United States. She then met in London with the Contact Group, made up of Russia and the Western nations. At the end of the conference, the Contact Group summoned Yugoslavia and the ethnic Albanian leadership to meet in Rambouillet for talks aimed at granting substantial autonomy to Kosovo within Yugoslavia and substantial authority to the West and Russia to police the agreement. If this was rejected, the Contact Group made it clear, NATO would begin bombing Yugoslav targets.

Unlike the Gulf War of 1991, decisions were being taken in London and Rambouillet with little public discussion. And if the public didn't know, neither did many in Congress.

Republican Senator James Inhofe of Oklahoma expressed his puzzlement over Kosovo at a January press briefing by his state's delegation: "The bottom line is we don't know for sure who the good guys and the bad guys are, and we have no business being over there."[22] Inhofe has many sources of information besides his state's leading newspaper, the 217,000-circulation *Daily Oklahoman* of Oklahoma City, but if he had relied only on the paper to inform him, as many of his constituents did, he would have found little coverage of the Kosovo crisis. The *Daily Oklahoman* printed the story deep in its inside pages, with an occasional mention on the front page and sometimes no mention at all. On January 29, when the Western European powers, the United States, and Russia agreed in London to bring the Serbs and Albanians to the conference table under the threat of NATO bombing, the *Daily Oklahoman* put the story on page 9 and allotted it four hundred words. On February 25, the day after the Albanian-Serbian talks ended without agreement, the paper carried five hundred words on page 17. And although it devoted many editorials and opinion columns during the two-month period to the shortcomings of Bill Clinton, whose impeachment and acquittal dominated the headlines, not a single editorial or column was used to explain what was at stake in the conferences deciding Kosovo's fate.

Oklahomans who turned to the evening news programs of ABC, CBS, CNN, and NBC as their sole or supplementary source of information were no better served. On January 29, ABC ranked the crucial London decision sixth in importance on the *World News Tonight* lineup and gave it two minutes and ten seconds. It led its evening news program with a story on the U.S. economy. CBS also led with the economy and put the Kosovo decision in third place, at two minutes total. NBC's twenty-second Kosovo coverage ignored the London conference and its findings and mentioned only local fighting. Only CNN led its nightly news roundup with the story, devoting eight minutes to the conference decision and the fighting.

The talks on Kosovo's future were allotted only 3 percent of the evening news time during the period immediately before and during the London conference, January 21 to 29. CNN provided the most thorough coverage of the four programs, but that still amounted to only 5 percent of the news time on its half-hour evening news programs, according to the abstracts of Vanderbilt University's Television News Archive, on which all these figures are based.[23] In the nine-day period that included the talks and the key announcements, ABC ran two stories on Kosovo; CBS, three; CNN, four; and NBC, three. Only once did a network lead its evening news program with Kosovo. Some of the stories were as short as twenty seconds and concentrated on the fighting or massacres, not the peace process.

In February, coverage of the Kosovo issues was much the same. The Rambouillet talks covered a longer period, February 6 to 24, and for their first week, the conflict with presidential impeachment news was even greater than it was in January. (On February 12, the day of President Clinton's acquittal, none of the networks could find room for a story on Kosovo.)

In the twenty-day period that included the Rambouillet negotiations and Kosovo stories just before and after them, ABC carried eight stories; CBS, ten; CNN, twelve; and NBC, seven. Coverage of Kosovo accounted for about 8 percent of the available news time; the story was played first on the evening news of the four networks fourteen times out of a possible eighty. What is at least equally important to the public's understanding is the paucity of the long, explanatory pieces on all the networks except CNN. The cable network filed nine of them during the twenty-day period; ABC, 4; CBS, 3; and NBC, 3. Only twice, on February 19 and 20, when the talks broke down for a time, did all four evening news programs take the time to explain what was at stake if they failed.

ABC, CBS, and NBC each devoted four to five minutes to such analysis; CNN gave the story and its implications twice or three times that.

It is not the aim of this book to measure the minutes and seconds of broadcast time or the paragraph inches and page placement of newspaper stories in order to come up with a formula that would quantify media, and hence public, interest or disinterest in a topic. But rough measurements are possible. If a foreign story is headlined on the front pages morning after morning and leads the network news evening after evening, it can be said to have the public's attention. If it is a short, routine account, buried down among the TV actors selling antacids or the columns of classifieds for used cars, then it doesn't.

The *Daily Oklahoman's* coverage of Kosovo was part of a survey I made of ten newspapers, chosen for geographical distribution and range in circulations.[24] I did not examine those national or regional newspapers that have remained committed to covering and analyzing foreign news but instead designed the survey to look at how the smaller papers use the foreign news sources that are readily available to them. All the newspapers I chose subscribe to the New York Times, Los Angeles Times–Washington Post, Knight Ridder Tribune, Dow Jones, or other news services, which gives them easy access to the same reporting and opinion that the bigger papers' staffs provide. But most of them made little or no use of these services, choosing to bury the Kosovo negotiations on inside pages as news briefs or skimpy accounts of a few hundred words. It was beyond the scope of my survey to include every one of the nearly fifteen hundred daily newspapers in the United States, and thus I can make no claim for the completeness provided by the monitoring of all the evening newscasts by the staff of the Vanderbilt Television Archive.

In the same nine-day period of the January negotiations that I examined for television, the ten newspapers surveyed carried a total of fifty-two Kosovo stories, about five per newspaper, or, on average, one every other day. Nine of those stories were on the front page. Only four papers carried editorials or op-ed analyses of the Kosovo situation.

In February, with the talks under way in Rambouillet and the Clinton impeachment out of the way by midmonth, the newspapers carried more news about the negotiations, but still not a great deal. Over the twenty days of the talks, most papers provided short daily stories about the fighting, the conference, or related events in Washington and Moscow. Most were in the range of two hundred to four hundred words, and most were on inside pages. Thirty-nine times, or fewer than four times per paper during the twenty days, did the story make page 1. More important than placement was the virtual lack of commentary. Only six times in the nearly three weeks of the Rambouillet conference did the ten newspapers run editorials or op-ed pieces commenting on the issues and likely outcome.

FOREIGN NEWS AND PUBLIC OPINION

Does any of this matter? There is plenty of evidence that it does, that thorough coverage of international issues leads to an informed public opinion, and that this in turn influences foreign policy decisions.

The most important example, so taken for granted that it usually escapes notice, is the cold war. For nearly half a century, American readers and viewers were so well informed about the threat of Communism that they gladly supported a huge defense establishment, gave their assent to two wars, Korea and Vietnam (even though most of them withdrew it late in the stages of the second one), and voted for presidents and legislators across party lines who would carry out such policies. When the Berlin Wall came down, the American public considered the job done and lost most of its interest in further developments in Russia and Eastern Europe.

South Africa is the best example of how quickly the media can influence public opinion on a foreign issue and how that opinion can be marshaled to change policies. After decades when few people outside South Africa paid attention to the struggle against apartheid, media images and news stories began in 1984 to focus the world's attention on the situation there. The then-new technology of satellite transmission, along with the skills of reporters like Charlayne Hunter-Gault of the Public Broadcasting System, created an instant presence for the world at the scene of the fighting and protests. The mistaken belief by the white minority government that letting the camera crews into the turbulent townships would show that the African nationalists were really terrorists made coverage easier, until the government finally realized how much harm it was doing to its cause. When organized protests began to grow in the black townships, daily newspaper and nightly television news accounts of the repression and deaths became a regular fixture for audiences in the United States.

Soon American readers and viewers were contacting their senators and representatives to call for economic boycotts and an end to the Reagan administration's attempts at conciliation. Aided by committed lobbyists like Randall Robinson of TransAfrica, the sanctions bills sailed through Congress. Within three years, the South African government was forced to release Nelson Mandela and begin the negotiations that led to multiparty government.

"The policy reversal affected by this congressional override illustrates the power of lobbies, advocacy groups, and influential private citizens to shape the course and outcome of the legislative process," former Undersecretary of State David Newsom wrote. But first, he stressed, the media were needed to draw the public's attention to the issue.[25]

In addition to the coverage of South Africa's rioting, funerals, and brutal police sweeps, there soon were new images on television screens of activists picketing in Washington, led by Robinson and members of Congress. Twenty-two congressmen and women were among the seven thousand arrested in the mass demonstrations outside the Capitol. The evening news programs for July 23, 1985, capture the intensity of the media involvement. CBS led its program with a four-and-one-half-minute report on the violence in South Africa, funerals, and embattled Reagan officials defending their policy. ABC gave South Africa second place and four minutes, including footage of the protests in Washington. NBC's nearly five-minute report from South Africa led the program, and in Washington, it featured opponents of the Reagan engagement policy arguing against its beleaguered defenders. In the end, even thirty-five of the conservatives in Congress, mindful of the votes of their black constituents, joined in the vote to override the administration's South Africa policy.

"Public opinion is certainly not infallible," the man most identified with its measurement, George Gallup, wrote, "but when the people have enough information about alternative policies, and the reason behind each, they usually have the good sense to pick the best."[26]

In 1966, during the early years of the Vietnam War, President Lyndon Johnson was so successful in his leadership of both domestic and foreign policy that sociologist Seymour Martin Lipset wrote that "the President makes public opinion, he does not follow it."[27] But two years later, after a constant barrage of media images from the Vietnam battlefields and mounting American casualty tolls, public opinion reasserted its independence from its leader (if it had ever lost it) and forced Johnson to abandon his plans for reelection.

Today, when the long-term threat of terrorism has replaced the uncertainties of the cold war, the world still has a need for the sustained reporting of international crisis points. There still are sporadic bursts of little wars and local conflicts, unrelated to larger terrorist movements, and longer-range threats of famine and human rights abuses that call for coverage. Journalists' cameras and notebooks remain a valuable weapon for preserving peace.

There are many signs, though, that the surge in coverage of international news that followed September 11 is abating. More than half the 213 editors polled for a Pew International Journalism Program survey said they believed foreign news would gradually subside to the modest levels it had in most papers before the terrorist attacks, although the same survey found no decrease in the surge of reader interest that followed September 11.

There is a danger that the diminished coverage will shut the public out of the decision-making process in foreign policy, thus making future Kosovos and Afghanistans more likely. Mary Robinson, the former United Nations High Commissioner for Human Rights, says the lack of coverage of foreign news in mainstream national newspapers and broadcasts could lead to a world in which foreign policy is created in a "news vacuum." In a speech before the Afghan crisis, she criticized the trend toward reducing complex issues to sound bites. The media must report vigorously on international issues, even at the risk of losing readers and viewers, she added, if diplomacy is not to be isolated from public opinion. "How will we counter racism, xenophobia?" she asked. "How will we create a climate of understanding? How will we advance other human rights?"[28]

The answers to these questions may lie in three trends that could be discerned in the media even before the events of September 11 put the need for better international coverage at the top of the public agenda. The first is the galloping technology of the Internet, satellites, and cable systems, which has created an array of new media and given new voice to traditional media. Cable news networks linked instantly to all parts of the world, Web sites that give those even mildly interested in an area an encyclopedia's worth of current information with a few key strokes, and online editions of newspapers that multiply readership and extend it across the nation and the world are some of technology's achievements. The second is the growth of immigration, including the nearly 60 percent increase in the Latino population between the 1990 and 2000 censuses and the effects of their interests and media on the larger population. Immigrants have always been interested in news of their home countries or regions, but in the past, little of this information reached the general public. Now, some Spanish-language television programs are going bilingual to attract larger audiences, and mainstream newspapers are printing more news of interest to large immigrant populations, which spills over to the rest of their readership. Organizations like *El Sentinel* of Orlando, Florida, and New California Media of San Francisco act as bridges between the two populations, translating foreign reports into English and distributing them on the Internet or in newspapers. Many other news organizations pick up foreign news from foreign-language sources in their communities.

The third is the effort by newspaper editors, not matched by many broadcast producers, to improve foreign coverage. Some are working on new methods of linking foreign stories to local issues. Other proposals involve spending more time and a little more money trying to make sense out of the world around the

United States through special sections or better use of the plethora of foreign material that comes into every editorial office every day.

One single but important trend is counterpoised against these three. It is the effects of the changes in ownership of most of the media in the United States—print, broadcast, and Internet—that focus the efforts of publishers and broadcasters to expand profits to satisfy stockholders rather than the public's right to know.

It's as though they're turning out hamburgers and must be able to find ways to take shortcuts and do it more cheaply. But hamburgers are not a public trust and hamburger makers are not protected by the First Amendment.
—*Publisher of a chain-owned newspaper*

2

GATEKEEPERS AND BOOKKEEPERS

The business side of both broadcast and print journalism has always had a role in determining what stories are covered and to what extent. But in recent years the managers have far eclipsed the editors in determining the content of the news, with profit replacing professional judgments of what is important, at home and abroad, for audiences to know. Money, in fact, is the reason most often cited by professionals in both print and broadcast to explain why foreign news is neglected except in times of great national crisis.

For decades, the networks made great amounts of money, if not from news, then from entertainment. Figures from those glory years are hard to translate into current terms, but percentages tell the story: a steady 20 percent in profits all through the period until the end of the 1990s. Such profits were as attractive to outsiders as they were to the networks' stockholders, and within the space of just a few months in 1986, CBS was bought by real estate developer Lawrence Tisch; ABC was sold to Capital Cities, a regional owner of newspapers and television stations; and NBC became part of General Electric. There were more changes down the road: ABC was next sold to Disney, and CBS, to Sony and then to Viacom.

"Members of the news media—particularly those in the newsroom—feel caught in a pressure cycle," a nationwide survey by the Pew Research Center found in 1999. "Working journalists say that business pressures undermine quality, which hurts credibility, which in turn causes lost audiences."[1] How this has affected foreign coverage was noted at the time of the survey by an editor at a respected Kentucky daily. Even though publishers may understand that international news is important, she said, her paper had an informal ban on letting a foreign story dominate the front page: "Our circulation director has told us in no uncertain terms that he sure doesn't want to see any of that international news above the fold because it sure doesn't sell newspapers."[2]

If you were a network news executive faced with the prospect of sending a new correspondent to India at an annual cost of $500,000 or adding an entertainment feature that cost little but was practically guaranteed to bring in viewers, what would you do? a broadcast veteran asked.

The Project for Excellence in Journalism (PEJ) conducted a survey of twenty years of network news programs, newspaper front pages, and newsmagazine covers and found that between 1977 and 1997, celebrity, scandal, gossip, and similar stories increased from 15 percent of the total coverage to 43 percent. The Committee of Concerned Journalists, an affiliate of PEJ, singled out the television magazine shows covered by the survey as concentrating on crime, personalities, health, and consumer news "to the exclusion of education, economics, government, foreign affairs and most of the traditional subjects of public debate." The committee concluded: "After more than a decade of refashioning the news to make it more profitable, journalism professionals believe that the news media have blurred the lines between news and entertainment."[3]

NEWSPAPERS

Closing foreign bureaus is an obvious result of such bottom-line considerations, but cuts across the board have an equal, if not larger, effect. Not many newspapers had foreign correspondents or stringers in the first place, but all still subscribe to wire services that supply them with huge amounts of news from abroad. In newsrooms across the country, staff reductions mean that wire editors do not have enough time to sort out the important and the interesting from the hundreds of wire stories they must consider every day. In many newsrooms, the labor-saving technology that was used to get rid of expensive page-makeup crews has put an added burden on the editorial staff, who must do the makeup themselves on their computer screens. "We now have editors with no time to edit," a wire service executive remarked.[4]

The staffs of the television networks also have had to replace national and international news with light pieces that are believed to attract younger viewers and thus bring in extra advertising income. Many radio broadcasters don't even have this choice. They work for the two huge conglomerates that now own one in ten stations in the United States and, with notable exceptions like the all-news stations in the biggest cities, consider news as something that interferes with schlock talk and the increasingly numerous ads.

Business interests have always driven news; on the first day on the job, every reporter or copy clerk hears about the need to cut costs. Most news organizations, however, also have a parallel set of arguments contending that journalism is an integral part of the nation's system of self-government and that service to the public is journalism's main objective. This argument has been stated eloquently many times by newspaper proprietors who needed no lessons on making profits. While teaching in China in 1985, I had T-shirts made for my twenty-two post–Mao era students, with Joseph Pulitzer's motto, "That the people shall know," and the Columbia Journalism School logo. The words of John S. Knight were posted on the wall of his first newspaper, the *Akron Beacon Journal*, in the nineteenth century: "We believe in profitability but do not sacrifice either principle or quality on the altar of the countinghouse." But in the twenty-first century, the countinghouse, in the form of Knight Ridder's profits-driven management, imposed such severe personnel cuts on the *Beacon Journal* that some of its reporters and editors say they can no longer adequately serve their readers. Part-time correspondents who reported from abroad for Akron's ethnically diverse readership were dropped from the paper, an editor said, and many local government issues simply are not covered.

The publisher of a successful newspaper, part of a large chain, gave his views in a background talk on what has happened to Pulitzer's and Knight's promises:

There's been a complete change in the way newspapers are managed. In the past several years, the pursuit of quarterly profits and the wish to satisfy shareholder interests and demands have replaced the traditional management system. It used to be that being the best in journalism was what mattered. That was when the leaders of the newspaper business were the publishers with strong family connections and commitment, many or most of whom had risen from or served in the editorial ranks.

Now newspapers are in the hands of the marketing people, and by focusing on a profit that is usually in excess of 20 percent and trying constantly to raise it, [they] have cheapened the quality of newspapers and, to an extent, their staffs. Where good people are employed, their initiative is often stifled. Obviously, [reducing] foreign news as well as other public affairs reporting is one way to cut costs. It's as though they're turning out hamburgers and must be able to find ways to take shortcuts and do it more cheaply. But hamburgers are not a public trust, and hamburger makers are not protected by the First Amendment. That was done for newspapers for a reason. Now the number of traditional newspapers, managed by someone with a high sense of obligation to the public, has shrunk to a very few.[5]

Jay Harris, the chairman and publisher of Knight Ridder's *San Jose Mercury News*, expressed the same sentiments more dramatically in 2001 when he resigned to protest staff cuts designed to increase profits. Although the chain's profits had grown 66 percent from 1995 to 2000, when the rate stood at 20.8 percent, management was demanding further increases as part of its plan to be in the mid-twenties in the next three years. But when advertising revenues decreased sharply because of the economic downturn, that would have meant laying off journalists. In a letter to the company, Harris said he could not dismiss staff members "without risking significant and lasting harm to the *Mercury News* as a journalistic enterprise." Harris said he thought Knight Ridder had abandoned the values it used to follow, and he quoted some of them:

> Much greater priority is given today to the business aspects of our enterprise than is given to fulfilling our "public trust." I fear that we no longer sense the same level of "moral obligation" to "excel in all that we do" and that our founders' commitment to publishing "high-quality newspapers" is no longer the powerful drive in the company that it once was.[6]

The *Mercury News*'s emphasis on foreign news was one of the key elements in the budget dispute. Steve Rossi, the president of Knight Ridder newspaper division, told Harris that surveys showed readers wanted more local news and that although local news did dominate the front page, "the inside of Section A is very heavily weighted toward foreign news. This may be something to reconsider."

In his response and resignation letter, Harris referred to the paper's position as Silicon Valley's leading journal:

> Given the substantial number of our readers, and residents of the community who were born in other nations, the equally significant number employed by global business, and the many readers for whom such news is a priority, I would recommend that the weighting is proper and should not be changed.

The Knight Ridder dispute galvanized the newspaper community across the country, putting into boldface type the contradictions that have defined newspapers since the start of the republic: quality versus profits. At another Knight Ridder paper, the *Miami Herald*, a former editor says the cost cutting that Ridder ordered there is the main reason that the paper, once best in the nation for its reporting from Latin America, "has deteriorated in both quantity and quality" of its coverage of the region. A new team put in place by Ridder never "really realized that Latin American coverage was THE thing that gave the *Herald* more than a regional reputation." Until 2000, the *Herald* had an Americas page, an open page each Monday and Thursday dedicated to hemisphere news, plus adequate space on other days to accommodate all the important Latin America news. "Now, on most days, it does not even have a separate roundup of Americas briefs."[7]

TELEVISION

Scaling back international reporting in individual newspapers affects only their relatively small number of readers. But cutbacks in the news and reporting staffs of the three main television networks hinders the entire country's access to news from abroad.

At CBS, budget-based judgments affecting the quality and quantity of foreign coverage are not new, the CBS executive quoted earlier observed.

> There's been a change from news to corporate management. This means that CBS is only a small part of the conglomerate, Viacom, that the news division is a tiny part of that, and that the newsroom, the producers, the correspondents an even tinier part of that. There are probably twenty-five layers of management over them. They don't care what they broadcast; they probably don't even watch. They care if it makes money. The old CBS management knew what went on the air, and it cared passionately, even if it didn't always agree.

The executive noted that the result has been a drastic decline in national and foreign coverage.

> News has been cut back in the past ten or fifteen years so that there are no longer enough people to cover these stories. Now we work at constructing, not covering, stories—a piece from this television news service, this piece of other footage, this wire service material. They put it together for someone to read who is three hundred miles from the story.[8]

CBS, which once boasted that it covered the world with its own correspondent and news teams, now must rely mostly on its London bureau, which, the executive admitted, is less a news center than "a listening post, a transmission point for news" gathered by other organizations. "The people who own my company don't care what goes out on the air. The value of the stock is the ultimate goal. [Viacom CEO] Sumner Redstone doesn't care what the evening news does. [CBS founder] Bill Paley cared."9

At ABC, Tom Bettag, the executive producer of *Nightline*, insists that audiences do care, despite what the managers say.

> Foreign news costs twice as much as domestic news. If you could get people to buy into that with focus groups that asked people if they cared about foreign news or health news, [and were told] "I guess I care more about health news," that gave them the ability to close down foreign bureaus, which became more and more expensive. But it's strictly an accountant sort of thing.10

Bettag says the new miniature video cameras and digital editing equipment have made those traditional bookkeepers' arguments invalid. "Suddenly the technology has wheeled around so that not only is it no more expensive but it is less expensive in this form," with smaller crews and simpler editing processes. "Now there is a huge opening for someone to do a number of foreign news programs."11

It isn't surprising that producers at the other networks, with the notable exception of CNN, have the same story of cost cutting and reduced coverage of international issues. They buy foreign footage to make up for the reporting no longer coming from their own bureaus and particularly to insure against missing a major event like a political assassination or natural disaster. But attempts to fill in the gaps with material supplied by the Associated Press Television News Service (APTN) or European teams have failed, one veteran said, because the feeds lack the personal presence of familiar correspondents. Those correspondents can do voice-overs from a studio far from the scene to describe the action that the viewers are seeing, but the impact isn't the same.

A producer in Europe for another network increasingly uses APTN's footage when its own crews are not immediately available for an important story, but this, too, has its drawbacks. "APTN serves as a wire service way to have first coverage of a breaking story where we don't have a crew, but it's important enough to get on the air immediately with," he explained, in the same way that the *New York Times* might use a wire service story on its front page for an early edition, before it can get its own reporters there to cover it. "The trouble with AP and Reuters television is that they get there, cover, and then move on to the next story. They can't stay in place for a full cycle of news that would including morning and evening programs in the United States."12

Broadcasters started with the same structure of personal and family ownership that newspapers did, but the two diverged sharply after the corporate takeovers of the networks in 1986. Although chains continued to swallow up newspapers and even smaller chains, until only 20 percent of U.S. dailies were independently owned, the four most influential papers in national and foreign news have remained under systems of ownerships intended to guarantee their continued independence.

In 1986, as the imprimaturs of founders William Paley, David Sarnoff, and Leonard Goldenson vanished from CBS, NBC, and ABC, the Sulzberger family agreed to a remarkable document to keep the *New York Times* under family ownership. The four descendants of the late publisher Arthur Hays Sulzberger, the son-in-law of *Times* founder Adolph Ochs, and their thirteen children signed an agreement never to sell their controlling shares of company stock to outsiders. The signatories, who included the then publisher Arthur Ochs Sulzberger and his son, the current publisher Arthur Ochs Sulzberger Jr., agreed to offer their stock to other family members before anyone else and to stick by the agreement well into the twenty-first century. Family members knew they were giving up their right to millions of dollars by promising not to sell their stock, but as Marian Sulzberger Heiskell told the family's chroniclers, Alex Jones and Susan Tifft, "We were all trained that the money that was made went back into the pot to make the *Times* that much better."[13] Nine years later, the younger members of the family confirmed these arrangements with a fifty-page document stating that the family's guardianship of the paper "will certainly always come first" and have precedence over "most considerations of individual welfare." The *New York Times* is "an organization ruled by a monarchy," Jones and Tifft commented. "Although the stock price and earnings mattered, it was not to the same degree that they did in almost every other corporation in the country."[14]

The death in 2001 of Katharine Graham, chair of the *Washington Post* executive committee, drew attention to the future of that privately held newspaper. "The business activities of the company will not be affected" by her death, a company spokesman declared. "Of course the company is not for sale." The Graham family members who survive her control all the Class A shares that elect 70 percent of the Post Company's board. Even if these shares are sold, the company charter mandates their conversion to Class B, or nonvoting, shares.

Mrs. Graham herself wrote about the importance of family ownership in a *Wall Street Journal* op-ed piece dated March 20, 2000, after another family-owned giant, the *Los Angeles Times*, was sold to the Tribune Company of Chicago. Although family ownership has never guaranteed quality, she wrote, "I don't think it's an accident that the newspapers best known for quality in this country are, or were until recently, family controlled. We have a responsibility to put long-term service to readers ahead of short-term financial gain."

Long-term service to readers can be expensive. The *Post's* Tokyo bureau, for example, costs $250,000 a year, excluding salaries, and foreign news generates little advertising revenue. "Public media companies can, of course, choose to invest in quality journalism at the expense of maximum profits," she wrote. "But the sad truth is that most have curtailed their reporting activities—especially abroad—in recent years."

The *Wall Street Journal* has been controlled for a century by the family of Clarence Barron, its third owner after Charles Dow and Edward Jones. Barron, founder of the financial magazine that bears his name, was succeeded at Dow Jones by his son-in-law, Hugh Bancroft, whose descendants own the majority of the *Journal's* stock today. Shares were sold to the public starting in 1963, but Clarence Barron's heirs retain majority control. A 5 percent share of Dow Jones stock belongs to Ottaway Newspapers, publishers of small dailies and weeklies, and an Ottaway family member, James Ottaway, sits on the Dow Jones board.

The sale of the *Los Angeles Times* to Chicago's Tribune Company was an example of the vulnerability of family ownership over the generations. As long as the one hundred-year-old line of publishers from General Harrison Otis to Otis Chandler was intact, the family provided an atmosphere of trust and faith in the newspaper, Otis Chandler told his biographer, Dennis McDougal. But after he left, as the last family member to serve as publisher, some of the managers began to devise ways of maximizing their own and other family members' profits. Although the ownership agreements placed restrictions on selling family stock, intermediaries working with the Tribune found loopholes, and in 1999 Otis Chandler's relatives—wealthy, conservative, and uninvolved in managing the paper—were persuaded to sell the *Los Angeles Times* to the Tribune Company. *Times* staff members say the sale has brought no change in foreign operations and are thankful at least that the new owners also are primarily interested in news rather than theme parks or aircraft engines. And through its ownership, the Tribune company has finally acquired the worldwide network of correspondents that its management was never willing to finance for the Chicago paper alone.

For more than three decades, Otis Chandler used the latitude that family ownership provided him to transform the *Los Angeles Times* from a pedestrian regional paper to one with wide influence in the nation and the world. When he was thirty-two and took over as its publisher in 1960, the paper had only a single foreign correspondent, a crusty former admiral named Waldo Drake. Chandler realized that if he wanted to compete with the *New York Times* as a national newspaper, he would need to expand his foreign and national bureaus quickly. Within five years, *Times* bureaus were planted around the globe: Tokyo, Rio de Janeiro, Mexico City, and Hong Kong followed Paris, Rome, and Bonn.

The United Nations, Moscow, Saigon, London, and New Delhi were next in line. Chandler and Philip Graham of the *Washington Post*, which was also expanding overseas at the same rate during this period, began discussions about sharing correspondents but decided instead on a joint wire service. Soon the Los Angeles Times–Washington Post news service was up and running, and the two papers sent their sales forces to newsrooms around the country to sign up clients. From two dozen at the beginning, the service grew to more than six hundred subscribers in the United States and abroad.

The service greatly improved the national and foreign coverage of papers unable to afford any or many correspondents in Washington or abroad. But it also had unintended consequences as one of the factors that led to the decline of United Press International. Editors could buy the supplementary coverage for less money than the UPI service cost, and as news holes shrank, so did the need for three versions of a single story from Brussels or Tokyo.

Most of newspapers' legal structures preserving family ownership are probably planned well enough so that they'll succeed in doing just that: preserving family ownership. This makes it more likely that the newspapers will continue their commitment to quality, even if it means lower profits. But this is not why these arrangements were made, and there is nothing to guarantee that they will end up doing any more than keeping the paper in the family, not keeping the paper excellent.

NATIONAL ASSETS

The emergence of four strong news organizations committed to covering serious national and international news, regardless of marketing surveys or budget analysis, served the nation well in the cold war, the dry period of the 1990s, and the crisis that started the new century, growing in importance as all the networks except CNN reduced their commitment. The *Los Angeles Times, New York Times, Wall Street Journal*, and *Washington Post* constitute a core of internationally minded newspapers with wide national circulation, leading positions on the Web, and news services that reach into the newsrooms of the best smaller papers. Each has correspondents in every major nation or region, and all strive to have their own correspondents cover the most important international stories, day in and day out.

In broadcasting, the Cable News Network and National Public Radio are the only organizations that match the international power and reach of the Big Four newspapers. ABC, CBS, and NBC still provide important coverage of the world, but without the global system of bureaus they once had, they must rely on others' reporting when major stories break abroad. CBS's 60 *Minutes* and ABC's *Nightline* have maintained their quality in both international and national coverage, although the future of *Nightline* is uncertain. PBS's *NewsHour*, which provides the greatest depth in foreign coverage, is limited by the same lack of a permanent presence abroad.

These newspapers and broadcasters are among the nation's many assets in providing coverage of international issues at levels commensurate with the United States' role in the world. The Associated Press connects every member newspaper and subscribing broadcast station, more than 4,500 in all, to world-wide resources. Most important, the United States is the world's leader in the technological innovation that has already brought widespread access to foreign news on the Internet and is certain to develop new ways of informing the public about international events.

The leading newspapers and networks have been recognized as national institutions by the government as well as the public. In 1945, when the United States was preparing for the final battles of World War II against Japan, the *New York Times* science reporter, William L. Laurence, was contacted by the War Department and made privy to the secret of the atomic bomb. A little more than two decades later, during the Vietnam War, a Pentagon official, Daniel Ellsberg, contacted Neil Sheehan of the *New York Times* to leak the documents that became known as the Pentagon Papers, which the *Washington Post* and *Boston Globe* joined in publishing.

World War II and the Vietnam War were the two high points of U.S. coverage of foreign news and, at the same time, the bases for expanding that coverage during peacetime. The end of the cold war brought a flurry of activity into the foreign news business. New correspondents were assigned to Eastern Europe as Communism began to crumble. With no more civil wars to cover in Central America, freelancers moved their operations from Managua or San Salvador to Berlin or Prague. But with the exception of Yugoslavia, post–cold war coverage became less interesting to American readers, and the increase in foreign news proved to be nothing more than a temporary spike.

The *New York Times* and its three main competitors, however, continued to look on events abroad as something that required continued, thoughtful, and thorough coverage, whatever the rise and fall of warfare or violence and often whatever the involvement of Americans. These newspapers' consistency in foreign coverage over the years, through periods lean and fat for Americans' interest in world events, is shown by the Pulitzer Prizes for international reporting they have been awarded. The *New York Times* tops the list with eighteen in the fifty-eight years of the international reporting category, followed by the *Wall Street Journal* with six,the *Washington Post* with five, the *Christian Science Monitor* and Long Island's *Newsday* with three, and the *Los Angeles Times* with two.

Despite the dozens of exceptions among the nation's 1,482 dailies, including the international-reporting Pulitzer winners *Dallas Morning News*, *Baltimore Sun*, *Miami Herald*, *Chicago Tribune*, and *Philadelphia Inquirer*, most other newspapers and the television networks have not kept pace with foreign coverage. Television's shift from thorough to facile coverage of foreign affairs will be examined later. But for far too many newspapers, in city after city, the story is familiar and dreary: news digests on remote pages in fat newspapers stuffed with recipes, new car reports, and gossip about the media and movie stars.

Many critics say that whether newspapers carry more foreign news is as irrelevant as the newspaper itself has become in the American media system. They cite polls showing that younger audiences have deserted print for electronic information, a factor that has hastened the national decline in newspaper circulation. Newspapers have been relegated to dinosaur status for decades, beginning in the 1920s when the NBC news broadcasts from David Sarnoff's crackling radio sets were said to be poised to eliminate the costly and inefficient bundle of newsprint thrown onto American front porches. Since then, television, cable, and the Internet have successively taken the place of radio as newspapers' likely nemesis.

But analysts of newspaper readership, including John Lavine of Northwestern University, maintain that the very diversity of news sources in the marketplace makes newspapers, traditionally a single institution anchored in a community for many generations, stronger than they have been since the golden days of the 1950s. According to Lavine, despite the decline in newspaper circulation, 85 percent of Americans read a newspaper in an average week. Newspapers actually benefit from the fragmentation of their competition, since "other media are chopping up their market and audiences at a rapid rate." Super Bowl Sunday draws 86 million television viewers, Lavine said, but every Sunday, newspapers have 132 million readers.[15]

Lavine's team conducted the largest survey ever of readers' preferences. It received completed questionnaires from 37,000 readers of one hundred newspapers, ranging from small-town papers with a circulation of ten thousand to big-city dailies like the *Chicago Tribune*, *Baltimore Sun*, and *Houston Chronicle*. At the top of their wish list, not surprisingly, stood local news, with lifestyle news—including health, travel, real estate, and food—in second place. But in third place, far above crime news, movies, business, and even sports, was a category labeled "how we are governed and global relations." Although the way the question was asked made it impossible to divide national and foreign news, details of the responses made it clear that this third-place category remains important. Readers said they wanted both quantity and quality in this category: more stories, and more of them written as features, accompanied by good color photography and bracketed by stand-alone opinion columns to help explain their meaning. Respondents said they had a personal need to be informed and "in the know," according to the survey's authors. This included "being informed about the world and the nation" by a source that readers could identify as "honest, trustworthy, helpful."

The four leading newspapers in international coverage certainly conform to this description, but so do many others, including those with bureaus or correspondents abroad: the *Baltimore Sun, Boston Globe, Chicago Tribune, Houston Chronicle, San Diego Union, Dallas Morning News, Newsday,* and the main newspapers of the Knight Ridder chain: the *Detroit Free Press, Miami Herald, Philadelphia Inquirer,* and *San Jose Mercury News.* The *St. Petersburg Times* and *San Antonio Express-News* have put new emphasis on reporting from Latin America, with David Adams covering the region from the *Times's* Miami bureau and Robert Rivard, a veteran Latin America correspondent, directing reporting as editor of the *Express-News.* Both won Cabot Prizes in 2002 for their Latin America coverage.

Another group encompasses papers without foreign correspondents that nevertheless make special contributions to foreign coverage, such as the *Des Moines Register, Louisville Courier-Journal, Sacramento Bee* and other McClatchy papers in California, *New Orleans Times-Picayune, Newark Star-Ledger, Kansas City Star, Omaha World-Herald, Portland Oregonian, Hartford Courant, Richmond Times-Dispatch, Providence Journal, St. Louis Post-Dispatch,* and Seattle's *Times* and *Post-Intelligencer.*

Two newspapers deserve a category of their own. The *Christian Science Monitor* has correspondents all over the world and, with three Pulitzer Prizes for international reporting, ranks above most of the nation's largest papers in that field. Its circulation of only about eighty thousand, however, means that the correspondents' work is not widely read, at least in the print version. *Monitor* managers have had considerable success in extending its reach through Internet and news service links, however, and were helped by the nation's need for background and explanation after September 11. *USA Today* is on the opposite end of the spectrum—huge circulation but few bureaus. As the *Monitor* is looking for ways to attract a larger audience, *USA Today* is seeking to broaden its world coverage.

As the foregoing list shows, size matters, but not always. Four of the five largest circulation newspapers in the nation are the leaders in foreign coverage, and the fifth, *USA Today,* is starting to compete with them. But some papers with high levels of foreign coverage have only a fraction of the circulation of these leading newspapers, like the *Fort Lauderdale Sun-Sentinel* and papers along the Texas-Mexico border, including the *Laredo Morning Times* and the *Monitor of McAllen*. Three large metropolitan tabloids, New York's *Daily News* and *Post*, and the *Chicago Sun-Times*, rank in the top fifteen in national circulation but pay relatively little attention to foreign news.

Ownership matters, too, but not always. Some small family-owned newspapers—the *Anniston Star* of Alabama and *Watertown Daily Times* of New York—are committed to more complete coverage of foreign and national news than are some far larger ones owned by chains. But chain ownership is not an automatic recipe for ignoring serious news. The locally owned *Omaha World Herald* and *St. Louis Post Dispatch* do a good job, but so do the Gannett-owned *Louisville Courier Journal* and *Des Moines Register*. Part of the reason may be that these latter two were very good papers before Gannett acquired them, which means traditions and expectations of good if not excellent performance among both staff and readers.

"Stories that really matter in the world may or may not be stories that move ratings or sell papers," Joseph Lelyveld, former executive editor of the *New York Times*, explained.

> You don't report on missile shields, Kosovo, energy technology, lobbying in Trenton or the drug war in order to build circulation. But if you build trust, your readers will understand that these stories matter to their lives. The focus groups beloved by some managers bent on what's likely to be termed "product enhancement" can't tell you what those stories are. And they're dangerous when they tell you what they're not, what subjects to steer clear of.[16]

I'm not a doctor, I'm not an aid worker. But I really do believe my words can raise awareness and hopefully the people that are qualified to change the world will pay attention to my words and make an effort.
—*AP Africa correspondent Ian Stewart*

3

GETTING THE NEWS FROM ABROAD

The news-gathering system that supplies American newspapers and television is worldwide, modern, efficient—and, except in times of crisis or war, greatly underutilized. Its mainstay is the wire services, whose correspondents cover all but a very few of the nations in the world. Millions of their words and billions of bytes of their images flow around the globe every day. Technologies transmit news with ever increasing speed, but the great strength of the news agencies is people. Computers are good at gathering and sorting information but are not good at distinguishing the new and noteworthy. The experience and standards of the men and women in bureaus large and small are as vital to the reporting process as is the raw information they gather. Internet users who thought they could be their own experts or rely on the work of other amateurs have largely returned to the professionals. The ability to judge the newsworthy, to analyze and explain, has been recognized once again for its importance.

The news agencies transmit images—still pictures for newspaper or magazine pages and, increasingly, video for television and Web sites. But their main product is words, words written on note pads or laptop computers and sent without great change into the computer banks of news organizations and thence into print.

Although the entry into television of the Associated Press and Reuters, the two largest news agencies, has helped make video news from abroad more accessible, the agencies are still heavily print oriented. "A newspaper correspondent is on the scene with a pencil and pad, or a notebook computer. To match that, there have to be at least four, and often five, television people," an American network producer in Europe explained.[1]

As network coverage of the world faded, both AP and Reuters expanded their television efforts. Their output now is a video version of their text wires rather than a broadcast network in the traditional sense. Satellite feeds, digital editing equipment, and small video cameras are the technical ingredients of the program, and the worldwide network of bureaus is the human ingredient. New editing equipment makes it possible for three or four people to do the studio work of thirty or forty. With a little training for the agencies' print reporters on video cameras, they can do an acceptable job of recording the news, and the producers and camera personnel who work on video full time produce quality comparable to that of the network crews. Satellites already in use for print and still photo transmissions can speed the footage from Reuters and AP bureaus to networks and stations around the world.

Reuters, which has equipped seventy-seven of its bureaus with television capability, files sixty news and sports stories a day for television. Some of them, like the AP's, appear on American television screens tuned to the networks or the local programs of large commercial stations. These television reports are produced in the same style as the written AP and Reuters dispatches: objective, succinct, and factual. For the most part, the correspondents are reporting from their home bases—rather than having been rushed in from half a world away—and they know and understand the issues.

In both video and text, the basic supply of international news to American outlets is much better than it has ever been. For decades, the news agencies were hampered by the slow speed of transmission (sixty-five words per minute) and weak links from distant parts of the world. Now the Associated Press alone files twenty million words a day. Newspaper subscribers can choose from service packages that range from twenty to fifteen hundred stories a day.

The United States' AP claims to be the world's largest wire, picture, and television service, but Reuters, the British-based international agency, competes with AP in all these fields, taking up the slack left when United Press International, the other main American news agency, was hit by management and financial troubles. Two well-regarded European news services, Agence France-Presse and the Deutsche Presse-Agentur, have expanded their international coverage and appear from time to time in U.S. newspapers. China's Xinhua, or New China News Agency, has more employees than any of the other news services, but despite the professionalism of many of its reporters and editors, it cannot be compared with them as an unbiased source of news. Russia's Itar-TASS gained independence but lost government subsidies after the fall of Communism.

The New York Times News Service is big enough to be considered in the ranks of all but the largest news agencies. It sends out 150 stories a day from

Times correspondents as well as those from Bloomberg Business News, the States News Service, the Hearst and Cox newspaper groups, and about twenty-five other newspapers, including foreign news providers like the *Boston Globe* and *San Francisco Chronicle*. The service has 650 customers in fifty-three countries. The New York Times Service and Los Angeles Times–Washington Post Service, with more than six hundred clients, have surpassed United Press International, once in the first rank, in coverage from abroad. Reuters has always been stronger in international news than the AP. It has bureaus in 163 countries; AP counts ninety-five bureaus in seventy-two foreign countries. Each has a far larger network of part-time or local journalists who file from other points to their bureaus.

Unbiased coverage is the raison d'être of the traditional news agencies, not only because it is a standard of the profession, but also because it is a selling point and, sometimes, a necessity for reporters' access to countries with authoritarian regimes.

The attacks on Washington and New York put Reuters in the middle of a dispute about what constitutes bias. Its policy of avoiding terms like "terrorist" in news stories was heavily criticized after the attacks on the World Trade Center, which cost six Reuters employees their lives. An internal memo noting that "one man's terrorist is another's freedom fighter" was condemned by clients and Reuters' own staff. But the agency stood by its practice. Using neutral terms helps it defend its reporters against charges of propaganda, the agency said, and gives them access to countries that ordinarily limit foreign reporting.

Jonathan Fenby, a former Reuters editor who surveyed the world's news agencies for the 20th Century Fund, noted that all the agencies began in business with the basic idea that "a single satisfactory report could be provided to a large number of recipients whose politics, editorial values, and publication schedules differed widely." This policy continues today, he said, "so that Agence France-Presse can provide the same coverage for subscribers in Peking or Pretoria." Or Peoria and other U.S. cities, I might add, which brings up the second of Fenby's basic practices for news agencies. Their standard procedure is to pin their stories on sources, usually avoiding the opinions of their reporters. "Demonstrably correct information is their stock in trade," Fenby says. "Traditionally, they report at a reduced level of responsibility, attributing their information to spokesmen, the press, or other sources."[2]

It's easy to understand why many wire editors on American newspapers are reluctant to use agency copy that is thus constricted, particularly when the neighboring style and entertainment pages are awash in anecdotes, gossip, and long descriptions of how the writers feel. It is possible to go beyond the limits of this strict "it was announced today" journalism, as the AP proved when it won the Pulitzer Prize in 2000 for its exposure of the No Gun Ri massacres of Korean civilians by U.S. troops during the Korean War. But the controversy over whether all of that story's supposed eyewitnesses were telling the truth made some at the agency wonder whether it wasn't safer to stick to the traditional kind of wire service reporting.

The expansion of the news services of the nation's leading newspapers pushed the traditional wire services in the direction of longer and more analytical reporting. The New York Times and Chicago Daily News had been transmitting the dispatches of their foreign and national correspondents since before World War II, using the revenue to help pay for the cost of their own coverage. The Los Angeles Times–Washington Post entry into the field was followed by many others, including a service founded by Knight Ridder which became KRT when the Chicago Tribune joined it. "What the supplementals offer is access to the reporting resources of some of the biggest U.S. newspapers," Fenby observed. "Smaller dailies can run coverage that would otherwise be far beyond their means, while the originating newspapers can offset part of their reporting costs."3

These supplements provide a single story rather than the running accounts offered by the news agencies, which suits some newspapers needing only one finished version of a foreign disaster or political event. But some smaller paper editors complain that too many of the stories they are given seem to be written primarily for the correspondent's own paper, with a larger news hole, and are often difficult to fit into their own more modest space. The New York Times Service instituted a shortening desk to prepare shorter reports for papers that can't handle the length of Times dispatches from distant places or don't consider them worth that much wordage.

Trust is the main currency of both the newspapers' supplemental services and the news agencies. It's become more important than ever in the age of the Internet, when wanderers onto Web sites don't have the assurance of accuracy and objectivity that a wire service report in a newspaper or broadcast has. Trust is nurtured by impartiality. The Associated Press tries to achieve both through its cooperative ownership arrangement, in which American newspapers (but not radio stations or foreign papers) are the owners of the organization and exert their ownership rights the way that powerful shareholders everywhere do. The AP's longtime chief executive, Louis Boccardi, reports regularly to a board made up of members large and small. A larger group, the Associated Press Managing Editors (APME), evaluates and monitors the AP's output.

Reuters has the special arrangement of a "founder's share," a block of stock that can outvote any or all the others if there is an attempt to take over the organization by "any one interest, group, or faction." Another safeguard for the agency's objectivity is a provision that no single shareholder can own more than 15 percent of the stock. For decades, United Press International had the anchor of ownership by the Scripps-Howard newspaper chain, but after it was cut loose in 1991, it went through a variety of owners and ended up the property of the Reverend Sun Yung Moon's Unification Church.

FOREIGN CORRESPONDENTS

Ian Stewart came from a family of journalists and never wanted to be anything other than a foreign correspondent. After journalism school and jobs at two newspapers, he bought a one-way ticket to China to start a freelance career that took him to forty countries in Asia and Africa. He covered wars and the victims of warfare until he became one himself in a nearly fatal attack in Sierra Leone in 1999.

Stewart began as a stringer, a freelance correspondent usually paid by the story or wordage, which was once measured by a length of string. Later, hired first by UPI and then AP, he wrote about Hong Kong's transition from British to Chinese rule, the refugees left in Afghanistan from fighting in the 1990s, and India's conflict with Pakistan in Kashmir. He had tea with the Dalai Lama and interviewed India's prime minister. Sent to Hanoi, he learned Vietnamese and put up with government wiretaps on his office.

In Africa, Stewart covered urban gun battles between government and rebel troops in the numerous insurgencies that swept the western part of the continent. He was assaulted by a mob and harassed and threatened by officials and anyone carrying a gun. In daily dispatches for the AP, he wrote about the fighting, but he also took time to write about the costs of war. Stewart was a war correspondent, but he was also a peace correspondent, writing about children, those who had been killed or maimed by rebel forces in a terror campaign and those as young as a nine-year-old he interviewed who had been coerced into fighting and hacking off limbs. "Sierra Leone is a nation whose next generation has been destroyed," Stewart wrote.[4]

In the town of Mansao in Guinea-Bissau, he talked to the grandmother of a baby whose mother had been killed in the fighting. The story he filed for the AP wire began this way: "He's a little boy, an infant born eight months ago in an impoverished, largely ignored West African country. Now, with the withered face of an old man, he's dying minute by minute." The doctor at the makeshift clinic said Adao, the baby, had malnutrition and dysentery. Plasma could save his life, but none was available. In the next room, an eighteen-year old woman was giving birth to a healthy baby girl. "Overwhelmed by the unfair juxtaposition of life and death at the clinic, I began to cry," Stewart wrote later in a book about his experiences in Africa.[5]

Stewart says he felt he had two jobs as a foreign correspondent: to cover the news as it broke and to tell the world about Adao and the many other victims of warfare. "I write for the general public so they will be appalled and get involved, and I also write for the Beltway in Washington," Stewart says. "We can't stop wars, but we hope our words and images can provoke people to do that."[6]

Only a few foreign correspondents have the grisly experiences that Stewart had, but in the current age of scattered insurgencies and terrorists, more and more are becoming used to the risks and dangers that often go with the job. Still, one correspondent can remain for decades in a comfortable corner of a foreign capital noting the rise and fall of cabinets and stock markets, writing about or filming new ideas, fashions, and plays, while another can lurch from crisis to disaster, from terrorist attack to revolution.

A correspondent can spend a tour of several years, as I did, to a country where *nothing happened*. The old German chancellor retired, and the new one was far less interesting. The Russians threatened West Berlin's independence but never actually did anything about it. The East Germans boasted of production miracles that we later learned were fabricated, but they also banned access to their country to prevent anyone's checking their claims. Minor war criminals were exposed; the big ones remained in hiding. We nevertheless wrote thousands of words on all these subjects and did our best to file them before our competitors did.

In another period, I covered the Black September civil war in Jordan, the death of Egypt's Gamal Abdel Nasser and the disorders that it set off, and the shipyard workers' uprising against Communist rule in Poland, all in the space of a few months.

Many correspondents grow restless trying to chronicle the minutiae of political and economic change in a stable society and agitate for transfer or at least rotation to the places where the bombs are going off. Others welcome the chance to chart long-term trends such as the rise of extremist movements that might shake the stability of those societies or the growth of innovation and productivity that would benefit them. These kinds of stories don't involve explosions or danger, but they can contribute as much to readers' or viewers' understanding of the world as can the accounts of who was firing at whom.

This is not to argue that thoughtful journalism is confined to the ranks of those who cover the parliaments and bourses of settled societies. Those correspondents and producers familiar with terror and war, like John F. Burns of the *New York Times* or CBS's Leslie Cockburn, supply the explanations of what caused the shooting to start and what will happen when or if it stops. They owe their insight to their close-up experience, for which there is no substitute.

Most foreign correspondents start out with the wire services. Bloomberg, the worldwide financial and general news agency founded by Michael Bloomberg before he became mayor of New York City, has joined the AP and Reuters in hiring for overseas posts. All but gone from the job market is United Press International, with its tradition of hiring young men and women abroad and paying them so little that in Paris, at least, a helpful black market money changer used to add value to their meager dollar salaries with a special franc rate for regulars.

That kind of romance is absent in Bloomberg's operation, with seventy-nine bureaus around the world producing information for Bloomberg's wire service, Web site, radio, television, and magazines, as well as the more than 150,000 Bloomberg boxes, terminals that provide investors with market news and analysis. This effort takes more than a thousand reporters—about half the number that Reuters and the Associated Press each employ, although exact comparisons are difficult because of different methods of counting. Reuters lists about 2,100 journalists, photographers, and cameramen around the world; the AP says its total worldwide staff is 3,700, two-thirds of whom are involved in news gathering. Across the world, there are probably six thousand to seven thousand journalists working for the international news agencies and broadcasters.

Bloomberg reporters and their counterparts in the other agencies have to know the economics and politics of the countries they cover. The best of them also soak up languages and insights into foreign society. This, combined with experience and luck, sometimes lands them jobs as newspaper correspondents or, more rarely, broadcasters.

Is it better to have correspondents based abroad, covering a country or region, or to send out fire brigades every time there is an earthquake or a government is overthrown? Those who favor the parachute approach argue that a good journalist can cover any story, that language difficulties can be compensated for by interpreters, that it's better to have close links to the home office and a feel for what people at home want to read or watch. Those who work out of the home office are more in touch with the needs and wants of their editors or producers as well as their readers and audience. They are also better able to play the role of adviser and advocate for their stories and story ideas, actions sometimes known as office politics.

Parachutists, those ready to go abroad—anywhere—at a moment's notice, often have in guts or skills the attributes to make up for their lack of local knowledge and languages. Their main advantage may be the familiar face or byline they bring to a story, which makes it more likely to be viewed or read.

The appearance at a scene of crisis of the three main television anchors is the high point of this recognition factor, as evidenced by the triple-anchor coverage of the pope's visit to Cuba in 1998, although it has become rarer for foreign events to appear in the general contraction of the space that their networks devote to news from abroad.

Those who want a correspondent on the ground base their arguments on expertise: having someone who has an array of sources and knows how the place works, politically, economically, and culturally. Their expertise gives these foreign-based correspondents an edge in disasters and coups, but it is most valuable in situations without a dramatic focal point, such as a slide into famine or an unmanageable burden of foreign debt, or plans for recovering from such afflictions. Correspondents based abroad have the advantage of living in the society of their country or region and, on the basis of this knowledge, being able to chart its long-term trends as well as the day-to-day actions in the government and economy. Those who know the language have another dimension, literature and the theater, to probe, and a decided edge in understanding the gossip, street, and market talk that are often as important as the pronouncements of officials. Nick Daniloff of *U.S. News & World Report* went to the Russian equivalent of PTA meetings in Moscow because his son was in a public school. His contacts with other parents were priceless in the closed Soviet society. They enabled him to report on the anger among ordinary Russians at the increasing toll of the Soviet war in Afghanistan, one of the factors leading to the collapse of Communism.

A third way of approaching foreign reporting, somewhere in between these two opposing practices, is gaining ground. Some correspondents travel, not to suddenly flaring trouble spots, but on regular and routine assignments that are part of a domestic/foreign beat. With the Internet, they can read the *Bangkok Post* or *Buenos Aires Herald* every day. Some can manage papers in local languages. All can follow BBC or CNN reports on their areas, read the output of the local news agencies, and check speeches and statements from governments and opposition. If their home office is in a big enough city, there are also lots of visitors from the places they cover to provide information for attribution or not. The *Portland Oregonian's* Rich Read, based in the United States, covers the Pacific Rim, a region of great importance to Oregon's economy. Yves Colon of the *Miami Herald* travels frequently to Haiti. The *San Diego Union-Tribune* supplies the same kind of coverage of the Mexican-U.S. border region with a two-person Tijuana bureau, frequent trips across the border by a reporter covering Baja California business, and a federal court specialist covering drug arrests.

Sandra Dibble worked as a foreign correspondent only a few miles from her home office. Her beat was Tijuana, Mexico, and her paper was the *Union*

Tribune of San Diego, close to the border. For eight years, Dibble covered politics, crime, and daily life from the Mexican side of the border, an assignment she continues now while based in San Diego. Her contacts and experience enable her to explain to her readers why the political changes in Mexico since the election of Vicente Fox have helped the crackdown on crime syndicates in Baja California, which for years was at odds with the central government. She also guides San Diego readers to art shows, concerts, and street food and tells how Tijuanans celebrate small victories like a family member's graduation from junior high school:"If you just saw the crooked fence, the dusty dogs and the neighbors banging on their cars, you might just keep going, very slowly, so your car wouldn't hit a rut," she wrote of one neighborhood. "Not a lot to celebrate, some might say. But here, barely a month goes by without some kind of festivity." Dibble says, "I feel like my job is—and should be—a cross between local reporter and foreign correspondent."[7]

Another great difference among correspondents is their basic approach to their jobs. They ask, Do my editors want me to follow the day-to-day flow of breaking news, matching or beating the wire services in their accounts of cabinet changes, strikes, or rioting? Do they want me to detach myself, write about sweeping but very slow changes in the countryside, get out to the villages, ignore the day-to-day doings of government? Or do they want me to do both—get out to the country but be ready when somebody plants a bomb in the prime minister's car? No American Express employee would ever go abroad with such a vague set of instructions, but foreign correspondents do. The preference of the correspondent also figures in this equation. Someone with a Washington background might be more comfortable dealing with the officials, legislatures, and embassies (particularly the American) of the foreign country's Washington, whereas someone who covered the environment or science might spend more time on the bigger picture of the country or region.

The cost of running a bureau abroad and the promotional value to the home office of having foreign correspondents can sometimes tempt editors to assign stories of little importance that the wires could handle as well. This practice limits the correspondent's time to explore issues that the wires don't often cover. But it shouldn't be a matter of either/or. The correspondent can't have a lofty detachment from everyday events, or he or she won't be able to understand the big picture. And when the usually desk-bound journalists of the wire services do get the time to report on a big-picture project, their familiarity with the day-to-day events is a great asset. They have a range of trusted sources to work with and the ability to fit small pieces of an economic or political puzzle into a story that describes and explains a national or regional trend—in refugee movements, industrial problems, or threats to democratic institutions.

Trust is of the highest importance in both the use of sources and the employment of stringers. In both cases, it's a reciprocal relation. The embassy political analyst or government official who provides not-for-attribution information to the correspondent knows its source will be protected—otherwise, no more information. The correspondent keeps this confidence with future needs in mind.

Stringers depend on repeated assignments or acceptances, filing either through the local correspondent or directly to the newspaper or broadcaster. One inaccurate element in a story is enough to cut off the relationship, not only with the correspondent for whom it was written but also the entire local press corps. Stringers can be of enormous help to a correspondent who must cover more than a single capital or region. Sometimes the region is so large that careful checking of the stringers' sources is impossible. In these cases, correspondents, and sometimes their editors, must trust the stringer. Usually their trust is justified; stringers are often respected and experienced local journalists who want to keep filing for the foreign media.

But there are many examples of stories that are filled with inaccuracies or exaggeration and in some cases complete fabrications. The news services and syndicates sometimes make mistakes in sourcing or quotes, but every foreign editor can recite a long list of freelancers who have concocted interviews and manufactured facts, as in the famous cases of a writer's fictional encounter with the Cambodian war criminal Pol Pot that appeared in the *New York Times Magazine* or the British television team that used actors and a concocted script to fake a Colombian drug lord documentary that made it to CBS's 60 *Minutes*. The *Times* magazine was deceived a second time in 2002 when a freelancer admitted that he had misrepresented the experiences of the title character in his article on slavery on Ivory Coast cocoa plantations.

A video journalist in Italy scooped the world with what were marketed as the first pictures of the Chernobyl nuclear meltdown. Both NBC and ABC bought the footage, paying him $25,000 for shots of a cooling tower in Trieste.

El Nuevo Herald of Miami was taken in by claims that Fidel Castro had a rare brain disease, purportedly made by a Cuban doctor who had defected to Costa Rica. The mistake was magnified when the *Miami Herald* picked up the story from its Spanish-language partner and ran it on the front page. It turned out that the informant could not have treated Castro, since she wasn't a doctor.

A Web site that claimed to be crusading against censorship offered a photograph of Princess Diana as she lay dying in the wreck of her limousine in Paris. The picture was a fake, but it was published in the Paris newspaper *France Soir* and widely distributed across the Internet. Those running the Web site said they knew it was counterfeit.

"The great frauds are perpetrated by those who parachute in for four hours," Tom Bettag of *Nightline* asserted. "If they stage faked scenes, you can pretty well tell [from raw footage]. But if it's edited, there are dangers inherent that are just massive," since skillful editing can camouflage fakery. "You can edit, sure, but how can you be sure that every bit of information is journalistic, or is it serving some cause?" a newspaper wire editor asked. He tries to check the clippings and résumés of prospective stringers as well as interview them before they go abroad, but often, he says, this process is neglected because of the urgent needs of breaking news abroad and the urge to have your own reporter on the scene.[8]

The power relationship between correspondents and editors is complex and, as with American Express employees sent abroad, dependent on many variables. The one basic element is that correspondents don't fire or recall editors but editors can fire or recall correspondents. Nevertheless, powerful senior reporters in the field have great leverage in discussions with the lower-ranking staff members who are the first gatekeepers for the arriving copy. Both can appeal to the higher-ups in the editorial structure, and thus the correspondent may win many decisions.

A newsmagazine correspondent whose career spanned the old days of slow and expensive transatlantic calls and the instant communication of the Internet says the old system provided much more protection from the interference from headquarters. "I'd be working on a story I'd developed myself, getting it ready to file, when the rockets would come in from New York, suggesting or demanding this or that angle," he said. "I could always tell by the timing that they'd just finished reading the *New York Times* and *Washington Post*."[9]

Editors and correspondents disagree on predictable lines whether it is better for the story ideas to come from headquarters or the foreign bureau. Most correspondents report a mix of varying proportions of assigned and original stories. In crisis areas, the daily briefings often dictate what is filed, whatever the preferences of the editors or bureau people. Veteran correspondents agree that the best way to avoid too much long-distance direction is to know your beat, work hard at your reporting, write or broadcast dispatches that will attract an audience, and, in the words of one bureau chief who has worked for both broadcast and print, "Overwhelm them with so many stories that they'll leave you alone."[10]

Without long experience in a foreign country and without the local bureau support that used to be available for the larger news organizations all over the world, it's difficult to do much investigative journalism abroad. There are multiple barriers of language, social systems in which openness is rare, and government and corporate policies that discourage access to information, particularly by an outsider. Some correspondents manage to overcome all these difficulties, almost always with the help of good local bureau support, familiarity with the country and language, and encouragement from home offices to skip some of the day-to-day stories in pursuit of those taking weeks or months to complete. "You deal with weak institutions and a labyrinth of secrecy," Sebastian Rotella of the *Los Angeles Times* says of his work in Latin America. "There's a paucity of facts and an abundance of versions."[11]

Rotella went to the Paraguayan-Argentinean-Brazilian border to investigate Ciudad del Este, a Paraguayan city of lawlessness where smugglers, Chinese gangs, and Arab merchants funding Hezbollah terrorists operated. "The polyglot mix of thugs epitomizes a foremost menace of the post–Cold War world: the globalization of organized crime," he wrote in 1998. As a result of Rotella's story, the United States' Federal Bureau of Investigation began working with police in the three border nations.[12]

The *New York Times*'s Larry Rohter sought out another part of the Brazilian jungle in 2002 to uncover what the government admitted were "contemporary forms of slavery." Rohter found that workers in timber camps and cattle farms deep in the Amazon interior "are held in unpaid, coerced labor" by ranchers who get away with the practice by bribing corrupt officials. Despite some efforts by human rights groups and the government that have freed a few thousand slave laborers, he wrote, Catholic Church activists put their number at 25,000, a fivefold increase in a decade.[13]

As the kidnapping and death of *Wall Street Journal* reporter Daniel Pearl showed, investigative reporting on terrorism is on a much different and more difficult level. No terrorist is going to give away his plans to a reporter. But with a well-staffed bureau, long in place, and a network of informants, someone who knows the terrorist might. Pearl's contacts with the man convicted of his execution, Sheik Omar Saeed, were part of his investigative efforts in the wake of the September 11 attacks. Two months before his abduction in Karachi, he had gone to a gem mine in Tanzania in search of al-Qaeda links. Many of the gems, called Tanzanite, will end up at Zales or Tiffany, Pearl wrote, "but it's a long way from these dusty plains to U.S. jewelry stores, and the stones pass through many hands on their journey. Some of those hands, it is increasingly clear, belong to active supporters of Osama bin Laden." Pearl also frequented miners' bars and cafés for his evidence. "Yes, people here are trading for Osama," a miner told him. "Just look around, and you will find serious Muslims who believe in him and work for him."[14]

Isn't investigative work like this a job for the CIA and other government agents? Journalists don't surrender their investigative and monitoring function to the CIA and other government agents at home, and many have succeeded in penetrating the layers of bureaucracy and crime.

Commitment is the key, whether the correspondent is based in the home office or in a distant bureau. Sources must be cultivated, political twists and turns monitored. Filing a daily story is the least of it—anticipating the next day's or month's story is work that goes on regardless of deadlines. Being a foreign correspondent is more than a full-time job.

Ian Stewart's commitment is what got him abroad in the first place and helped him work his way from stringer to West Africa bureau chief for AP. It's what made him take one more trip into Freetown on the day that rebel soldiers opened fire, hitting Stewart in the head and killing his Associated Press colleague, television producer/cameraman Myles Tierney. Stewart, who was flown to London with a bullet lodged in his brain, was given only a 20 to 40 percent chance of survival.

But he did survive and slowly recovered. The story he wrote about his experiences was given an award for feature writing at the Associated Press Managing Editors' convention. In that story, he told how he hoped to go back overseas when he was well enough to do so but was pessimistic about the impact his work might have on readers: "Myles, David [Guttenfelder, the AP photographer] and I were naive to hope our reporting could make people care about a little war in Africa. In fact, Freetown might never have made your daily newspaper had it not been for the death of one Western journalist and the wounding of another." He concluded: "Will I risk my life for a story again? No, not even if the world cares next time."[15]

"Do you still feel that way?" Ed Jones, editor of the *Freelance-Star* of Fredericksburg, Virginia, asked during the award ceremony.

"Actually, I don't," Stewart said. "It's changed. I think I wrote that a little bit early." Far from having it ignored by the world, he said, "I've seen that our reporting really did raise some flags and make people aware that it was something to pay attention to. And I'd like to think that was the beginning of raising awareness at the UN, with the United States, with Great Britain, to get some involvement that started the ball rolling."

Jones asked Stewart why he had wanted to be a foreign correspondent.

"I wanted to change the world."

"Do you want to be a foreign correspondent still, for that same reason?"

"I do. I want to get back to work. I want to make the world a little bit better, a little bit more peaceful. I'm not a doctor, I'm not an aid worker. But I really do believe that my words can raise awareness and hopefully the people that are qualified to change the world will pay attention to my words and make an effort."

Words like Ian Stewart's tell more than do countless studies about what constitutes the purpose of the news business. Is it directed by the goals of the marketing people, executives who don't care whether the product is hamburgers or information for the public? Or is it there as a public trust, with profits a necessary but secondary consideration? Is the media's main role to inform, educate, and enlighten their readers, viewers, and listeners or to produce 20 percent plus margins for their stockholders? Should foreign correspondents be concerned that opinion polls regularly rate journalists far below elected officials, ministers, nurses, and pharmacists?

The thousands of men and women who report from abroad, many in dangerous situations, none very well paid, and all subject to the major and minor restrictions and annoyances of life in another country, answer these questions every day with their own commitment.

CHANNELING THE FLOOD

It might surprise readers looking for better foreign coverage in their local papers that the complaint in many newsrooms is that they receive too much copy rather than too little. Editors senior enough to have complained about the old slow tickers now say they can't keep up with the thousands and thousands of words that flow across their computer screens. Even the wire services' frequent advisories of stories to expect, some say, are often too much to handle.

With news from Asia arriving all night and news from Europe and Africa replacing it in the morning, followed by Latin America, these editors must deal with the unexpected and unplanned event in a way their colleagues on city or regional desks seldom have to. The contrast comes out at editorial meetings, like one I attended at the *Seattle Times*, where every local and regional reporter or editor had his or her story idea, with a set of city and county meetings, trials, and hearings to guide them. At the state and national levels, the day's schedule of the governor, president, legislature, or Congress could be penciled in.

There was confident chitchat among a dozen department heads about what was going to be reported, written, and photographed. "We're going to have good color on that schooner launching . . . the cocaine cure programs advertising on television need to be looked into . . . something on health today for certain from Washington."

This familiarity and predictability stopped dead when it was the turn of the foreign staff. Aside from long-running crises involving Americans, everything was open. The unknown news could be a hostage taking or a little-understood and hard-to-explain economic collapse in Asia. The wire desk was also in a perpetual quandary on how to cover whatever was going to happen abroad. The city desk can assign reporters to anticipate breaking news. Only a few of the largest newspapers have to worry about whether to fly a correspondent from Delhi to the Gulf. But as a foreign desk editor on another paper noted, he and his colleagues must ponder, every time the news of a big breaking story starts to come in, "How will the wires handle this? Will I be able to get a summary or wrap-up from the *Washington Post* or *New York Times?*"

The only foreign editor with complete control over the placement of news from abroad works for the *International Herald Tribune*, in which every story is a foreign one. Every other foreign editor must bargain, fight, and compromise to get his or her place on the front page or other sections where readers are more likely to see it. Foreign editors come in a variety of titles, depending on the size of the newspaper, including wire, national and foreign, and assistant managing editor/foreign. What they have in common is a comparatively modest position in the table of organization and, as visits to many newsrooms show, comparatively little weight in the decision-making process. Some foreign stories make the first page without question: an election in Israel, a major disaster, unusually grave violence in Northern Ireland. Some, like bus wrecks in Bolivia, are always destined for remote pages to fill out columns. Most of the daily run of foreign news falls in between these categories, and often the best work a foreign editor or foreign staff member can do is to make these stories attractive and interesting. "Editors want the background that explain news events abroad," a wire editor said. "They want something that can speak more directly to their own readers, tell them what it means in human terms, what it is like. The wires promise to do this, but they don't very often." This means that editors have to step in to provide context themselves. "My time can best be spent by sorting out the great number of supplemental services plus two main wire services, and particularly in working with stringers, filling in the gaps in their stories, passing along suggestions and story ideas," an editor on the two-person foreign desk staff of a metropolitan newspaper said. "What I like to do best is craft stories, cutting down the thirty-six-inch stories filed by the supplemental services to half that."[16]

Both editors said the best way to win the arguments is to present well-told stories that can stand up in the competition against the local material that dominates their papers.

It's not surprising that foreign editors like the idea of having as many reporters covering the world as city editors do covering their local beat. But local reporters are relatively cheap, and their needs do not include housing, interpreters, and transmission expenses. Using part-time correspondents saves money but has its limitations and sometimes problems. Simple economics—although the cost of a bureau abroad keeps rising, it is said to range between $250,000 and $1 million—usually rule out sending out full-time correspondents.

Foreign editors say there is a gap in coverage that isn't properly filled by any of the vast resources they have, including the wire services and the big-paper news syndicates. It is the ability to discuss story ideas, assign projects, or encourage suggestions from a reporter or stringer abroad. With a correspondent in the field, the process is simple. Without that, it becomes a matter of patching together arrangements.

"Editors want, above all, a kind of sourcing that transcends the usual spokesmen in the capital and political leaders," a foreign editor with experience as a correspondent abroad explained. "Sometimes syndicated material does this. But neither the syndicates nor the wires are able to respond to the ideas and queries of the editor."[17]

The solution often is finding a stringer. A good man or woman in the field, the editor pointed out, gives the paper a closer-to-the ground approach and can often provide tie-ins between events abroad and interests of the newspaper's readers back home: "The best way is to build up your own corps, either on your own or through sharing with newspapers of the size and general outlook of your own." Some sharing arrangements have worked well, but others have broken down in conflicts over which editor assigns which story and how they handle local angles for multiple readerships. Wire editors agree that the AP provides too much detail and too many little stories but disagree as to whether it should limit its coverage to big-picture summaries. One editor would like "a story that puts—once a week or once a month—the Kosovo situation into perspective so we can understand what that means." Another thinks it's necessary for his staff to keep closely informed every day about trends and processes abroad, but to shift to the longer view, if possible, when a major story breaks. "I think we are going to be missing a bet with a lot of our readers if we are not on top of daily news developments." he said. "The best way to do that, for those of us who are fortunate enough to get supplemental wires, is with a story that breaks with enough time so that supplemental wires can do it. We will almost always use the *Washington Post* or *Los Angeles Times*."[18]

The sheer volume of daily copy makes it difficult for the staffs of smaller papers to make these kinds of judgments. Most of the nation's newspapers don't have foreign editors or even national editors. The task of sorting through the national and foreign news often falls on the copy desk in small papers, on a staff of one or two. Many copy editors also make up the pages on their computer screens. The paper's top editors choose what goes on the front page, but the copy editors often decide which foreign stories to run in the space left to them. Editors concede that with the limited pay and recognition given to copy editors, they're unrealistic to expect them to become foreign experts, although many do, nevertheless. Getting the paper out is what they're paid to do, and sending on the made-up page forms, whatever their content, takes top priority. The help wanted ads for copy editors in *Editor and Publisher* show that many managers are seeking a makeup person first and a professional who cares about story selection and structure second. It's the final legacy of the fight for automation of newspaper production that, beginning in the 1960s, pitted crafts unions against management and was supposed to save large sums of money that would be plowed back into news coverage. The *New York Daily News* had about 750 editorial and advertising employees and 250 typographers in 1990, when it was torn by a bitter strike. At the end of the conflict, the typographers were gone, and the white-collar employees who remained took over the chores of production through computer systems. Across the nation, union members lost their jobs or were bought out with severance benefits. There were great savings in costs, but the consequence was that the work of production was transferred to the journalists. Where staffing is adequate, this means pushing a button to send a story into the system rather than taking a sheet of paper out of a Royal or Underwood. Where it isn't, it means neglecting some of the professional duties of journalists: selecting, editing, querying about, and rewriting copy, whether local or foreign.

Copy editors greeted the technological changes at first with resistance, looking on the new systems as a way of saving the company money, not necessarily extending deadlines or improving the content and appearance of their papers. Then, as the systems became more widespread, they began to see the benefits, particularly of no longer having to worry about a sometimes sticky back shop that slowed down or messed up late-breaking stories.

At the heart of the problem is pagination. In the old days, copy editors edited, added, subtracted, rewrote, and wrote headlines for individual stories, marked their positions on dummy pages, and sent them down to the composing room to turn into type. Now the makeup or design is done on copy desk computers. Most agree that pagination has increased the amount of work for the copy desk; some estimates say by as much as 20 percent. Publishers, who write the paychecks, have greeted this phenomenon by either keeping copy desk staffs constant and making them produce more, or hiring or training specialists to handle the pagination, just as they do for the other specialized needs of the paper. "In effect, pagination shifts makeup work done in the back shop into the newsroom," the University of Oregon's John Russial, a former copy editor, reasoned. "It can save page production time and it certainly saves money overall but, by most accounts, does not save time in the newsroom. In fact, it typically takes up more time. The burden lands squarely on the desk."[19]

George Krimsky, a news consultant who reported and edited foreign news for the Associated Press, claims that this affects the selection process for foreign news.

> In a lot of smaller newspapers we see that with increased pagination duties, they're not reading all the wire stories—they're just looking at the digest and depending on the digest for what their big international story will be. They're not scrolling through the whole wire because they haven't got time anymore.[20]

One solution is to have the AP and Reuters, as well as the supplemental services tied to the big newspapers, provide the advice on importance and timeliness that small newspapers do not have the resources to provide themselves. This editorial service has two components. The first, long established, tells the wire editors what new stories and developments are coming and when, with updates every few hours throughout the news cycle. This is generally welcomed in newsrooms, although some wire editors complain about a plethora of advisories on stories they don't intend to use anyway. The second is recommending an order of importance, which is welcomed by some harried copy editors and resented by others who see the system as outsiders imposing their news judgment on the local paper. The television sets tuned to CNN, after all, keep a running account in most newsrooms of what's going on in the world. One argument for the rating system is that it protects inexperienced copy desk staff from skipping a major story that might be on the front pages of other papers the following morning. An argument against it is that if followed too closely, it would take too little account of local readers' interests. A major story about trade with Asia is more likely to make page A1 on the West Coast than it is on the East; and the reverse can be true about Ireland and the EU.

"We've been engaged for a long time in trying to make international news understandable to a U.S. audience," Tom Kent, AP's deputy managing editor, noted. "It's an ongoing process and not always an easy one. We are trying to provide more explanatory copy; we're trying to gauge the moment at which a story suddenly is likely to attract attention and giving people a point of entry to that story at that time." As an example, he cited the European Union's introduction of the euro. The new currency unit had been discussed for years, but when a summit finally made the decision to adopt it, AP editors decided reader interest would be high enough to warrant a Q and A feature, something they probably wouldn't have felt was necessary a few years earlier.[21]

Kent said the AP is responding to editors' concerns about less space for foreign news by supplying two versions of important stories. An example was a

2,700-word account of the challenges facing the Arab world, with details and comments from many capitals, which was also sent out in a thousand-word version. "We think it was worth 2,700, but we also moved a thousand word version, and there are many international stories that are moving at five hundred words or less," Kent said. "We realize those are some of the realities about putting out a newspaper."[22]

Brevity alone is not the answer to getting foreign news before readers, even in the era of sharply reduced available space. "We probably have a better chance of getting well-written, five-hundred- or six-hundred-word features that say something about West Africa into papers than we do a three-graph brief about the latest thing in Togo," Kent said. "You are looking for something that means something, and I would be willing to trade away five briefs to get in a story and a picture and a graphic that a reader will actually remember."

Krimsky says the competing and sometimes conflicting demands on the wire service staff means that it is constantly stretched in a lot of different directions.

"The AP is under an incredible amount of pressure to do the feature story, the human story, the analysis story and the for-the-record story that some people regard as necessary but sometimes dull," he said. "Do that as well as file radio spots, keep the TV services informed." Correspondents in the field, he added, "are quite well aware of the need for more grass roots, people-oriented stories—and to a certain extent they feel they are providing them and that editors are missing them." With wire and copy editors on smaller papers tied up with pagination and other tasks, he pointed out, not everyone sees all these human interest stories from abroad. The news budgets and advisories that flow over the wire during every cycle have been little help in drawing attention to them because their emphasis is on the big news of the day. The grassroots story has begun to get more attention in a redesigned news digest that draws attention to good, well-written accounts that wouldn't necessarily make the front page.[23]

The main problem for foreign news in most American newspapers is the competition with local news for space. "Foreign news is often the first to go when a space crunch happens," an editor who has worked on three medium-size papers admitted. "Smaller space means shorter stories. So while you'll have thirty inches plus sidebars and photos on the local story du jour, you get thirty inches for your two top foreign stories. Not enough space for the stories that step back to take a broad view, so we end up with bus crashes, coups, and earthquakes." But still the foreign copy keeps rolling in, he adds: "Many papers have so many sources—AP, New York Times, L.A. Times–Washington Post, Cox, et cetera., that it's ridiculous—maybe a dozen stories, and more than a thousand to choose from."[24]

Some wire editors are interested enough in foreign news to take the time to select stories, even if it means a great deal of extra work. Some would frankly rather be editing movie reviews or out covering local politics. "Editors wouldn't appoint a copy editor who knew or cared nothing about sports to be the sports editor, or someone ignorant of business to head the business page," this wire editor said. "So why do they take someone from the copy desk who may or may not care about national and foreign and put him or her in charge of choosing the few stories the paper will run on those topics?"[25]

One reason for this lack of attention is that the top editors in many small papers say their franchise is local, not world or even national. It's an argument with two complementary sides. Their readers already get their national and foreign news from CNN or the traditional networks. But only the local newspaper—not the understaffed local television stations, not the Internet, not the nationally distributed editions of the *Wall Street Journal* or the *New York Times*, really covers local news.

Institutional forces are also keeping newspapers in the traditional practice of scattering a little foreign news in the front part of the paper and limiting the number of pages set aside for the background stories available from the wire services and syndicates. The explosive growth of inserts—the glossy ads for food, home improvement, computer, and gardening stores that fatten the dimensions of newspapers on Sundays and other days aimed at consumers—has considerably reduced the space for news. Unlike advertisements in the body of the newspaper, even full-page ones, they provide no place for news on their pages or adjacent ones. Chris Peck, a former *Spokesman-Review* editor in Spokane, said that when he joined the paper in the 1970s, an average weekday issue probably would have run forty-eight to sixty pages. With so much of the advertising now shifted to the inserts, he said, that day's issue was thirty-two pages. Publishers welcome inserts as ad revenue; editors dislike them because they have reduced the size of the news hole. But both agree that if local newspapers didn't carry them, the insert companies would find other ways, mail or direct delivery, to get them to consumers.[26]

Another limitation on the amount of foreign news papers can print is the advertisers' preferences for placement in the news sections. The department stores like to be in the A section, with the national and foreign news. As retailing moves from Main Street to outlying malls, some many miles from the newspaper's home city, department store ads shrink, and so does that paper's national and foreign news hole. Replacement space is hard to find in the rest of the paper. Ads for tires and bars usually accompany the sports news. Small local businesses want to be next to the local news. "These are old patterns that are hard to mess with, particularly if there is no driving force for change, and usually indifference or hostility instead, since change is expensive," a small-town newspaper editor said. "And local news is attractive. We [newspaper staff members] usually have no other background. We easily understand it. We have our own people covering it. And we think, and probably have studies to show, that it sells ads, familiar and repeated ones in the same section."[27]

Editors like James B. Johnson of upstate New York's *Watertown Daily Times* reject these arguments. Johnson packs his front page with national and foreign news, maintains a bureau in Washington, and uses his weekday and Sunday columns for ample explanation and analysis. The paper's *Sunday Weekly* carries articles on national and world issues like water shortages and immigration instead of publicity for celebrities, the main content of many weekend magazines across the country. Johnson says that his staff of two wire editors can concentrate on the news because other editors handle the pagination work. For a readership close to the Canadian border and near the site of Fort Drum, home of the Tenth Mountain Division, which was sent to combat in Afghanistan, international news is a public service, Johnson maintains. But the *Daily Times* does much more than run Canada or army stories. Its unusual policy of putting national and local news on the front page and local news on the back gives it space to cover issues Johnson says people want and need to know about, like U.S.-Chinese relations or ethnic conflict in Macedonia. The family-owned paper, with no corporate profit targets to meet, devotes far more space to news and less to advertising—70 to 30 percent—than most chain papers do. This means Watertown readers can find full accounts of the Bush-Putin talks or Middle East violence in their own *Times* without having to buy the one from New York City. *Editor and Publisher* calls the paper "among the best of its size in the country."[28]

"Who limits the news hole? The publisher," insisted a journalist who returned from freelancing abroad to become a wire editor. In papers large and small across the nation, the real limitation on foreign news coverage is money. More money in the personnel budget would permit hiring more journalists to select, to rewrite, to localize better foreign news stories. Decisions to add extra pages to accommodate more news and background would also mean extra expenses, although advertising might expand in a better newspaper to make up for it. In any case, the decisions lie with management, not the men and women who watch the world's events every day on their computer screens.

MAGAZINES

Close relatives in the print family to newspapers, newsmagazines have experienced a similar drop in coverage of news from abroad, a similar surge after September 11, and a leveling off since then. *Time, Newsweek,* and *U.S. News & World*

Report did more than cut foreign bureaus and slim down their foreign sections in the 1990s. They transformed themselves into consumer and lifestyle magazines, following the advice of marketers who showed that covers on foreign subjects and even nonscandal Washington topics cause newsstand sales to slump dramatically. The same "end of the cold war" that caused or gave newspapers an excuse to lighten up their pages with entertainment, health, and recipes and the same advertising malaise that came with the recession is blamed (or credited) for the changes in the magazines. Audit Bureau of Circulation figures show that all three weeklies lost circulation between 1996 and 2000: *Time* and *Newsweek* by less than 2 percent, but *U.S. News* by more than 8 percent.

Newsmagazine editors say their commitment to foreign news remains high and that nothing in the world that should be covered is neglected. But sometimes when bottom-line priorities get in the way, adjustments are made. Before September 11, after rumors of downsizing to less than weekly publication, *U.S. News* publisher Mortimer Zuckerman told media buyers that his magazine would remain as is, although it did have plans to scale back its coverage of foreign news because of waning interest. *U.S. News*, he said, would concentrate on better-selling news like college rankings and the nation's top hospitals. Shortly thereafter, its bureaus in Beijing, Moscow, and Latin America were closed, and the "World Report" logo on its cover became even less a guide to its contents.

September 11 caught the newsmagazines in their consumer mode, although they quickly deployed correspondents to cover the crisis at home and abroad. *Time* set up a "terrorism" search button on its *Time.com* Web site to help with background, but its only offerings were the stories written after the tragedy plus a few odd bits and pieces three or four years old, about terrorism in Greece. The site thus served as a reminder of the news you can use that had filled the pages of *Time* and the other newsmagazines when they might have been paying more attention to international issues.

By contrast, Britain's *Economist*, which has a growing circulation in the United States, was able to point on its Web site to a series of stories in recent years about the threat of Islamic extremism.

The shrinkage of foreign news in the news magazines is a lesser loss for average readers than is the same trend in their home newspapers. These readers can shop around and find replacements for *Time* if it has gone too fuzzy. But they can't drop their local paper in their search for foreign news because of the local and state news it still carries.

One alternative they turn to increasingly is *The Economist*, whose international focus is apparent from cover to book reviews. Even its coverage of the United States is from an international point of view. *The Economist* publishes sixty-five pages of world news and analysis every week with a very low fluff index, although in 2001 even its editors conceded the need to restyle its makeup a bit because "the modern decision-making reader has little time to wade through dull-looking prose." Like Reuters, the other British-based provider of world news, *The Economist* has a corporate arrangement aimed at guaranteeing its editorial independence by preventing any individual or organization from acquiring majority control. "Other publications within any category you can think of are domestic plus international," *Economist* editor Bill Emmott observed. "But we see ourselves as global." *The Economist's* circulation in North America accounts for 300,000 of its 760,000 readers worldwide. Although *The Economist* has experienced a circulation growth of nearly 70 percent in the last decade, it still reaches only a fraction of *Time's* U.S. circulation of four million.

Time's covers after September 11 showed a clear switch from celebrity to international subjects, and its inside pages, along with those of the other news-magazines, managed to accommodate both serious news from the world along with personalities and entertainment.

Newsmagazine managers may have been discovering what the editors of the nation's top newspapers had known and practiced for years: that it's possible to combine the very best of international and national news reporting with the lighter stories that attract more readers and advertising.

The relevancy of *Nightline* is just not there anymore. —*Disney Corporation executive*

Nightline is not the end of the story. The future of the evening news programs on all the networks has now been put in doubt. —*Senior producer, television news*

4

BROADCASTING

The praise of the nation and the critics for the performance of television news on September 11 and the fight against terrorism that followed was still at a high level half a year later. Although international coverage on the evening news shows had decreased from its peak as the fighting in Afghanistan quieted down, it continued in full measure on some magazine shows, and above all on ABC's *Nightline*. Afghanistan was *Nightline*'s kind of story. The program began in 1979 as an outgrowth of a special nightly roundup on the hostage crisis in Iran, where radicals occupied the U.S. embassy and held fifty-two members of its staff captive for more than a year.

Nightline and its anchor and managing editor, Ted Koppel, seemed to be on their way to another shower of awards from broadcasting's highest arbiters. In the more than twenty-one years the program had been on the air, he had been awarded no fewer than thirty-seven Emmys, six Peabodys, ten duPont-Columbias, nine Overseas Press Club Awards, and two Sigma Delta Chi Awards from the Society of Professional Journalists. Harvard University gave him a lifetime achievement award for excellence in journalism. He and *Nightline* were also honored by *Broadcasting Magazine*, the *Washington Journalism Review*, the Broadcasting Hall of Fame, and the government of France.

In March 2002, *Nightline* received yet another honor: the George Foster Peabody Award, its seventh, for its coverage of the World Trade Center attacks and subsequent crisis. As the jurors at the University of Georgia declared, *Nightline* is "a truly remarkable institution demonstrating the medium's capacity to serve a vital social function, offering the best in long-form news programming for more than 20 years."[1]

That same month Koppel, and the nation, learned in the pages of the *New York Times* that the program's corporate managers think that "the relevancy of *Nightline* is just not there anymore." This quotation came from an anonymous executive of the Disney Corporation, which owns ABC and *Nightline*, to explain why the company was trying to get rid of Koppel's program and replace it with David Letterman's late-night comedy program. It wasn't that *Nightline* didn't make money for Disney. It had earned the network half a billion dollars in its two decades, and it still pulled in five million viewers every night. But if Letterman agreed to leave CBS for ABC, he could earn the network much more, since he appealed to a younger audience and could attract more advertising revenues, Disney executives told the *Times's* television writer, Bill Carter.

Koppel and his producers charged the network with harming the program with its deal making and demanded from Disney "a clear and unmistakable signal to all of our loyal viewers interested in the robust future of network television news that *Nightline* can count on serious corporate backing." No such signal was forthcoming.[2]

Disney's plan to replace substance with comedy could be compared with a decision by the *New York Times* to remove the op-ed page, with its regular columnists and guest experts, and substitute a page of jokes and cartoons. The new page might attract more readers, particularly those in the sought-after eighteen-to-thirty-four age group, and thus raise profit margins. But it would be hard to promote it as a public service.

ABC's parent appeared to have no difficulty in dealing with such a paradox. In the days after September 11, it had pointed with justifiable pride to its performance of *Nightline* in the crisis. Half a year later, the same managers used terms like "sound business management" to explain why they tried to jettison the program. "I'm proud of what we did," one executive told the *Times*. The first chapter of the *Nightline* story ended when Letterman decided not to move to ABC, in part, he said, because of his admiration for Koppel and the program. But despite conciliatory statements on both sides, Disney management made no promises to keep the program in its 11:35 P.M. slot or even on the air at all.

The eventual outcome of the *Nightline* dispute is unknown, but the issue has underscored the dividing line in the three major networks and the nation between advocates of public service and advocates of maximum profit.

"*Nightline* is not the end of the story," a senior producer at another network predicted. "The future of the evening news programs on all the networks has now been put in doubt. The same arguments they applied to *Nightline* apply to them. They are very expensive to produce, and they could be replaced with something that could earn more money." The attempts to dislodge *Nightline*, she noted, were taking place at the same time the industry was full of rumors about possible cost-saving mergers of one of the networks and CNN. Under such arrangements, star anchors might stay on the evening news with their role reduced to hosting and introducing the footage produced by CNN. Reports of salary cuts forced on ABC network correspondents and negotiations on reducing Peter Jennings's pay, she said, lent credence to this scenario.[3]

Television executives were also moving on other fronts that might impact the quality and quantity of the news their viewers receive. Federal courts and the Federal Communications Commission (FCC) have been heeding broadcast industry arguments against rules limiting their ownership and consolidation possibilities. One court struck down rules that prevent cable and broadcast stations in the same market, and another eliminated the FCC's rule limiting the market share of cable companies. The old prohibition against newspaper and television station ownership in the same market seemed likely to disappear, along with one preventing the networks from owning local affiliates that reach more than a third of the national viewing audience. Industry analysts said large media organizations like Chicago's Tribune Company and Viacom, which owns CBS, were likely to try to acquire more stations in big cities.

Making it easier for large corporations to own more media outlets, a spokesman for Consumers Union and an alliance of other consumer groups claimed, "will trigger a wave of mergers that would compound the economic pressures already weakening journalistic quality. Hundreds of newspapers would quickly merge with TV stations and by the time the dust settled, the number of independent owners of major local news media would be slashed by almost one-half."[4]

PUBLIC SERVICE AND PROFITS

Broadcasting got its start in the 1920s in the same way that most newspapers had—founded and expanded by private entrepreneurs, providing a public service but also depending on advertisers for revenue and profits. The founders, William Paley of the Columbia Broadcasting System and David Sarnoff of the National Broadcasting Company, considered public service a good way to promote their business, and in the early years of radio, they were right. Listeners were fascinated by the immediate access to news and even the speeches by public figures that the two networks broadcast. Paley, Sarnoff, and their sales forces converted this interest into ad sales.

New Deal regulations soon added another layer of protection for public service. The Federal Communications Commission was created to ensure that the public benefited from the free use of the airwaves that CBS, NBC, and the smaller networks and individual radio stations enjoyed. When television came along in the 1940s, the FCC's power to define broadcasting in the public interest was extended to cover it.

Television news bloomed after World War II, bringing footage of events from around the world into American living rooms. At first, the news was a few days old because of the need to send film thousands of miles by air cargo. Then, in time for the Gulf War, came satellite feeds and, in time for the Afghan war, the instant videophone images that brought viewers to remote battlefields.

Early television's black-and-white footage superficially resembled the dense black-and-white columns and headlines of the newspapers of the day, but television was a far more powerful means of bringing the world to people at home. It provided action, not accounts of action, and its audience no longer needed the expressive powers of print reporters to describe political rallies, wars, plane crashes, and new ballet stars.

The pictures still needed explanation and interpretation, though, and here the austere columns of type in the good newspapers usually did a better job, although one of the most telling commentaries of the Vietnam War was delivered in a few words by Walter Cronkite: "It seems now more certain than ever that the bloody experience of Vietnam is to end in stalemate . . . with each escalation, the world comes closer to the brink of cosmic disaster."[5] Cronkite's words impressed the nation because viewers had seen him so often in the anchor chair introducing the terrible pictures of the war, an exposure that no one in the print world could achieve.

Foreign news on television was an enormously expensive operation, with logistical systems spread across the globe to report the news and to take, process, and ship pictures from distant scenes of conflict or, occasionally, of progress. Even when videotape and satellites simplified the process and dramatically speeded up transmission and broadcast, the costs remained high: $2 million a year for a foreign bureau, $5,000 a day on location for a team.

As long as the networks considered their news divisions the pride of the company, costs didn't dominate management's thinking. News programs were not supposed to make money, and if they lost more than they should, well, they kept the corporate flag flying with awards and commendations.

The networks aspired to the standards of the *New York Times*. No one in the federal government had granted network correspondents access to the Manhattan Project for a preview of the atomic bomb, as they had the *Times*'s William Laurence, but the TV journalists did get their share of government leaks, including the information on which CBS based its documentary "The Selling of the Pentagon." CBS News covered the cold war with the team of foreign correspondents originally assembled in wartime London by Edward R. Murrow. It established bureaus around the world feeding the news to Cronkite. NBC kept pace with Chet Huntley and David Brinkley and a worldwide news-gathering effort that was considered first among the networks. ABC, which entered the competition later as a spin-off from NBC, managed to catch up with the older networks under the leadership of Leonard Goldenson and news president Roone Arledge, with a corps of younger correspondents and the veterans Howard K. Smith and Harry Reasoner.

At the same time that network television was emerging as a national medium with the linking of the East and West Coasts by coaxial cable, newspapers were beginning to use technology to go national, too. The *Wall Street Journal* established satellite printing plants, and the *New York Times*, a West Coast edition. The *Washington Post* and *Los Angeles Times* took more modest steps into national circulation. All three of the newcomers also hired correspondents and editors to match the efforts of the dominant *New York Times* and the faltering *New York Herald Tribune* in coverage of the world.

Sarnoff and Paley gave their editorial staffs and network correspondents the latitude and resources they needed to make them worthy competitors for the best of the nation's newspapers. The advent of television created a whole new branch of CBS News, a staff that grew from fourteen to nearly four hundred in the six years after 1950. CBS's reputation of being the "Tiffany Network" was based in part on good public relations but also on fact. As Sally Bedell Smith wrote in her not uncritical biography of Paley, "CBS shaped and influenced American society to a greater degree than its rivals. CBS told us in immediate and revealing terms about war," from Murrow to "a succession of grim images from the rice paddies of Vietnam."[6]

For many years after the Vietnam War, cost was considered no object in opening bureaus or sending news teams to nations many viewers had never heard of. The three networks held their own with the top newspapers through Vietnam, the decolonization of Africa, and the Soviet collapse. But television reporters began to find that post–cold war coverage was becoming increasingly hard to sell to the producers in New York.

Their hugely expensive news operations caught the eye of executives, first in their organizations and then in the larger conglomerates that took over their ownership in the 1980s. For a long time, news divisions had been exempted from the demands imposed on all other network departments to present budget projections at the start of the year and turn in profit statements at the end. News was unpredictable; no one could tell what political crises, natural disasters, or violence might have to be covered in the year ahead. And coverage cost money that could never be recovered by the advertising sold during news programs. For decades, this equation was accepted in the broadcast business as one of the costs of public service—required by the Federal Communications Commission—and of maintaining a competitive advantage over rival networks, a relationship that shifted from one to another over the years.

Selling ads for entertainment programs brought the networks huge profits that easily balanced the costs of covering the news, but one result of the sale of all three networks in the mid-1980s was that the new owners lacked their predecessors' commitment to news. If entertainment was the basic money earner and news the leading money loser, it seemed reasonable to the new management to cut news and expand entertainment. In contrast to their predecessors, the developers, manufacturers, and movie executives who made those decisions had no history of commitment to public service.

"We may have passed through what will be come to be known as the golden age of information," Ted Koppel recalled in his 2000 book *Off Camera*. "There was plenty of money to go around, and it was produced exclusively by entertainment programming. News and public affairs were not expected to generate revenue, and so there was little pressure to cater to the lowest common denominator."[7]

The golden age was the victim of three related events in the middle 1980s. First, the Reagan administration all but eliminated the FCC's requirements for broadcasting public service programs. Second, the networks became the property of corporations that focused on shareholder profits and neglected public service. Third, the winding down of the cold war made news managers less interested in covering foreign stories.

Under a president who had campaigned for less government, the Federal Communications Commission relaxed to the point of extinction the half-century of rules holding that broadcasters, in exchange for the free use of the public airwaves, had to serve the "public interest, necessity, and convenience." The idea was based on earlier federal legislation regulating public utilities. New Deal logic extended the regulation of the water and electricity lines to the airwaves. But the Reagan team saw it otherwise.

Mark S. Fowler, Reagan's appointee to head the FCC, held the radical view that the *public's interest* is what constituted the public interest; in other words, watch or listen to whatever you want. The broadcasters were as delighted as a school class when a substitute teacher decides to drop the math and composition and lets the students play their CDs. It meant no more measurement of public affairs programming, including political and foreign news, to satisfy the government.

The signal to the networks was given early in the new administration, when in his first statement of objectives, Fowler called for "an unregulated, competitive marketplace environment" for all communications. "The FCC is the last of the New Deal dinosaurs," he declared, promising release from the regulatory straitjacket and the provision of services that the public wants, "whether Washington likes it or not."[8]

In a speech in 1982, Fowler made the clearest distinction between his policy on broadcasting regulation and that of his predecessors, which he called the "trusteeship approach":

> In exchange for the opportunity to operate exclusively on a frequency, broadcasters were expected to demonstrate a level of public service. . . . In exchange for the license, promises were made to carry news and public affairs programs and to fulfill community service obligations.

> As Chairman, I have urged the Commission to move away from this trusteeship concept. Under it, the Commission made rules dictating how the broadcaster was to serve the community. Instead I advocate a marketplace approach. Under it, the Commission will defer to a broadcaster's judgment about how best to compete for viewers and listeners, and how best to attract and sustain the public's interest.

Then Fowler stated his central thesis: "Under this rationale, the public's interest defines the public interest in broadcasting." Instead of government regulators, he continued, the success or failure of broadcasters in the marketplace, their programs and their schedules, is the real measure of public interest or, in his new formulation of the term, the public's interest. Fowler said the change was justified because of the proliferation of cable and other outlets meant that the major networks no longer had a monopoly on broadcast information.[9]

The networks instantly saw the value of what had been accomplished. They turned their efforts even farther away from the traditional definition of the public interest toward what *they* perceived was the public's interest and began to cut foreign coverage and other costly public affairs commitments. Although the language of the 1934 act remains in the FCC's rules, no one pays much attention to it.

The second change was the acquisition of the three major networks by new owners that made them part of larger corporations. Only in the case of ABC, which was bought by a regional corporation that owned newspapers and TV stations, did the new management have a background in or commitment to news. But that arrangement ended with its 1996 sale to Disney. CBS's purchaser, Lawrence Tisch, was interested in selling off parts of the company to pay back his investment, which he did handsomely before the entertainment conglomerate Viacom eventually became CBS's owner. General Electric, which bought RCA and hence NBC, was interested in making the new properties as profitable as its aerospace and plastics divisions.

Richard Wald, a news executive with both NBC and ABC, sketched out the following account:

> Television, when it started as a network news operation, 1950–1954, roughly, it had no money and it was a sop to Congress and it operated on a shoestring. Then there came a period when television by itself made huge amounts of money. [Network news operations] were deliberately designed not to make a profit. It was not expected and not wanted.

> This was a piece of the proof that networks were built for the public interest, convenience, and necessity, the wording of the Communications Act. You went from not having a hell of a lot of money and the commercial pressures not being the same to having a huge amount of money. And then in one year all three networks were sold to corporations that were fiscally prudent and were careful about how they did their internal budgeting. All three networks went through the wringer and became far less expansive in terms of their money. And so the internal fiscal—the budgetary pressures—mounted and changed the world.[10]

Three years later, the cold war ended, the third factor, and with it the running story of the Soviet threat, which had kept squads of broadcast teams stationed around the world. The networks did not take long to get the message. In the week that the Berlin Wall fell, they rushed extra crews to Berlin to chronicle the drama, preempting news magazine shows usually devoted to crime and celebrities. Every one of these historic programs finished with lower ratings than the gossip shows they had replaced.

The new owners of all three networks first proclaimed the special place of news and then proceeded to demolish it with drastic cuts. When Tisch was taking over CBS, for example, he announced: "We will spend any amount of money whenever it is needed to maintain our standards of quality and to meet any new public service needs. We will respond to an unexpected event today or tomorrow by spending whatever it takes to provide the appropriate coverage."[11] But according to Richard Salant, former president of CBS News, the new owner told CBS management to cut deeply into the news budget. It fired more than three hundred news employees. "Although there was an expectation that quality would not suffer, it did," Salant wrote in his memoirs. "Both NBC and ABC also reduced their news budgets during this period."[12] Tisch saw the value of his investment increase from $980 million to $1.4 billion in two years.

CBS news anchor Dan Rather responded to the first round of Tisch's staff reductions in a *New York Times* op-ed piece headlined "From Murrow to Mediocrity?" "We have lost correspondents, producers, camera crews. That means we will cover less news. We will go to fewer places and witness fewer events. We are determined that our new corporate management not lead us into a tragic transformation from Murrow to mediocrity."[13]

Not to worry, Tisch replied a few weeks later:

> Involvement in covering the great issues of our time and finding ways to use the power of television to keep the American people better informed are among the challenges most important to me personally.[14]

When Warren Buffet became a major shareholder in the Capital Cities takeover of ABC, he told his partners they needed someone like him who would treat ABC in the same way that the Sulzberger family treated the *New York Times* or the Graham family the *Washington Post*. But in the first two years of the new management, ABC fired three hundred of its 1,450 news division staff and watched its share price increase by 22 percent.

General Electric, the new owners of the third network, NBC, also made an initial pretense of public service. Former NBC News president Lawrence K. Grossman wrote that he was instructed by the new management "to confirm, if asked, that GE had given its solemn promise not to interfere with the work of NBC News. The news division was to retain its independence and integrity under the new owner as it had under the old." Grossman said the instructions were in response to concerns expressed by Ralph Nader and others about the independence and integrity of NBC news under GE. He was confident, he wrote, that these fears were unfounded. NBC's previous corporate parent, RCA, had kept its hands off news, and the new managers "had given me their explicit assurance that GE would do the same. Despite all the assurances, GE wasted no time making its mark downsizing and downgrading the quality and character of NBC News."[15]

General Electric CEO Jack Welch and NBC president Robert C. Wright seemed puzzled that NBC or any other network news had a responsibility to the public that came ahead of its obligation of making money. Instead, their responsibilities were to their shareholders, not the public, they believed.

FCC chairman Fowler supported this position. He took the view that television sets were no different from other appliances: a toaster with pictures, he said, in what might have been a reference to the classic Murrow condemnation of television's superficiality.[16] Appliances, Fowler inferred, needed no government protection for what was broadcast to them. Welch liked the appliance idea, too. He told his new associates at NBC that his consumer appliance plant in Louisville was reorganized to make 15 percent more appliances with

60 percent fewer people working there. He wondered why NBC had so many correspondents across the nation and around the world when so few of their reports could be squeezed into the twenty-two minutes of nightly news. NBC News, he said, must become efficient, and in tandem with Wright, Welch began a series of cuts of news operations, fifty staff members at a time, eventually adding up to the 25 percent or more reductions the other networks were carrying out.

The Welch and Wright idea of public service was to manufacture reliable products, not subsidize money-losing television news programs. GE's airplane engines were a good example, Welch told the media writer Ken Auletta. If they failed, that was a true disservice to the public.[17] In addition to this responsibility to the public at large, Welch and Wright had a particular responsibility to earn money for their stockholders, an idea that went against the grain of the news culture, not only at NBC, but at all the other networks as well. News was something different and special. The public owned the airwaves; it was the task of the networks to pay back the public for its use of the airwaves with serious coverage of the issues before the nation. If that earned money, well and good, but if it lost, well, news had always been insulated from the bookkeeping departments in all the networks. After the 1980s, this line of argument found few defenders.

In Grossman's view, the result of the pursuit of profits was a critical decline in broadcasting stories about the economic, political, and social issues about which the American people had a right to be informed. Instead, Grossman wrote, "network news divisions now turn over the greatest part of their resources to the production of tabloid style prime time magazine shows and 'reality' TV."[18]

Network producers and correspondents say that the changes of ownership meant an immediate change in the ways they did their job. Before the mid-1980s, the potential news value of a story, not the potential costs of covering it, determined assignments. Bureau chiefs and their crews worried about getting to the scene of coverage, arranging for satellite transmission, and fighting for space on the evening news against many other equally active bureaus around the world. CNN correspondent Jim Bittermann remembered that "money became a factor in everything" during his days in Paris for ABC.

> Until 1985, I can't ever remember having had a discussion with a producer about the costs in covering a story. We just didn't think about it. When the money pressures came, things started changing. How much is it going to cost? How many camera days are we going to spend? Can we deliver a story in just two days rather than three days?[19]

Rick Kaplan, former head of CNN's news operations, said that the tight budget means "you know you think twice before you send crews out—not so much on the money you'll spend but in a very real way on the ratings." Producers, he mused, "must wonder: 'is this the story that will get me audience return—will I have a low rating?' because too many low ratings and you're dead."[20]

Executives high and low defended cuts in foreign coverage or simply denied that anything important was taking place. David Westin, taking over from Roone Arledge as the chief executive officer of ABC News in 1998, told Reuters he intended "to maintain or expand overseas coverage," although he could point to no immediate plans to add bureaus.[21] Dan Rather insisted in a 2000 interview with the industry journal *Inside* that "we have shored up our international coverage. We run more international pieces and I think the pieces are sharper, better focused, better written than we had for a long time."[22]

But as media consultant Andrew Tyndall's measurements of network news broadcasts show, in 1989, the year of revolution in the Soviet world, foreign news took up about 25 percent of the time on the leading network, ABC, but only 12 percent in 1996. NBC fell to about 8 percent in the same period, which is where all the networks except CNN entered the twenty-first century.[23]

Before September 11 changed both these figures and the public perception of the value of knowing about the world outside the United States, foreign news gathering was considered in the executive suites of the networks in New York as a costly nuisance. Without American involvement in a foreign story, there was only a slight chance that it would be covered. Even situations with thousands of Americans on the ground, as in Kosovo or Bosnia, needed another ingredient: violence, drama, conflict involving Americans directly. Fortunately, those elements were usually absent from the American missions in the former Yugoslavia, and stories about KFOR or IFOR were as rare as explanatory pieces on the Japanese economy or AIDS in China.

In contrast, magazine shows cost far less to produce, do not require staffing permanent bureaus in distant places or sending correspondents chasing to even more distant parts to cover breaking stories. Unlike breaking news, they can be fashioned in-house to supply the drama that is popular with audiences and be laced with whatever amount of violence their producers feel necessary to depict. Such stories are not fiction but rearranged, burnished and dramatized fact, and they differ from a breaking political or disaster story as much as a men's magazine story differs from a news report off the AP or Reuters news wire. Arranging facts already in-house is far cheaper than seeking them in all corners of the world. And since the television magazines draw lots of advertising and can charge premium rates for it, they usually are moneymakers.

It costs between $500,000 and $700,000 to produce an hour of a news-magazine, according to the television critic Marc Gunther. This must be compared with at least $1.2 million for a prime time entertainment hour, and news-magazines are nearly as popular with audiences as entertainment is, particularly in the summer, when the sitcoms are rerun. The cost of a thirty-second advertising spot on magazine shows ranges from the $250,000 CBS can charge for 60 *Minutes* to the $100,000 for the run-of-the-mill shows on other networks. All these rates are higher than those generated by the evening newscasts, although only the rates for 60 *Minutes* compare with the best of prime-time entertainment.

"I do worry that sometimes we do stories that might be seen as appealing to audiences that we don't necessarily do our best work on," Andrew Heyward of CBS News conceded in a 1999 panel discussion on news.

> In this environment, we're still expected to deliver important journalism at the same time we're expected to make money, and, to the degree that there are stories that are selected that don't necessarily represent the best of us but that are an attempt to maximize audience, I sometimes regret that. But I could say that doesn't happen terribly often.

Heyward insists that the world of Walter Cronkite wasn't all that perfect, either: "The definition of news has broadened substantially. You could make the argument that some of that broadening has not necessarily been to the public benefit, but by the same token, in the Cronkite era, there were vast changes going on in America that were woefully undercovered," including social movements and the environment. "The evening news broadcasts remain remarkably traditional and responsible and quite conservative, given the tabloidization and trivialization of much of television," Heyward added.

> Despite pressures to make a profit, the network evening news [programs] have remained very sober and they do many many stories that are "uncommercial" in nature. Night in and night out the editorial choices that are made by those programs are not the most commercial choices and thence not designed purely for audience maximalization. If they were, you'd have extremely different shows than you have now.[24]

The profit pressures have increased with the introduction of new methods of measuring audiences. With instruments that record minute-by-minute viewership as the programs are broadcast, producers have an immediate impression of what's popular and what's not. The effect is most noticeable, producers say, when a gossip or entertainment item on a newsmagazine show is followed by one that looks at national or international issues and the needles that show audience numbers drop precipitously. The system isn't refined enough for anyone to pull a segment off the air if it isn't popular enough, but the results are considered carefully when it's time to put together the next magazine show. Producer Rick Kaplan explained that "the real tragedy of the minute-by-minute ratings is that you sit there and watch what the audience is doing. Unfortunately, that happens a lot in magazine shows and news shows."[25]

The Committee of Concerned Journalists surveyed the news magazine offerings and concluded that "prime time network news magazines have all but abandoned covering traditional topics such as government, social welfare, education, and economics in favor of lifestyle and news-you-can-use" entertainment categories. Citizens can still turn to the newspapers for news about government, foreign policy, and domestic policy, the survey's authors added, but television has become an uncertain provider of such information: "News magazines which once concentrated heavily on coverage of ideas have moved heavily toward celebrity." And the traditional network news programs have "become a hybrid of all the others."[26]

News you can use may help you with your diet or your next car purchase, but it offers little of utility for the major issues that Americans face when making up their minds about who will occupy the White House or lead the Congress or what challenges the United States can expect in its relations with the rest of the world. The truly useful news is the kind that was long provided by American news organizations that took seriously their mission to inform the public on matters of national import, whether domestic issues or responses to events abroad.

The answer that those seriously interested can always buy a serious newspaper or journal is dodging the issue. If ABC News can proclaim that most Americans get their news from it, it should be the responsibility and duty, somewhere in the hierarchy, that this outlet, too, is a consistent and regular provider of the important news you can use.

As Koppel wrote in *Off Camera*, instead of expanding to meet this additional task, news divisions were cut back and quality declined. "Those with the inclination can find everything they want and need in print, on NPR, or on the Internet. But the networks, which still reach the largest audiences, are cutting back on stories they might once have felt an obligation to cover—especially foreign news."

The most accessible media are devolving into the least useful and daring. The educational and economically deprived in our society, who used to receive at least some exposure to information they might not have selected for themselves, but from which they might have received some benefit, are now reduced to watching only what we believe they want; and we have little confidence in their appetite or range.[27]

THE VIEW FROM RIVINGTON STREET

From a jumble of cables and a wall full of screens in his apartment-office on New York's Lower East Side, Andrew Tyndall watches the world every evening on the three networks and measures, for network executives, advertisers, and the occasional scholar, the content of and changes in their news. He has watched foreign news decline from a high point of 25 percent in 1988 to the 8 percent he measured before September 11, and like many in the business, he wishes the trends would turn back and head the other way—not for the advertisers, not for the anchors, but for the public.

Tyndall was warning in the 1990s that the networks were neglecting important stories vital to U.S. interests, above all the rise of Islamic fundamentalism and its increasing resort to violence. He still says that the networks should turn to some neglected international issues closer to home. Tyndall uses the "near abroad," the Russian term for the former Soviet republics close to the old homeland, but he doesn't mean this region. "We've got our own near abroad," he says: the countries close to the United States, above all Mexico and Cuba, but also Canada and Latin America, all places where not enough is being reported for American network audiences. The bodegas and fruit stands in Tyndall's neighborhood show how near this abroad is to New York, as it is to most other U.S. cities.

"If the network headquarters were in Dallas or Houston, you can bet we'd already be seeing this kind of coverage," he asserted. Tyndall's list of undercovered stories are linked, although not exclusively, to the near abroad. They include the environment, the war on drugs, immigration, and globalization. None can match terrorism in dramatic impact, but all are important to the daily lives of Americans, Tyndall argues—our safety, the air we breathe, our jobs, our children.

Aside from these, the big foreign stories are still covered, but the medium and small ones are not, Tyndall says, and this means that American audiences aren't getting a complete picture of the world around them, but only a patchwork of crises, terrorism, and natural disasters. And all the while the networks are neglecting the foreign topics that really impact people's lives. "As a result, public opinion has less information to base its decisions on."

Tyndall's weekly bar charts record how many minutes are devoted by ABC, NBC, and CBS on their evening programs to the ten top stories. Before September 11, when the bar charts went off the page, if foreign stories ranked at all, it was usually at the bottom of the chart, in the four- and five-minutes range (out of a possible weekly 855 for all three networks). In 1988, when Tyndall began to keep score, foreign stories were regularly represented by long bars of sixty minutes and more. It's a simple matter of economics, Tyndall asserts. "Domestic news costs a lot less to cover."[28]

Walter Cronkite, speaking at a fifty-year tribute to his career in 2000, said that today's broadcast journalists are superb but are constrained from doing their best by the corporations that have taken over the three networks since his retirement. "They're better than they've ever been, better than they were in my day; they've had more practice, more experience," he observed.

> The fault I find is in management. Today we have the mega-mergers, the mega-ownerships and these people are solely in business for profit. As such, [news departments] are directed to make higher ratings, greater profits, cut costs, and this is not the way to produce the best news broadcast. Their first objective should be serving the people.[29]

It is enormously costly to cover a foreign story, and it is difficult to justify this expense to executives who can see from Nielsen ratings that people want entertainment, anyway. "If we're to have foreign news, let's have it on an innocuous magazine show, pampered pigs in Britain or something to do with the royal family," a network producer who puts together such shows on a morning program suggested.[30]

In 2001, with heavy expenses for crisis and war coverage and a sharp decrease in revenues from commercials, network news still made money: $300 million a year for the leader, NBC, but only $30 million for third-ranked ABC, with CBS somewhere between those figures. Most of the profits came from the three networks' morning news shows, which attract not only larger audiences but the younger ones prized by advertisers.

But as the newspaper industry was also finding out at the turn of the twenty-first century, just any profit won't do in a corporate system in which shareholders want regular increases. Rumors of mergers and acquisitions, the end of the current formats of the evening television news on the three major networks, were endemic. As the *Nightline* decision showed, executives have no trouble at all with repeatedly questioning the value of expensive news operations, national and foreign, that appeal to an even older class of viewers. Thus reports circulated of an operational merger between CBS News and CNN, or between ABC and CNN.

VIEWS FROM EUROPE AND ASIA

"It costs $2 million to keep this bureau open every year even if we would never cover a single story," a network producer in Europe stated. "We go out with a producer, correspondent, camera person and sound person. If you're editing on site, there's also an editor. That's very expensive. When we take editing equipment, our excess baggage often weighs half a ton." Are shortcuts possible? Producers can serve in a pinch as correspondents, but their strengths are their local or regional knowledge and contacts and not their on-air presence. "We've tried just sending a cameraman to cover stories," the producer said. "We got wonderful pictures but he ignored what people were saying."[31]

CNN claims to be more correspondent driven and less subject to direction from headquarters. Its rivals in the field agree with this assessment but contend that it sacrifices professional quality by not having a full team and sometimes putting locals on air, and sometimes, they say, this sacrifices accuracy.

Watching those programs on visits to New York is usually a disappointment for the network's foreign staff: "We're unhappy about the impact that it makes, whether the incredible number of commercials or the trivial stories about health, and a little appalled to see how small the international contributions are."[32]

It's not from lack of trying; story ideas are constantly proposed. Network crews abroad understand the ground rules that stories must have a very strong American angle. But no one at headquarters was interested in the strong American angle of U.S. troops in the Balkans, since the routine of keeping the peace had little drama or violence. The producer concluded:

Their attention span is too short to consider stories of what might happen, to go into a developing situation that hasn't reached any really dramatic stage yet, to anticipate—we know these things and these issues, but that kind of story isn't wanted. It has to be immediate, it has to be if not sensational then a headline.[33]

Since it started in 1968, 60 Minutes has moved with a different rhythm, trying to anticipate the national and foreign issues that might make headlines in the future and explore them, with its own special mix of careful preparation and

confrontational interviewing, ahead of the other television and print journalists. In the process, it has broken every record for ratings of a news program
and has been a consistent money earner, the basis of its independence from
network pressures to follow the pack. "When the pack isn't there, you can
really dig a little bit," producer Leslie Cockburn, a veteran of 60 *Minutes*'s
international reporting, noted.

Nearly a year before the terrorist attacks, 60 *Minutes* was alone in broadcasting a carefully documented story on the threat to the United States of Pakistan's political instability, terrorist training camps, and ties to the Taliban.
Cockburn and correspondent Steve Kroft used a camera concealed in a video
photographer's scarf to film the terrorist training camp footage of "America's
Worst Nightmare" and interviewed President Pervez Musharraf as well as
Muslim extremists to tell the story. In Pakistan, Kroft pointed out, "the gener-
als who seized power are beholden to Islamic radicals who revere the terrorist
Osama bin Laden."

Interviewing some of the radical leaders, Kroft and Cockburn found support
for Taliban policies like bans on women working outside the home and anyone
watching television. There was also "openly lavish praise of Osama bin Laden."
One extremist Muslim leader compared bin Laden with Abraham Lincoln.

Musharraf told Kroft in an interview that there was no danger that the
approximately 100,000 Pakistani militants who had fought in Afghanistan
would take over in Pakistan, but Kroft concluded: "The country could fall into
the hands of Muslim fundamentalists, one of the few cohesive forces" left.

Kroft and Cockburn said that 60 *Minutes* gave them the time they needed on
both ends of the story: preparation and production. Cockburn, who has been
covering South Asia since 1985, conducted scores of interviews before Kroft
went on camera. Weeks of editing were waiting after their return, the antithe-
sis of the way that a story gets on the evening news. "The evening news has a
lot to get in," Kroft said. "We do storytelling, almost like short little movies.
There's something magical about twelve or thirteen minutes. You can really
shrink an hour into that time. People will watch if it's interesting. Part of it is
the implicit promise that something different is going to happen" if you continue watching.

The use of hidden cameras has been a point of contention for 60 *Minutes* and
other programs, criticized as spying or deceiving sources, but Kroft and Cockburn defended their use in filming "America's Worst Nightmare." "If you do this
kind of work, there's a certain amount of risk," Kroft explained. "You have to
believe that it's important to talk to these people to understand what's out there.
In the middle of a compound with a lot of people heavily armed, with a group

capable of sending suicide bombers, you make a decision, and think it's worth bringing in a hidden camera."[34]

LOCAL TELEVISION NEWS

Local news had its golden age of international coverage, just as the networks did, and watched the golden age end for the same reason: the cost of foreign coverage and the belief that it did little to improve ratings. Beginning with the Vietnam War, some of the larger television stations in the United States sent correspondents abroad to report on hometown people in the news or to compete with network coverage on major stories.

"The big stations went into foreign coverage enthusiastically in the 1980s and stayed in it until the recession of 1991," recalled Charles Kravetz, who was the news director of WCVB in Boston. "It was very expensive, and there were some who thought they could do a better job than the networks, which wasn't the case." But while the foreign news trend lasted, it was satisfying to its exponents and its audiences, Kravetz thinks.

> It was an attempt to make local stations more like good local newspapers—to give a complete account of the news in the nation and the world, not just the local shootings and fires. It was argued that there was no reason to turn this other important kind of story over to Dan or Peter.[35]

But as the local/foreign wave subsided, that's what happened, except that Dan, Peter, and Tom, too, were spending less time on the important stories.

Another surge of local news exposure was cut loose in the mid-1990s with the entry of Rupert Murdoch's Fox network into large cities across the nation, in many cases replacing the traditional network affiliations of long-established stations. A new Fox station meant as much as two additional hours of news each day for local viewers. But the competition in this case stayed local: the new players simply produced more fires, crime scenes, and other standard fixtures of local news.

On many stations, September 11 brought a return to foreign news, or at least to local angles on foreign events. There was a run on stories about local Muslims and Afghan exiles, police and national guard security measures, and the vulnerability of airports, nuclear reactors, and ports. Notre Dame's WNDU-TV, which covers northern Indiana and southern Michigan, put together a list of Internet sources for its own staff coverage and then decided to share them with the users of its Web site. They included Jane's, the British authority on the world's military and armaments; a military analysis network of the Federation of American Scientists; the Federal Emergency Management Agency; and the *Sydney Morning Herald*'s Web site, "A great place to start if you're looking for information on Afghanistan, including history and analysis of current events."[36]

Many larger stations, like Chicago's WMAQ, provided war and terrorism summaries for their late-night news, some of them done in-house and others using feeds from the networks. Miami's WTVJ-TV used two veterans on its staff, Ike Seamans, a former NBC Middle East correspondent, and anchor Willard Shepard, a reserve air force major who served in the Gulf and Bosnian conflicts. But many more stations stayed on their regular diets of local news, sports, and weather.

Before and after the terrorism attacks, two interlocking arguments have favored this local emphasis. The first half of the argument is that local stations report and broadcast local news because no one else does—not the networks, not CNN. The second half is that the network coverage of foreign and national news makes it unnecessary for the local stations to do so. After September 11, many stations arranged to switch to CNN when other major crises hit. Local stations aren't like local newspapers, which carry the news of both their town or city and at least a little of the world. Instead, the stations could be thought of as a local newspaper wrapped up in the national and foreign sections of the *Washington Post* or *New York Times*, since most local stations' news programs feed into the networks' broader coverage on the morning or evening network news.

In such a situation, a local station wanting to intersperse its accounts of fires and municipal problems with news from abroad has to decide whether to devote the extra staff time or money to footage from a network feed or the services of APTN or Reuters. "The money isn't there, and their surveys tell them the ratings wouldn't justify it," a print editor who has worked with small stations explained. An exception can be made for a foreign story of special interest to the city or region, like a kidnapping or combat death of a local person or a event affecting a large ethnic population, but this doesn't happen on a regular basis.

For stations from Chicago to Amarillo, in the broad swath of the Central time zone, the main networks' 6:30 P.M. Eastern time evening news programs are broadcast at 5:30 P.M., in the middle of the local news. This is a good argument for not trying to preempt their national and foreign coverage on the 5 P.M. local newscasts that precede them or the 6 P.M. ones that follow them. In the Mountain and Pacific time zones, the 6:30 Eastern time evening news programs are taped for later broadcast.

Some local television journalists say unequivocally that local should stay local rather than attempt to cover the world or nation but should use any extra staff time and money to provide time for reporters to do their work better. Stations "ought to cover their city councils rather than do vanity pieces from abroad," a reporter in Oregon maintained. "There are neglected areas of their own communities that are more important to cover than featury foreign stuff." Boston news director Charles Kravetz, an advocate of international news, criticizes local stations that pull footage of gory violence or disasters from their satellite feeds and broadcast it, without any context, just for the shock effect.

As the Afghan war wound down, there was a flurry of postings on television journalists' Web sites complaining that some stations were grandstanding by sending teams to Afghanistan. "What possible advantage value can a local affiliate add to the coverage?" one asked in the Water Cooler chat room on *SpyTV.com*. "Sending reporters to dangerous places in foreign countries where there is no law, no infrastructure and a bunch of raggedy yahoos carrying AK-75's JUST so you can say you have someone there is irresponsible," another e-mail said. "Save your money and put them on a local story," another respondent said. "Let the national newscasts cover" the foreign news.

Nevertheless, quite a few stations do some enterprise reporting that might seem hard to justify under the conditions just cited. At the local level, foreign news coverage wins regional awards and sometimes gets national recognition. It costs money, but nothing like the expense of having correspondents abroad. There is usually a connection to regional interests or ethnic groups. KRON in San Francisco, an ABC affiliate, did a five-part series on the Japanese economy and its links to the Bay Area. Dallas's WFAA, with an audience that includes many military and defense installations, sent its own team to cover the Gulf War—with distinction. WTVJ-TV of Miami, where many Haitians live, focused on the conflicts in Haiti. Chicago has a large population from Central America and an even larger one of Catholics, part of the reason that its CBS outlet, WLS, sent correspondents to Honduras to report on the victims of poverty and disaster and to the Holy Land to accompany the aging pope. But when WBBM, another Chicago station, tried to change from nearly full-time frivolity to seriousness in its local news, in an experiment that was closely watched across the nation, the new course lasted less than a year. It used longer segments, more investigative reports, and more prominent play for national and international stories. Ratings rose at first but then began to fall again, until the program lost 20 percent of its audience. WBBM general manager Walter DeHaven called the program "very, very stern" and said the station would try for a lighter format but still feature serious coverage. Carl Gottlieb of the Project for Excellence in Journalism said the program didn't do enough to entice an audience: "The broadcast did some things well while falling down in areas like local relevance."[37]

Edward Seaton, editor of the *Manhattan Mercury* in Kansas and former president of the American Society of Newspaper Editors (ASNE), sees no sign of any effort in the broadcast industry to think about new ways of bringing foreign news to audiences in the way his newspaper editors have begun to do. With the notable exception of CNN, he says, "when this issue comes up among network broadcasters, they just shake their heads."[38] Foreign news was not on the program at a recent convention of the ASNE's broadcast counterpart, the Radio-Television News Directors' Association (RTNDA). RTNDA's background material for news directors and reporters devotes just two pages to covering the world (compared with nineteen for the dangers of lead paint).

Even when the opportunity is presented for foreign stories with plenty of local tie-ins, most of the nation's local news programs fail to exploit the links. Two major stories involving Americans broke in 2001 before the World Trade Center attacks. The downing of the American spy plane in China and the submarine collision with the Japanese ship off Hawaii raised defense issues to third place in a study of local news conducted by the Project for Excellence in Journalism. But the depth and local links that the news staffs across the country might have provided was lacking in about half the stations surveyed. In contrast to the stations that made some effort to make specific connections to local viewers, an equal number were "likely to simply pass along the latest updates without explaining their local effects." The study concluded: "The locals mostly duplicated the networks rather than supplementing them with more nuanced, original coverage." Andrew Tyndall, writing in the same study, noted that the spy plane incident made the networks' coverage of defense, economic, and foreign affairs spike up to 39 percent of their content, compared with only 16 percent for the same period on the local broadcasts.

RADIO

Radio news, the forgotten branch of communications in a world dominated by television, the Internet, and newspapers, is making a comeback, mostly on the public airwaves. Both commercial and public radio news have been benefiting from the technology revolution, using satellite feeds and the Internet to recapture audiences lost to other media. Constantly improving technologies have also been important factors in establishing the connections that radio journalists need for effective gathering of foreign news.

In this way, radio is returning to the roots of its success in World War II. Radio correspondents were able to compete with their far more numerous and seasoned newspaper colleagues because the factor of speed was on their side. Edward R. Murrow's famous live broadcasts of German bombing raids on London were delivered to their audiences instantly. That put his CBS broadcasts hours ahead of the newspaper correspondents' reports and days ahead of the newsreels, that era's equivalent of television news, which had to be flown across the Atlantic.

CBS had prepared for the challenge of World War II by putting a solid news organization in place from the beginning, hiring veterans from print news, Ed Klauber of the *New York Times* and Paul White of United Press, to head it. At first largely confined to domestic news, CBS's focus gradually spread abroad as war approached in the 1930s. The finest performance of CBS's marriage of technology and journalism was in its coverage of the German march into Austria in 1938, when it was able to draw on the reporting of Murrow, William L. Shirer, and others in the world's first roundup of correspondents (managed by the world's first anchor, Robert Trout, in New York), switching live from country to country. The *World News Roundup*, one of the few remaining standouts of CBS radio, is still on the air.

No figure like Ed Murrow stands out in radio today, but current developments in technology compare with the strides made during the Murrow era. One directs radio broadcasts over the Internet into those little speakers next to the computers in American homes and offices. The other uses satellites to beam broadcasts directly to radios, in both cars and buildings. Both developments are important to a revival of radio news and its international coverage.

Satellite radio and a monthly fee of $10 to $13 provide clarity and variety, the two elements often missing in standard AM and FM, for car and home radios. Two enterprises, Sirius and XM, have spent a combined $2.6 billion to launch satellites, make deals with car and radio manufacturers, and entice the public with promises of up to fifty channels of news and talk (as well as a like number of music channels) free of commercials and with digital-quality sound, available coast to coast.

Sirius at Rockefeller Center and XM in Washington have built the first new radio studios to come along in decades. XM employs more than forty reporters and editors, a figure that instantly places it in the nation's top five radio staffs. The outside services teaming with one or the other satellite organization sound like a national media directory. XM works with *USA Today* to produce round-the-clock news and talk and with BBC World for international news. The rest of XM's twelve news channels include sports, financial, and Spanish services from CNN. Bloomberg provides Sirius with a new nationwide financial news service, and C-SPAN's radio version goes out on the Sirius satellites. National Public Radio (NPR) has links to those satellites with its new special programs, NPR2 and NPRNow.

The heads of both companies compare the change to the coming of cable television. There may be some truth to this. Broadcasting means reaching as wide an audience as possible. Cable narrowed this by focusing on individual interests, charging a monthly fee to compensate for the loss in revenue that a wider audience would provide. When foreign news is that special interest, the two satellite organizations provide a great range of options.

The Internet carries the broadcasts of about a third of the nation's AM/FM radio stations, and one in every five computer users reports having used these streaming audio services. Most stations simply stream what they're broadcasting on the airwaves, but Washington's all-news station WTOP has hatched a special one, WTOP2, available only on the Internet. WTOP2 specializes in the kinds of news the Washington community wants, above all about government's plans and doings for the federal employees, military personnel, and retirees from both who make up most of its audience. Its foreign news is also Washington based: a background story on the U.S. base at Guantánamo Bay, Cuba, for example, after prisoners from the Afghan war were sent there, or the Defense Department's plans for future overseas deployment.

A survey commissioned by the Radio-Television News Directors Association found that 17 percent of Internet users are using it for radio broadcasts, although it did not determine whether they listened to news or rock and roll. "The delivery of radio news on the Internet has just begun, but it shows considerable potential for growth, particularly as wireless Internet services become more widely available," the survey concluded. RTNDA warned that local radio stations face competition from both the Internet and the new satellite broadcasting.[39]

While the investors and the digital engineers work this all out, old-fashioned all-news radio, some of it so old-fashioned that it's on AM, not FM, is doing well in providing a ready source of foreign news in metropolitan areas where there are enough listeners to support such ventures. With the help of the Associated Press, more news is on the way even to places with few people. All-news was invented in the 1960s and hasn't changed a great deal since then. Only about forty stations across the country use the format, including two in New York and two in Los Angeles owned by Infinity, a part of Viacom, the parent of CBS. There is some dispute about what constitutes a pure all-news station, since talk has intruded, but stations like Boston's Infinity-owned WBZ, even with evening talk, still provide plenty of news during the rest of the day.

WILM in Wilmington, Delaware, is even more old-fashioned. First, it's one of the two independent all-news stations left in the country, and second, it has a news staff that prepares and broadcasts a mix of local and international news. WILM's emphasis is on the local, but it has room for weekend features like reports from Radio Nederland and Deutsche Welle, the German broadcaster, and CBS's national and international news throughout the day.

The catch in all-news, or part-news, is the cost. Big-city stations need large staffs of reporters and expensive equipment to roam their streets and suburbs and experienced editors to cope with national and foreign reports. Talk, however, is cheap, depending on the talker, and music is even cheaper. But the all-news stations can charge more for their ads, since their listeners are considered to be more desirable. Surveys show that they listen more closely, and they're supposed to have more buying power. All-news listeners are an attractive audience for advertisers because of their above-average education and income, and the news format makes it easier to accommodate those advertisers. News is delivered in short bursts rather than the long narratives or arguments of talk shows, which means more commercials can be interspersed. News stories also are shorter than recorded music, hence more ad time. And even though New York City's two all-news stations rank only sixth and seventh in ratings, they are among the highest grossing in the nation, according to *Duncan's Market Radio Guide*. The top station in the country is Chicago's WGN, heard all over the Midwest on the AM band.

AP's All News Radio (ANR) is an attempt to take the big-city idea to smaller places where the relative paucity of listeners determines how much or little can be spent on the station's own news gathering. It offers a twenty-four-hour clock of "news," including national and foreign, business, sports, and weather. Local stations have the option of letting the clock run or interrupting it with their own news—if they have any. ANR also has another channel to provide longer versions of important stories, in much the same way that CNN's correspondents and anchors fill out the headlines broadcast on its partner Headline News channel.

Talk may be cheap, but it's often infuriating, according to AP's sales force, and this is a financial consideration for stations. High-class advertisers sometimes don't want to be associated with extreme or controversial talk show hosts or music. This is not a worry for AP's All News Radio, which promises "straightforward, balanced reporting that enhances an advertiser's image."

There are about ten thousand commercial radio stations in the United States, more than six times the number of daily newspapers, but unlike the papers, many of them don't carry any news at all. Radio, like television, has taken advantage of the FCC's relaxation of public affairs and news requirements for use of the airwaves. With only the free market in charge, it makes sense to most station managers to play records and broadcast DJ banter, which are cheaper and more popular than news. But the free market got a jolt on September 11 when listeners across the country searched their dials for news of the attacks on the country. Some stations hastily arranged newscasts, and others simply plugged into the sound of Peter Jennings.

If there is less news, there is more advertising. The communications scholar James McChesney points out that since the telecommunications act was revised, advertising on radio has increased 50 percent, which means up to eighteen minutes per hour. He calls the 1996 deregulation "a textbook case of how to destroy a medium."[40]

Buffalo Evening News media critic Anthony Violanti agrees. "Instead of a public trust, radio's future is decided by accountants and businessmen. Stations now have 35 percent to 45 percent returns. Could they accept only 30 percent?" Radio industry advocates say that far from causing the decline of news, a single owner of many stations can improve it by combining newsrooms that serve them all better. "Consolidation may lead to a revival of radio news," RTNDA president David Bartlett insisted.[41]

As the communications act moved through Congress, the broadcast industry lobbied strenuously for the right to consolidate ownership of radio stations. Its argument for relaxing the rules of ownership was that local radio stations were already competing with cable systems, including the new cable audio services, and would be facing XM and Sirius. Restricting ownership left individual station owners unable to raise the immense amount of capital they would need to compete, claimed the National Association of Broadcasters.

In the end, the 1996 law did not do away with the public trustee obligations for broadcasters, but it also did not specify what they were or extend them. Its main point repeated FCC Chairman Fowler's deregulation policy from more than a decade earlier, that a competitive environment is equated with the public interest, is convenient, and is a necessity.

Just how big the chains of radio stations have become is disclosed in the annual reports of the two biggest, Infinity and Clear Channel. Viacom's ownership of Infinity and CBS gives it more than 185 stations in thirty-five markets, including the many CBS-affiliated radio stations across the country. The flagship is the all-news WCBS in New York, a main source of news up and down the East Coast with its fifty-thousand-watt power, which competes locally with all-news WINS, also owned by Infinity. In Los Angeles, the KCBS station is part of the group as well as another competing all-news format, KFWB.

In numbers, if not in influence, Clear Channel makes Infinity seem like mom and pop with crystal sets. It operates about 1,170 radio stations in the United States and has interests in or owns another 240 in other countries. It estimates its U.S. listenership at 114 million. The music or news formats of such behemoths obviously span the entire range of American radio. Their employment statistics sound like the glory days of U.S. Steel, with more than eight thousand people working for Infinity and more than seventeen thousand for Clear Channel. Their combined sales of more than $5 billion, with annual double-digit increases, seem more like those of the most successful of the New Media, not the old media they represent.

But what Clear Channel and, to a lesser extent, Infinity stations do not have is very much news. In the 1990s, hundreds of news staff members lost their jobs when the FCC's relaxation of ownership restrictions let loose the consolidations in the radio industry. They were replaced by syndicated services, in which as many as a dozen stations get their news not from reporters but from an announcer disguised to sound local. "The company's Programming Dream Team helps transfer the sound of big market programming to small market stations, and uses technology to keep the flavor local," Clear Channel's Randy Michels explains. Audiences prefer this sort of pretext to real news, he insists. "If we have anything to say about it, newspapers will soon be useful only to those training puppies."[42]

Despite what appears to be the drying up of radio news sources of all kinds, a survey by the Radio-Television News Directors Foundation (RTNDF) found that 81 percent of the radio listeners polled agreed that radio news broadcasts were a welcome way to catch up on the day's headlines. "News is an important reason why people select a radio station and is second only to music as a reason for picking a particular radio station," Mark Thalhimer of the RTNDF wrote in the American Radio News Audience Survey of 2000. But as the details of the survey made clear, respondents were not seeking a Murrow-like view of the world. The most popular item of news they listed was the local weather forecast.

The survey found that although television remains the dominant news medium, most people have greater contact with radio during the day. About a third of adults listen to radio news when they get up, and more than three-quarters of commuters listen to radio news on their way to and from work. In the workplace, radio supplies people with most of their news.

Many of them tune into CNNRadio, an offshoot of the cable news network that in recent years has increased the number of its affiliates from sixteen hundred to two thousand. The broadcasts are no-nonsense summaries of the top foreign and national stories, every half-hour, twenty-four hours a day. CNN also streams the audio of its television programs to listeners on Web sites.

The time spent listening to radio is prodigious, a fact directly linked to the growing amount of time that Americans spend in their cars in commuting. It averages to three hours of listening time per weekday, roughly half of which is devoted to news and talk.

Talk is popular, but the RTNDF survey indicated that it also may have helped reduce the trust people have in radio as a medium. Asked about accuracy and bias, those surveyed placed radio fourth, after national and local television and newspapers, a result that the analysts said may reflect the likelihood that "listener impressions of radio news have been colored by the strong voices and on-air personalities inherent in talk radio."

The survey's conclusions of what kinds of news programming listeners preferred were hardly a vote of confidence for the dominant broadcast corporations' elimination of newsrooms and the substitution of technical gimmickry for reporting. "Heavy listeners to all-news radio, talk radio and/or National Public Radio are among those most likely to agree strongly that the quality of radio news is improving," the survey said. More than half praised the general content and objectivity of public radio, with opinions like "It keeps me informed about what's going on in the world around me" or "I like the way they present the news. They spend enough time on each issue. It's not usually condensed." Or "The stories are varied. The foreign news is interesting and they go more in-depth."

PUBLIC RADIO

The giants of commercial radio news have been overtaken by National Public Radio (NPR), which started three decades ago as an unprepossessing collection of college FM stations. Public Radio International (PRI) and the British Broadcasting Corporation have joined in the movement to restore news and public affairs to the public airwaves. NPR serves sixteen million listeners every week with programs heavy with foreign news, exceeding the audiences of network radio and even network television's morning news shows. NPR's success in compensating for commercial broadcasting's shortcomings in news hasn't been matched, however, by its television counterpart, the Public Broadcasting System (PBS). Its main news program, *The NewsHour with Jim Lehrer*, wins awards and praise for its attention to foreign and other substantive issues but attracts only a fraction of the commercial networks' news audiences. Many critics have suggested that the *NewsHour* would be far more effective if it used the worldwide correspondents of NPR and the producers of public broadcasting's other strong component, the *Frontline* documentary series.

NPR News started in 1970, three years after Congress created the Corporation for Public Broadcasting (CPB). Its aim was to link the scores of noncommercial stations across the country, including many established as early as the

1920s, to broadcast lectures for university audiences. But with the introduction of the afternoon news program *All Things Considered* in 1971, the network became a hub-and-spoke operation rather than a chain from station to station. The hourly newscasts and the morning, evening, and weekend news shows all emanate from Washington. Individual stations supply their own news, some, like WBUR in Boston or WPBA in Atlanta, with large local staffs; others, with part-timers, students, or volunteers who read the local wire.

NPR opened its first foreign bureau in London in the 1970s with the help of a foundation grant and since then has added another twelve: two in Latin America, two in the Middle East, four in Asia, and four in Europe. When its freelance contributors are counted, NPR has reporters in more than twenty nations. Foreign editor Loren Jenkins, a former foreign correspondent for United Press International and the *Washington Post*, at which he won a Pulitzer Prize for his coverage of the Middle East, says the goal is another bureau every year.

As important as the network of correspondents is the editing in a small cluster of cubicles in NPR's building in downtown Washington. Jenkins and foreign specialists like Martha Wechsler, who has reported from Russia and Eastern Europe, and Ted Clark, a longtime State Department reporter who now follows developments in Asia, use e-mail and telephone contacts to keep abreast of developing stories and plan coverage. Jenkins usually represents the foreign desk in the editorial meetings that map out space on *All Things Considered* and *Morning Edition* and says that unlike the situation in many news organizations, international is seldom a hard sell.

The general meetings are preceded by frequent departmental meetings, described by one staff member as usually chaotic, in which the foreign department decides what to cover. Foreign editors say NPR's budget of what foreign news to follow probably depends too much on what is in the *New York Times* and *Washington Post* every morning, but they do develop their own stories in tandem with correspondents in the field and are open to freelance contributions. What not to cover—such as a single wire service report without corroboration from another source—is every bit as important. A story from the Middle East, for example, based on diplomatic sources or another formulation that makes it hard to check, waits for broadcast until another service carries it. NPR's own correspondents, including part-timers who may file only infrequently, are subjected to this checking and double-checking. These stringers are most successful if they're personally known to the foreign desk, a staff member says. They're urged to try to combine the views of an expert in the field with their own reporting; often the expert is provided by NPR from the ranks of the Washington think tanks and universities.

Audience surveys commissioned by NPR show that this commitment to accuracy is one of the main attractions to listeners, although some conservatives complain that the experts and viewpoints are too often too liberal for their tastes.

The liberal-conservative argument has been a part of NPR history since the beginning. If commercial radio news has been diverted from serving as a source of serious information, including foreign news, because of the concern with ratings, public radio has had to fight another battle for the approval of a narrower audience: Congress and the White House. Republican leaders have cut its appropriations over the years for a variety of reasons, most of them contentions of biased reporting. NPR was only one year old when President Richard Nixon vetoed the congressional appropriation for the Corporation for Public Broadcasting.

Former Speaker of the House Newt Gingrich sought the privatization of public broadcasting; former Majority Leader Bob Dole labeled public broadcasters as cheerleaders for the liberals. Congress has passed these cuts in budgets, which are usually scaled back in later negotiations, but criticism from the right has been a constant accompaniment to public broadcasting's growth.

But grow it has, despite all the opposition, and perhaps in part because of it. The calls for zeroing out or privatizing public radio led to the creation of individual station endowments and a national endowment fund that exceeds $6 billion. NPR has six times the 104 stations it started out with in 1971. Audiences, estimated at two million in 1973, have increased eightfold.

NPR's funding is complex. It used to get money directly from the Corporation for Public Broadcasting (CPB) but now sells programs to the local public radio stations, which pay for them in part with CPB money they receive directly and in part from the fund-raisers that interrupt their programs. Most public radio stations get the bulk of their funding from their listeners or underwriters.

NPR thus receives no direct operating funds from the government, but it does compete for grants from CPB's radio programming fund as well as from other federal agencies, including the National Science Foundation, Endowment for the Arts, and Endowment for the Humanities. Slightly more than half of NPR's funding comes from payments from stations, with the rest supplied by corporations and foundations. Only the stations may beg for funds, but NPR has a new foundation that accepts contributions to help put the system on a sounder financial basis. This new foundation is also designed as an additional firewall between grant givers and those who decide what goes on the public air. NPR's news policy manual already states that "grants must not be so narrow in concept as to coincide with the donor's area of advocacy or interest." This policy is reviewed every time the issue comes up, with senior management making the final rulings.

NPR attracts more listeners for its *Morning Edition* program than any of the three television networks' morning programs does individually and also more than the second- and third-ranked shows, *Good Morning America* and *CBS This Morning* combined. This means that 8.8 million American listeners get a daily mixture of foreign and national news at some time over a two-hour period in the morning. NPR staff members concede that much of the credit for the ratings is that millions of Americans are commuting in their cars during the morning shows' times and are unable to watch television. But they could be listening to other radio stations that provide less news and information.

Public news radio is getting even newsier. Many of the larger NPR stations are switching to all news and talk, using satellite feeds from NPR and other syndicated services. More than twenty-five have eliminated jazz and classical music, the traditional format for public stations between the big news shows, and describe themselves as strictly news stations. These include some of the most important in the network: San Francisco's KQED, Philadelphia's WHYY, and San Diego's KPBS.

Planning is under way for a noontime news show that would fit into this all-news and talk pattern. It would be based on the successful elements of *Morning Edition* and *All Things Considered*: headline roundups during its broadcast hour, interspersed with correspondents' reports.

Another strong news and public affairs connection for NPR stations is American RadioWorks (ARW), an independent team working with NPR and Minnesota Public Radio. ARW's Stephen Smith and Michael Montgomery won first place in the 2000 duPont-Columbia Awards for their report on a Serbian massacre in Cuska, a small town in Kosovo. War crimes prosecutors called it the most extensive investigation of any atrocity in Kosovo by any Western organization. ARW's other documentaries include investigations of the diamond-smuggling traffic and Muslim views of the United States.

"Massacre at Cuska" begins with the story of a twenty-seven-year-old woman who watched the Serbs enter Cuska at dawn one May day, killing and burning, and cuts quickly to Dragan, a young Serb militiaman who took part in the attack. "We waited all night for the signal to attack," Dragan says. "We went house to house, clearing people out. We concentrated on killing rebels from the Kosovo Liberation Army. If we decided the guy was KLA, we often executed him on the spot." [Smith and Montgomery's investigation showed there were no KLA fighters in Cuska.]

"The challenge that we had is that investigative reporting is often based on documents, on paper trails, money trails," Smith said. But all were absent in

Kosovo. Instead, he and Montgomery used scores of interviews with victims and, eventually, perpetrators.

> We had at least three sets of stories—the stories of the victims, the stories of perpetrators who were willing to speak to us, and the pictures left by retreating or dead Serbian militia men. We used those pictures to get a sense of who the units were and who the commanders were.

The next step was tracking them down for interviews.

The team was able to spend time at a rate unheard of on commercial networks. It took four trips to the region over more than seven or eight months to do the interviewing and cross-checking of stories that resulted in the hour-long report. "What was unusual for us was to be able to talk to these guys," Montgomery said. "Even in the last set of interviews, I don't think we were expecting to get a confession from a man who told us in detail about lining up thirteen men and machine-gunning them."[43]

Bill Buzenberg, executive producer of American RadioWorks, says its documentaries are aired both in their full hour length and in twenty-minute versions that fit into a segment of *All Things Considered*. "Even though everybody knows documentaries are dead, and nobody wants to listen to an hour," he said, "public radio needs this." American RadioWorks is public radio's largest documentary unit, a collaboration of individual public radio stations as well as NPR and MPR. It's supported by an array of grants—from CPB, The Promise of Justice project, the U.S. Institute for Peace, and George Soros's Open Society Institute.

Minnesota Public Radio (MPR) is the creation of Bill Kling, who went to work for the network when it started in 1967 and now has a staff of about three hundred. MPR is best known for *A Prairie Home Companion*, but with an endowment of more than $100 million, it has a formidable news operation. With seventy journalists working in St. Paul and in the thirty public stations in or near the state, it has a larger news staff than any other operation in Minnesota, commercial stations included. It starts and ends the day with international news from the BBC.

THE WORLD

NPR stands alone in the morning, but in the afternoon and evening, with the advent of *The World*, the broadcasting of foreign news has become competitive.

The program was launched in 1996 for three reasons: to step into the gap left when most American commercial radio stations, newspapers, and the Rather,

Jennings, and Brokaw programs started devoting more space to talk and health remedies; to gain a better foothold for the British Broadcasting Corporation's World Service programs in the United States; and to provide an alternative to the relatively skimpy foreign news coverage the NPR programs were then carrying. The World attracts an audience of 1.3 million for its hour, five days a week, of news, commentary, geoquiz, and world music, with seventy thousand listeners around its home base of Boston and more than 100,000 each in San Francisco and Los Angeles.

Although its audience figures are far below NPR's, The World's success can be measured by its impact on its rival. When The World started, NPR had two permanent foreign bureaus, in London and Moscow, and covered the rest of the world with part-time freelancers. Now it has a score of foreign correspondents in Europe, Latin America, Africa, and Asia.

The feed that goes out at 3 P.M. Eastern time from Boston's WGBH studios is the product of a day's work in the crowded World newsroom, work that is both helped and hindered by time differences. Being six hours ahead of Europe is a plus; being a half-day behind Asia is a minus for breaking stories, and World staffers have less time to develop domestic stories than do their counterparts on evening programs or the next day's morning newspapers. Calls placed at the beginning of office hours in Washington sometimes aren't returned by airtime.

Although The World contains its share of breaking news, deadlines are not its chief concern. "Connecting the events and trends in the world to listeners in the United States" is the program's main purpose, executive producer Bob Ferrante explains, "and doing it without making the connection too obvious." The top BBC producer in the mixed U.S.-British team, managing editor Jonathan Dyer, notes that his job is "telling stories about people," stories that a taxi driver might hear and repeat to a passenger.[44] Cohost Tony Kahn says the program aims for the "driveway effect," a story so compelling that a listener arriving home stays in the parked car after a commuting trip to hear the end of it on the car radio and then repeats it to someone at home.

If The World can provide even one or two of these stories a week, Kahn adds, it's worth all the effort for the rest of the five hours of reporting and programming.[45] Does this mean that every foreign story has to have an American involved or affected? "It's not just Americans; it's human terms," Dyer says. "We don't need to follow Americans everywhere on balloon trips to get interest in foreign nations. But every story should have its human dimension. We need to tell our stories so well that they'll get repeated."[46]

World producers discuss international events at their daily early-morning meeting with all the authority and precision of a State Department or think tank team of analysts, but they know they must stay away from old formulas of covering foreign events through speeches and communiqués. This is what Ferrante calls "forced nourishment of listeners," giving them what the producers think they ought to know, whether they're receptive or not. Most listeners get enough of that in college, he says, which is one reason there was such a falling off in interest in foreign news once the danger of the cold war abated. But well before the September 11 terror, Ferrante saw an upward curve in Americans' interest in foreign news. He traces it to the collapse of the Asian economies in 1998, when *The World* was just getting started. "Americans suddenly became very interested in Indonesia and Japan when they realized how their 401k's were being affected. Then they began to look around and saw how many of the consumer goods they owned and were buying were made in some other country."[47]

Journalists who report for *The World* find it as hard as others do to explain the rise and fall of distant markets and currencies to the average listener, who the program's producers define as a college-educated, middle-class man or woman who usually tunes in while commuting, but not for the whole program. But good storytelling can pull in a listener to absorb the other issues of a foreign economy; for example, a *World* piece on how Indonesia's corruption and disorder made it easier for poachers to kill endangered chimpanzees. Another story focused on the successes of foreign organic farmers in the American market, where they undercut U.S. producers because of lower wage levels. The first Arab summit since the Gulf War was handled not as a collection of speeches and statements but for its effect on Americans, reported through contacting experts in Washington.

All this is covered by two overlapping sets of correspondents: the eight to ten regulars who work primarily for *The World*, and the scores of BBC World Service journalists in every country or region who contribute when called on. Both crews are supervised by a staff of thirty-five in Boston, who assign, edit, and communicate through a network of computer and telephone contacts. Six of the Boston producers and editors are BBC staff members.

The program has underlined the friendly and not so friendly rivalry between NPR and Public Radio International, which, along with the BBC and WGBH, sponsors *The World*. Most listeners don't know the difference, but NPR is the older sister, formed in 1971, and PRI is the newcomer, started in 1983 by Minnesota Public Radio and three other state public networks. NPR is owned by its member stations, whereas PRI is run as a nonprofit under a board of directors and operates independently of the stations it serves. With the number of public radio stations likely to remain at about the current 640, both public networks are competing with each other, not only for listeners but also for funding. Executives of both networks deny that this means a rush to the lowest common denominator; on the contrary, a PRI funding consultant says, quality sells, particularly with foundations. But so do numbers of listeners. Each now claims about seventeen million, but this count includes the entertainment, quiz, and music shows as well as news. Stations benefit from the competition, since each gets to compare *The World* with *All Things Considered* and decide when and where to place one or both for maximum listenership.

Ferrante was at NPR when Iraq invaded Kuwait to start the Gulf War and thinks that this event made NPR's reputation as the professional source of foreign news. A decade later, he says, September 11 did the same thing for *The World*. The terrorist attacks gave the program a chance to show an expanded national audience how quickly it could move in covering and explaining a major crisis, and a good part of the new audience has stayed with the program. PRI offered *The World* free to any station that wanted it, and twenty immediately plugged in. Twelve of those stayed to become subscribers.[48]

The World's success in covering the attacks and the war in Afghanistan is based on a combination of the British-American crew in Boston and the BBC's decades-old connections in the region and the country. *The World* excelled at getting stories out of Afghanistan in the chaotic early days of the fighting. On one crucial day in the battle for Kandahar, *The World's* Lisa Mullens was able to interview Hamid Karzai, the tribal leader who was leading some of the anti-Taliban forces inside Afghanistan and who later became prime minister. *World* producers made their contact through the BBC Pashto Service, an institution in Afghanistan for many decades, through royal, communist, and Taliban governments. Karzai used the service regularly to broadcast to his countrymen before the Taliban were defeated and when Mullens's call came through was glad to switch into English to reach audiences in the West.

The interview underscored the BBC's role in this public radio competition for foreign news. It is both a partner with PRI in *The World* and a stand-alone producer of news broadcasts, radio and television, used by many public stations in the United States.

BBC World has always been the Voice of Britain, paid for by the Foreign and Commonwealth Office, and for much of its life has been immune from the budget cutting and pressures to expand its audience that have afflicted other BBC branches. BBC World's audience was ensured as long as the Iron Curtain stayed up, and since the cold war ended, the continuation of dictatorships, war, and censorship around the world has made it equally necessary. Audiences have reached an all-time high of 151 million for its broadcasts in forty-two languages, despite jamming by China, Iraq, Libya, and other nations whose rulers don't like what the BBC says about them.

BBC correspondents know their territories, their customs and traditions, their political figures, and usually their languages. This is because most of them are not parachuted in for a few days of crisis coverage but spend months and years on the scene. Cost-conscious American networks can't or won't afford what the British taxpayers can. Americans who tune in on public radio and television or find *News.BBC.co.uk* on the Internet are the beneficiaries.

The BBC, an "always on" service like CNN, is a staple of many public radio stations, which sometimes schedule its broadcasts early in the morning, before the NPR and PRI programs cut in, and sometimes at noon, when those hungry for news as well as lunch can spend an hour catching up on the world through a British perspective. As public stations switch from music to more news and talk, the twenty-four-hour BBC feeds are a good way of filling up other holes in the schedule. No one has to run and find a shortwave set to do this; the BBC has stayed on top of technology to keep its voice heard. More than one hundred nations pipe it into their FM systems from BBC satellites. And if you missed the BBC at lunch, it's there on the Web—one of the most visited sites for news of any kind.

More than a decade ago, BBC's World Service decided that shortwave broadcasting, its main means of transmission since the 1920s, was going to be superseded by newer technologies and that it was time to change its emphasis. Worldwide satellite connections made it possible to beam BBC World programs directly to FM stations in Europe, Asia, Africa, and the United States. For many years, college students across the nation have shared with Czech listeners in Prague and Chinese in Hong Kong the experience of clear, local reception of the BBC on FM. But the one-size-fits-all BBC news programs never attracted sizable audiences in the United States. So the BBC executives took a closer look at large markets around the world and decided to provide broadcasts tailored specifically for them. This brought special programs for post-apartheid South Africa and Nigeria and, for the United States, *The World*. When Nigeria moved from dictatorship to democracy, BBC World gained 3.3 million listeners. Despite its technological advances, most of the BBC's listeners still tune in on old-fashioned shortwave, a reflection of the technology on the receiving end in China, Egypt, and Kenya.

The BBC World Service's financing by the British Foreign Office has raised some questions about *The World's* objectivity, staff members say, but none can recall a conflict of interest since the program went on the air. *The World*, like the World Service, is free to report criticism of any government, including the British.

"Royal Charter" wouldn't have been a popular term in eighteenth-century Boston, but the one that keeps the government away from making editorial decisions is welcomed at *The World*. It gives the British government a say only in what languages the World Service broadcasts. Editorial control thus stays with the BBC, "allowing us to be editorially independent and impartial in our reporting on world affairs," as an editor put it.[49]

The BBC thrives on crises, although it tries to do the background reports that explain and sometimes predict them. Its government connection gives it a monitoring service that taps into the broadcasts, news agencies, and press of scores of nations, many of them dictatorships highly resistant to independent reporters. These monitoring reports help journalists, both inside the BBC and outsiders who subscribe to the service, to read speeches, budget debates, and economic figures as an early warning of what future crises might be worth covering.

PUBLIC TELEVISION

CBS visionary Paul Kesten had an idea at the end of World War II that his network should stop trying to compete with its rivals for a mass public and concentrate instead on an elite service that would attract fewer people but be able to seek the highest quality, whether in entertainment or news. The network never got started, but it might have looked something like the public radio and television networks that now broadcast across America from more than a thousand stations, about 360 of them television.

Kesten, who was CBS founder William Paley's vice president, envisioned an audience of ten million or fifteen million for a CBS that would become "the one network that never offends with overcommercialism," that presents "an important forum for great public figures and great public issues" as well as "thoughtful and challenging presentation of the news and the issues growing out of it."[50]

In his memoir, Paley says he turned down the plan because it was tantamount to giving up the fight with NBC for the nation's viewers. But just as Kesten's ideas might have been a description of the future public broadcasting, Paley's response is a good description of what happened to the commercial networks. "To survive, CBS had to give the majority of people the kind of programs it wanted to hear in popular entertainment."[51]

Public television has survived alongside its commercial rivals since its inception as a few loosely connected stations in 1967, and it now reaches 100 million viewing homes at least once a month. But its prime-time statistics are far below those of the commercial networks, 2.2 percent of the national viewing audience.

Like NPR, PBS's news programs provide something that the commercial networks cannot or will not. Its *NewsHour with Jim Lehrer* is the only hour-long broadcast evening news program and the only one in which analysis and discussion of the day's news play a dominant role. *Frontline* is television's best documentary series, with little competition from the main networks and cable outlets. And yet PBS could do much more. Ideas for reform or revolution have come and gone over the years. A general label that fits most of them was offered by a PBS producer at a ceremony to accept yet another journalism award: "Become more like NPR." More like NPR, he explained, by covering national and foreign news with a strong network of correspondents to provide better context for the panel discussions, by experimenting with freelancers and their innovations, by integrating some of the good investigative work of *Frontline* into the regular news programs (as NPR does with the American RadioWorks documentary unit).

The Public Broadcasting Service, a linkup of individual stations, began in 1973, but only in 1990 did it obtain the power to schedule for all stations. PBS is less a network than an interest group of the public television stations across the country. The commercial networks have affiliate stations that used to accept all the networks' offerings and still accept most of them. PBS members have a wider latitude, although the realities of individual production expenses mean that most of their programs come from the Big Three stations, Boston's WGBH, New York's WNET, and Washington's WETA, which produces the *NewsHour*. PBS has an annual budget of about $315 million; only about $20 million of which goes to the *NewsHour*. About a third of it is raised by local stations from their viewers in fund drives. Another third or more comes from underwriters, including foundations as well as corporations that benefit from spots hardly distinguishable from commercials. The final third is provided from sales of books, videos, Barney toys, and a grudging contribution of less than $50 million—about 14 percent of the total for this "public" broadcasting effort—from the federal government.

With Bill Moyers's new weekly program, *NOW with Bill Moyers*, PBS has two regular news and public affairs programs to compete with offerings from the main networks and cable news. Two others, *Washington Week in Review* and *Wall $treet Week with FORTUNE* , called the "W's" by the PBS staff, are more discussion than news, although they sometimes do break stories.

The NewsHour with Jim Lehrer does what no other television program does: five nights a week, for an hour, it subjects the major stories of the nation and the world to a dual process of reporting and explaining. Its efforts have been rewarded by many Emmy, duPont-Columbia, and Peabody Awards. ABC's *Nightline*, which attracts many more viewers, acknowledges its debt to the *NewsHour* as a model for its mix of spot news and expert discussion.

The day begins with a meeting of Lehrer, who is the program's managing editor, with his executive producer, Les Crystal, and his deputy, Linda Winslow, along with senior producers Michael Mossetig, Jeffrey Brown, and others. The

NewsHour usually broadcasts four segments during its fifty-five-minute show, each running up to seventeen minutes (nearly the entire twenty-minute news hole of the commercial networks) but some as short as seven minutes. Most come from the daily morning meeting, although some are planned a week or more ahead at a long-range meeting.

The reporting usually is accompanied by some other organization's footage. The *NewsHour* has access to three video providers: APTN, ITN, and ABC. Narration is supplied by a member of the small team of subanchors in the program's studios in the Virginia suburbs of Washington. These journalists are augmented by others from member stations around the country. They then take turns anchoring the second phase, sitting down with the experts or their video images from other stations, to discuss, analyze, and sometimes predict what will come next. In newspaper terms, the *NewsHour* is a combination of the front page and the op-ed columns. Along with *Frontline*, it stands out in an era when the commercial networks rarely venture beyond a seconds-long sound bite to present the viewpoints of experts or adversaries in the leading issues of the day.

But public television cannot match the blanket coverage of the world and the nation provided on the radio by *Morning Edition* and *All Things Considered* And for years, public broadcasting executives have tried to figure out ways to transfer NPR's wider appeal to television.

NOW with Bill Moyers, a weekly magazine show, is the latest effort. NOW is produced by NPR and the New York PBS television station, WNET, with a production staff that includes Juan Williams of NPR. Moyers scans the world for stories which have included close-up looks at Afghan refugees, the Zimbabwe elections, and NAFTA. One long segment described the complex relations among the major tobacco companies, the smugglers who have made cigarettes an international currency, and the money laundering of drug rings. It was the result of six months of investigative work done with *The Nation* magazine and the Center for Investigative Reporting.

NOW's aim is to describe "the rest of the world on its own terms, the way the rest of the world sees itself and the way it sees us," according to Stephen Segaller of New York's WNET, which produces the program. The discussions of such a program began before the World Trade Center attacks, but after that, he said, it became all the more obvious why it was needed.[52]

Collaboration with NPR had also been planned for *Public Square*, a ninety-minute weekly PBS program that was described as the *All Things Considered* of television but never got beyond the pilot stage. Yet another attempt, this one using the reporting staff of the *New York Times*, was *National Report*. Aimed for the 11 P.M. slot occupied by local news, the program planned to use the resources of the *Times* as a better way of filling airtime than the usually nightly diet of fires and murders. *Times* reporters would have discussed the stories in the next day's paper, focusing on what was likely to develop in the next news cycle. Although the idea was backed by *Times* publisher Arthur Sulzberger, who appointed Washington editor Michael Oreskes to oversee it, it failed to attract enough funding. So Oreskes and *Times* reporters turned instead to commercial cable and *Frontline* with investigative stories.

Many other ways of gaining ground on the commercial networks and cable have been planned and then abandoned. The most promising from the standpoint of international news was a morning news program that was to be broadcast before the *Barneys* and *Mr. Rogers*, using the talents of former NBC foreign correspondent Arthur Kent. The program, *World Watch*, was to have four, fifteen-minute segments, which stations could broadcast separately or in their entirety. Essentially, the program was a morning plug-in of ITN (Independent Television Network), the British network that provides much of the foreign footage for the evening *News Hour*, with Kent, a Canadian, as the London anchor to give it a less British image. *World Watch* never got out of the planning stage, apparently because major stations like New York and Boston either could not fit it into their schedules or objected to the ad-like sponsorship statements that the program's producers thought were necessary to attract financial support. The same objections by some member stations had scrapped an earlier plan to team with the *Wall Street Journal* in a program featuring its journalists.

In addition to the *NewsHour*'s daily measure of coverage through foreign footage and experts, there has been a marginal increase in the contributions of its own correspondents. Elizabeth Farnsworth, who works out of San Francisco, has reported from Africa and the Middle East, and Paul Solman of WGBH Boston, from Cuba. A British freelancer, Simon Marks, sometimes works as a special correspondent from Moscow and other datelines.

The *NewsHour* doesn't keep track, but executive producer Crystal estimates that 35 or 40 percent of its content is international, which refers to both foreign stories and Washington stories with international ramifications. The great majority of them are talking heads, but the program begins in the opening summary with footage from around the world and nation to illustrate the main stories. "Nowadays it's possible to get very good footage from [ITN and other services] on short notice and combine it with the views of experts in our studio," Crystal observed.[53]

The other approach is sending correspondents abroad to do long pieces, such as Farnsworth's trip to Africa to report on the AIDS epidemic and other social issues and economic correspondent Solman's two-part series on Cuba. "The growing gulf between those with and those without access to dollars may well prove to be the core of the country's dilemma," Solman reported. "Can Cuba, or any planned economy for that matter, encourage the free market and resist it at the same time?" As part of a four-part series of segments on AIDS in Africa, Farnsworth reported from a hospital in Malawi that in some parts of the continent, one-third of all adults are infected. "Seventeen million people in Africa have already died of AIDS," she said, and another 25 million have the disease. "This is not an African problem. It is a world problem," Malawi's vice president, Justin Malewezi, told her.[54]

Fred de Sam Lazaro of Minnesota's public broadcasting, who was born in India, travels around the subcontinent as a *NewsHour* correspondent, specializing in health and population issues. Lazaro has done *NewsHour* segments on AIDS, women's issues, and business enterprise in India as well as stories from Africa and China. He reported from India that the tradition of favoring male children has led to both infanticide and five million annual "sex-selective abortions." Sonograms to determine gender are illegal in India, but corruption circumvents the law. As a result "almost one in five potential female children is aborted in some parts of India."[55]

Crystal maintains that the two basic ingredients in this kind of reporting are using their own correspondents and keeping down the cost. The *NewsHour* is fortunate to have talent and to be able to take advantage of the new technology to save money. Farnsworth and Lazaro have extensive backgrounds in foreign reporting. Solman, although new to the international field, is an experienced economics and business reporter and told his Cuba story from economic as well as political aspects. Solman's budget for that trip, excluding salaries, was $15,000, according to Crystal. Farnsworth and her crew spent three weeks in Africa for $60,000 on top of their salaries. Solman took a single cameraman/producer, Alex Waugh of Boston's WGBH; Farnsworth, a slightly larger crew. "Digital technology makes it possible," Crystal said.[56]

With scores if not hundreds of freelancers equipped with the technology in distant parts of the world, or ready to go there, and good story ideas, why doesn't the *NewsHour* open its airtime to this new wave? First, this technology has limitations. "You can't—at least not yet—cope alone with the shooting, the editing, the script, getting there, getting set up for interviews—by yourself," Crystal says. "Giving the reporter too much to do dilutes the quality of the reporting." Add to that the inexperience of many young freelancers, in both ordinary journalism and the special needs of the *NewsHour* (the demands of fairness, always getting the other side's point of view). Few freelancers are able to meet these standards, Crystal says, no matter how inexpensive their operations or imaginative their story ideas.[57]

Marks, the British freelancer who works out of Washington for a variety of programs, including the *NewsHour*, has absorbed the program's practices and taboos so thoroughly that he's almost seen as another staff member, according to a *NewsHour* producer. "Many freelancers have agendas not readily apparent in their story outlines," the producer stated. "Others are honest about their advocacy, but that means we can't use them on this program. And some have past histories of infractions large and small, if not outright fabrication, then staging scenes in distant settings to make better pictures and hoping no one will know the difference."[58]

So the technology opens possibilities, but mostly on the side of easier and less expensive access to stories abroad. It does nothing to change the key issues of reliability, accuracy, and fairness. In fact, by making the journalist the only witness to the story that he or she is shooting, it can produce less accurate accounts than might have been provided with more supporting players.

Crystal says the *NewsHour* would like to be able to afford more reporting from abroad. The program costs of $20 million a year are limited by the grants the *NewsHour* can dig up. As a result, what covering a story is going to cost is a far larger factor than it is in the freer-spending commercial networks. The *NewsHour* hopes to raise some funds earmarked for foreign reporting. Although its policies forbid funding for specific fields of coverage, in order to steer clear of political advocacy, foreign affairs is a broad enough topic to be acceptable. More use of the new technology and more reports from the field might fit into a future expansion of programming, Crystal points out. "What this would do is not supplant the talking heads but give them more immediacy and interest. It certainly doesn't cheapen or sensationalize to have reports from the field. It adds the wonderful possibilities of television to a subject in a way studio discussions can't."[59]

In the small world of public broadcasting, the *NewsHour* must compete both with newcomer *NOW with Bill Moyers* and *Frontline*, both of which are staking out new territory in the coverage of foreign news. Within hours after the terrorist attacks on the World Trade Center and Pentagon, *Frontline* was ready, on both public television and the Internet, with an updated version of its year-old documentary "Hunting bin Laden." Its Web site provided information in great detail on bin Laden's activities and previous American responses to them, and its new material asked and answered questions that were on many people's minds: "What price might [the United States] pay for his martyrdom? What would be the effect on America's relations with the peoples and governments of the Islamic world? And how will America's declaration of war against global terrorism affect U.S. society, politics, and Americans' understanding of themselves and the world?"

"Hunting bin Laden" was followed by seven hour-long documentaries in the three months after the attacks, exploring previous terrorist actions, the role of Saudi Arabia and Iraq, potential cracks in the antiterrorist coalition, and "the biggest failure of U.S. intelligence since Pearl Harbor," as "Looking for Answers," broadcast a month after the attacks, charged.

No commercial and certainly no public documentary unit could have done so much in so little time to meet the viewing public's needs without producers, writers, camera crews, and editors already in place. *Frontline's* impact on Americans' understanding of the world was greatest in the weeks after the terrorists struck, but it has a long record of programs exploring the international themes that are given only cursory examination by other media. They include the dangers caused by Russia's lax protection of nuclear stockpiles, the roots of the Tutsi-Hutu conflict, and, in a four-hour series, the failure of the U.S. war on the international drug trade.

The standout of those pieces, however, was the 1999 "Hunting bin Laden," which most viewers got to see first in the updated version broadcast after the attacks. Those who watched the documentary the first time around would have been warned of the threat to Americans that bin Laden represented. The U.S. ambassador to Kenya, Prudence Bushnell, whose embassy was attacked by al-Qaeda in 1998, told *Frontline* that "for two nights after the bombing, I was plagued by the question: what's the point?" Later, she said that in taking responsibility for the attack that killed 213 people, "Mr. bin Laden explained the point. The point, he says, is 'I hate Americans, and I'm going to kill you.'"[60]

Frontline expanded its offerings in May 2002, with *Frontline/World*, which has been described as a PBS 60 *Minutes* with several short segments in its hour rather than the single subject of the traditional *Frontline*. Fanning, the executive producer of *Frontline*, calls it a new way of presenting "the thousands of stories that need to be told in the world, need to have a place somewhere on television." Describing the genesis of one such story, he said he talked to the *New Yorker* writer William Finnegan about going to Bolivia. Finnegan, who has written about South Africa, Mozambique, and other developing countries, spent a week there with David Murdoch, a producer/cameraman, and returned with footage about a confrontation between the multinational Bechtel Corporation, which had a government contract to supply water, and villagers who had built their own system and refused to pay high prices for the Bechtel water. Finnegan's reporting, augmented by the views of specialists in Bolivia and the Bechtel Corporation, provided insight into some of the conflicts of globalization. In *Frontline/World*, he added, "we'll present segments clustered around a single international issue or idea, from terrorism to human rights." Other reports in the *Frontline/World* pipeline include a story on illegal arms trafficking from eastern Europe to Africa, terrorism in Sri Lanka, and the effect of television on the isolated Asian mountain kingdom of Bhutan.

Frontline producers think that parts of their works in progress or stand-alone shorter pieces would be a natural fit for the *NewsHour*, but thus far, little has come out of plans to work together. An independent producer who has worked for *Frontline* and knows the *NewsHour* operation well says she sees little likelihood of much cooperation. "They're two very different cultures," she said. "*Frontline* is far more aggressive in presenting its point of view. The Lehrer show always has to get both sides. It's a pity they can't work together, because PBS resources are so limited." A *Frontline* staff producer agreed. "They want more control, they want to have their regulars and their regular routines, and sometimes our stuff doesn't fit in. We think it could help them attract bigger audiences without relaxing the very strict editorial control that everyone agrees makes their program so solid and reliable," he explained. "Change will come," he added. "But it's going to come slowly."[61]

PART 2

THE TRANSFORMATION
OF FOREIGN NEWS

As long as a guy in a cave can kill your brother in an office tower in
this country, Americans are going to be interested in foreign coverage.
  —*Stephen Gray, Christian Science Monitor managing publisher*

5

EVOLUTION, NOT REVOLUTION

How quickly change will come to the *NewsHour* is difficult to predict. But
all concerned agree that new approaches to foreign news coverage are in store
for every newsroom, print, Web, or broadcast, across the nation, driven by
technology, demographics, and the new view of the world that has existed
since September 11, 2001. Part II of this book explores the likely nature of that
change.

In the past, many of the innovations in the media were revolutionary. The
developments that brought more news from around the world to the American
people were based on single inventions or improvements in technology: the
rotary printing press, which created mass-circulation newspapers, and broadcasting, which could report the news as it was happening, first on radio and
then on television.

By contrast, the changes in the last years of the old century and the first years
of the new one are evolutionary and diverse. Only the creation of the Internet
in 1991 stands out as a milestone similar to that of radio or television. The other
changes are as varied as the sudden growth of immigration in the United
States, the invention of cable news and the development of national newspapers, Americans' growing awareness of the international links in their communities, and the realization of editors across the country that they must do a better job of relating readers to the world outside their borders.

Some of these changes are institutional and planned in advance, as when
investors open twenty-four-hour cable news outlets in cities and regions across
the country to tap markets not served well enough by local and network broadcasts or when leading newspapers spend many millions of dollars to create electronic editions with a global reach. Many more are individual. Thousands of

families in Mexico or Venezuela decide to go north to escape poverty or political unrest, which leads to a need for news from their homeland in the new land. Some editors and managers are determined to finance correspondents' trips abroad, to send reporters to explore ethnic communities, or simply to make better use of the information that flows into their computer systems from every region of the world. And some young freelancers create their own foreign assignments and work with shoestring budgets and new technology to catch the interest of audiences back home.

The technological innovations of the twentieth century were centered in the big cities, where the broadcast networks were headquartered and a mass readership prompted the invention of the rotary presses that made possible million-plus tabloid circulations. The twenty-first-century evolution is spread across the country, from a little Spanish-language station in Washington State with its own foreign correspondents to a news service on the edge of Boston's Chinatown that provides PBS stations across the country with Internet stories about the day's events. It includes a newspaper in Anniston, Alabama, that sends a reporter to Russia to write about common problems of military toxic dumps; a newsroom in St. Louis where special sections explain what's behind the day's headlines; a freelancer in India who takes her own videos as she interviews ostracized women AIDS patients, and a reporter in Omaha who writes about conflicts in his city's Sudanese refugee population.

These changes are working out against a backdrop of elements that don't change, including the commitment of the nation's leading newspapers and news agencies and of CNN and some network programs—above all, 60 *Minutes* and *Nightline*—to invest in expensive coverage abroad.

But these traditional sources of foreign news are also transforming themselves, most dramatically in their Internet presence but also in cross-media cooperation like the *New York Times* partnerships with ABC, PBS, and cable channels as well as NBC's and *Newsweek*'s alliance with Microsoft in MSNBC.

"To some extent, we are suggesting a reinvention of the way editors approach international news," according to Edward Seaton, a former president of the American Society of Newspaper Editors (ASNE). From readers and editors across the country, Seaton and his editor colleagues rounded up ideas for improving foreign coverage. Some call on editors' sense of responsibility: "an uninformed public offers opportunities for demagogues and enemies." Others play on their news sense: "There are many engaging stories beyond our borders. And a lot of them have local and regional angles."[1]

"The internationalization of business, science, government, etc. has broadened the definition of 'local' and knocked down some of the walls between home, country, and world," former AP foreign correspondent George Krimsky wrote.[2] "More of the papers are becoming aware of who their readers are," Aly Colon of the Poynter Institute in St. Petersburg, Florida, says. Colon teaches new ways of reporting on ethnic communities. As the foreign-born populations of American cities grow, he explains, the media have begun looking at the new groups in ways they never did before. Reporters who get to know their communities and go beyond superficial reporting of them are performing a valuable service to all their readers, not only those in ethnic neighborhoods. "Even though you're not writing from abroad, it's still a foreign story," Colon said. "What has changed is that the readers and viewers themselves have become a part of foreign news. You see Koreans in your community. You associate with them in business or in schools, and you want to read about them. These people have good stories to tell."[3]

Andres Oppenheimer, whose columns appear in both the *Miami Herald* and *El Nuevo Herald*, its Spanish-language partner in the Knight Ridder organization, notes that the huge increase in the number of Latinos in the American population is bound to lead to a reexamination of foreign policy, with more emphasis on the region they came from and less on big-power issues like Russia and China.

"Our news isn't just *about* New England, but *for* New England," Iris Adler, executive editor of New England Cable News of suburban Boston, noted. Accordingly, the station, the largest regional cable outlet in the country, covers foreign stories in which its audience is interested or involved, including one on slavery in Sudan that grew out of contacts with Boston's venerable Anti-Slavery Group.

An airline terminal in any American city presents a snapshot of the way that this evolution has progressed. At the entrance are the ubiquitous vending machines for *USA Today*, designed to put its front page at eye level, like a television screen, and imitating TV in color and graphics. Inside, the Cable News Network broadcasts from real television monitors, with perhaps a regional cable news channel alongside. Passengers with laptops are accessing *MSNBC.com* or a newspaper Web site. Those hungriest for up-to-the-minute news can get little bulletins on their pagers or cell phones.

Of all the innovations, the most important ones are those that have made news portable. *USAToday* combined the ease of use of a local paper with nationwide availability that later broadened to much of the world. The Cable News Network and its regional versions introduced the idea that news is not a static event that happened today or yesterday but a force in flux that can change constantly over a twenty-four-hour period and then begin another cycle of change. The World Wide Web extended the reach of every newspaper in the country, in readership and geography, and was of unique importance to the *Christian*

Science Monitor, a respected paper with heavy commitments to a reporting presence in the world that was hard to sustain through traditional circulation. We next examine these three developments.

THE CHRISTIAN SCIENCE MONITOR

The *Christian Science Monitor* has tried using a variety of other media to compensate for its long-term loss of circulation. Backed by the First Church of Christ, Scientist, it first tried broadcasting the *Monitor* and freelance correspondents' reports on MonitoRadio, a service used by two hundred public stations in the United States and heard around the world on shortwave by audiences in the millions. *World Monitor*, a monthly magazine, had space for longer stories from abroad than those that would fit into the daily paper's limited news hole. But both proved too costly to maintain. *MonitorWeek* was a well-edited insert section sent to smaller papers that might not have the staff to handle foreign and national news from the wire or syndicates but could use the section without any editorial work. Again, *MonitorWeek* turned out to be too expensive for papers trying to survive the 2001 recession, despite the increased interest in world events after September 11. The most ambitious project was Monitor Television, a program available on the Discovery Channel that was praised for its thoughtful coverage of international affairs but failed to attract audiences large enough to justify the millions in losses it incurred.

Now, *Monitor* editors say, the Internet has given the paper its best chance to return to its position as a premier source of foreign news. The newsprint paper, which appears five days a week, is on the Internet every day, and its paper circulation of eighty thousand has expanded to two million Internet visitors every month. "The number more than doubled (from an average 600,000) right after September 11," a *Monitor* editor said. "That wasn't surprising, but we were a little surprised that they stayed there and then added another million." Hitching the thin tabloid newsprint version of the *Monitor* to the Web offers another outlet for the work of its correspondents—nine foreign bureaus and about twenty-five stringers—and their concise and carefully backgrounded pieces. "As long as a guy in a cave can kill your brother in an office tower in this country, Americans are going to be interested in foreign coverage," the *Monitor*'s managing publisher Stephen Gray maintains.[4]

Explanatory journalism is the hallmark of the *Monitor*, a strength born of necessity because of the leisurely distribution and delivery system with which the paper must work. Production starts swiftly, with the day's paper electronically transmitted to printing plants near Boston, Chicago, and San Francisco, but the papers go to post offices for mailing rather than to front porches or newsstands and so may arrive two or three days after publication.

Since with this system the *Monitor* can't compete in breaking news, it competes instead with the story behind the story: how a crisis started and what is likely to happen next. *Monitor* stories are seldom limited to an official statement or an announcement of economic ups or downs. They use broader sourcing and supplement the news of the day with the events and issues leading up to it.

When correspondent Danna Harman interviewed President Ali Abdullah Saleh of Yemen, readers learned in the first five paragraphs about Yemen's location, recent history, special role among Arab nations, and importance to the rest of the world. "Yemen is the only Gulf Arab country that has embraced multi-party democracy," Harman wrote, also listing education for women, free elections, and televised parliamentary debates. In this way, the background merged with the news elements of the story because Saleh told her that the best way of fighting the root causes of terrorism in his country and the region was to develop the economy and democratic institutions.[5]

Freelancer Shai Oster described working conditions in the Chinese factory towns around Hong Kong, where peasants who have left their villages live twelve to a room and make $100 a month. He found "a complex balance between what the Western media call 'exploitation' and what many workers here consider a kind of liberation" from rural poverty. He mixed statistics of labor law violations with conversations that revealed why so many have left their villages to come to the factories: "These are small-village youths who wanted a little adventure. The money is important. But they wanted to develop themselves, meet different people, maybe strike it rich."[6]

The *Monitor's* Cameron Barr won an Overseas Press Club award in 2000 for his account of the brutal path of the Indonesian army's Battalion 745 in East Timor. He spent a week retracing the battalion's retreat from the territory after the East Timorese voted for independence in 1999, interviewing witnesses to the soldiers' murder of as many as twenty civilians. Barr described how the army targeted pro-independence activists as well as carried out random killings. "We won the vote, but they still killed our families," the widow of an activist told him.[7]

"We try to tell stories in human terms, working on both the connections to our readers and the narrative skills that make these topics readable," explained world editor David Clark Scott, who used to be a *Monitor* correspondent in Mexico City. "People may not understand the chaos in the countries we write about or its causes, but they do recognize the connections to their own lives and families, as, for example, when they read about children put in danger."[8]

Narrative techniques draw readers into stories, in much the same way they are drawn into well-written books or short stories, Scott continued. For example, Danna Harman introduced her interview with the Yemeni president with images of the white smoke of frankincense and the gold and silver equestrian statues in his palace. Images and quotations are supplemented with explanatory material to trace the background of a situation or the causes of a conflict. Harman's story included the views of specialists who were less sanguine than the president about the chances of success for Yemen's progress to democracy. Oster's story contained statistics from human rights activists. This sort of backgrounding is the joint work of the correspondent in the field and the *Monitor's* foreign desk editors, long known for their care in checking and shaping stories. Budget cuts have meant that an editor usually can no longer spend a day on a single story, as was sometimes the case in the past, but the time spent is still considerable.

Monitor editors say the focus on explaining the world to their readers goes back to the precepts of Christian Science's founder, Mary Baker Eddy, who started the newspaper nearly a century ago with twin commitments to public service and an international outlook. The *Monitor's* approach (and dismal bottom line and circulation figures) seems more like that of a think tank or a university. With its motto of "to injure no man but to bless all mankind," the *Monitor* takes readers to the jungles of Southeast Asia as well as the parliaments of Europe, trying to help them understand the world outside their hometowns without the distortion of commercial or political aims. Its approach is based on the idea that when citizens have access to the truth, they can make the right decisions for themselves and society.

A *Monitor* editor, commenting on the industry-wide push for profits that is causing an outcry among journalists, said that of course his newspaper loses money, a situation that most could not afford. But he expresses the same sentiments in a busy newsroom that a professor might in a seminar:

> We tell the truth, stay away from hype because we really feel a commitment to our profession and its standards. We check facts. We don't go out with one report, or with rumor. We try to make stories interesting but we don't do it with cheap shots. It's a calling we can be proud of, even at the cost of [individually] not making as much money as we might otherwise.[9]

At least one of the *Monitor's* four front-page stories every day is international. Editors can't recall the rule being broken for many years. On September 12, 2001, a Moscow dateline shared the main news about the attack on the twin towers and the Pentagon, with the lead insisting that only one man, Osama bin Laden, had the motive and the means to carry out such an act.

Seen in this sense, covering foreign news is one of the litmus tests of professional and ethical conduct in journalism. It's the news that people should have but cannot be forced into. Instead, they must be persuaded, through the power of the story, that it is both interesting and useful. The two ingredients of this kind of journalism are the imagination to undertake stories that transcend the routine and the skillful narratives that establish the links—if not to Americans, then to fellow human beings. The costs of war or poisoned air and water are the same for Americans and other nationalities.

This can't be done entirely by interviewing peasants on dusty village roads. A backbone of fact and analysis is needed as a link back to the foreign capital and perhaps Washington. Poisoning the water or cheating the rubber workers is more than a local story. Every foreign desk helps round out stories with facts and opinions difficult to get in the field, and some encourage the use of ordinary people and their views. The *Monitor* has been the most successful at combining these elements to produce good narratives and thorough explanation, all condensed to fit into its limited space. Although it wasn't intentionally designed in this way, these techniques turned out to be perfectly suited to the Internet.

Associate editor Tom Regan, who helps run the Web site, sees the *Monitor's* success on the Internet as not only good for the paper but also a clear and positive sign that Americans' interest in foreign news is not declining as the effect of September 11 wears off. The trend is based on the two powerful factors of technology and demographics, he says, and is thus stronger in the long run than any corporate attempts to pare down international coverage for the sake of saving money.

"Young people have grown up on the Internet," he pointed out.

They turned to it on September 11 as their first reaction, the way older people turned to television or radio. Then they found that besides the breaking news, the Net provided them explanations. They discovered newspapers—which few of them read—in their electronic form, and have come back to them regularly.[10]

Regan reported that the *Monitor* has benefited greatly from these "surf and drill" practices, in which Internet users search for interesting sites and then dig into the links they provide. In his own *Monitor* column on the Web, he has introduced visitors to hundreds of other sources around the world, which is one reason they keep returning to the *CSMonitor.com* site. "And they're discovering the printed paper, too. I've had a couple of thousand e-mails that tell me 'didn't know about your paper' and 'glad you're still in business.' September 11 really changed the outlook on the importance of foreign news" to this young audience.[11]

"'The *Monitor* has become a brand,'' Stephen Gray, the publisher, stated. "It's a brand for expertise and trust. Our reporting out of the Middle East has been the best for years, with no onus attached to the Christian in our name and plenty of use and praise from Muslims in the United States and in the region." After September 11, two Arab newspapers were among the new subscribers to the *Monitor's* syndicated service.[12]

USA TODAY

USA Today was derided as the fast food of journalism when it started in 1982. It was a nationally circulated paper with no foreign correspondents, minimal coverage of international affairs from wire services, and a tendency to look on the weather and sports as the most important events to bring to the attention of its readers. But the paper grew in many ways in the next two decades: in circulation, to lead all others in the nation; in profitability, after several money-losing years; and in performance, as its reporters and editors of national stories began to hold their own with their more experienced competitors and sometimes even surpass them.

Foreign news remained the exception. With its only local news crowded into a page of briefs that provides "news from every state," *USA Today* had the space for more international news. But for years, in keeping with founder Allen Neuharth's admonition, to "help make the USA truly one nation," still carried on the editorial page, *USA Today* editors concentrated on the United States. They favored short items of spot news from Washington or longer accounts of trends across the nation in health, housing, traffic, technology, and the family. The world was mostly dealt with by snippets of information from the Associated Press. Its parent, Gannett, had a news service but, like *USA Today*, no permanent presence abroad. Gannett executives used to dismiss criticism of the paper's lack of foreign bureaus by repeating the paper's name: *USA*, which meant its focus, and *Today*, which meant breaking stories and not much depth.

In the 1990s, the paper began to open bureaus abroad at a time when others were closing them, to send more correspondents out on international assignments, to extend its audience by developing a powerful and much visited Web site, and to contribute stories to XM, the new satellite radio system. Such decisions seemed to go against the corporate practices of Gannett, which is renowned for penny-pinching in the cause of pushing its profits, already the highest in the industry, even higher.

USA Today editors say there is no conflict between higher earnings and making the paper better. They defend the early *USA Today* as not nearly as shallow as its critics contended but concede that as the paper advanced in quality, so did the quality—and the income—of the advertising.

Elisa Tingley, the world editor, has another explanation for USA Today's broadening of its coverage: the unexpected way in which the paper has developed in its second decade. "We were supposed to be the second read to your local paper, a kind of printed television, with the colors, graphs, and maps. Instead, we became the only paper that many of our readers rely on, whether they're staying at home or traveling. And that meant getting more serious."[13]

Circulation managers began to profile the readers more closely and found out that many who picked up the paper at airports or hotels were engaged in, and interested in, international trade, finance, and travel. Getting serious meant becoming more concerned about putting the United States in its international setting in USA Today's reporting. Printed in thirty-six plants around the nation and abroad (most using Gannett pressrooms), USA Today has the speed of transmission to print late-breaking stories and the distribution system to get the papers to readers.

It hired good journalists from other newspapers and promoted other good ones from within Gannett as it opened bureaus in Hong Kong, Berlin, London, and Mexico City and began to build a second tier of stringers in the field and reporters sent out from its headquarters in northern Virginia. Language skills were not among the criteria for staffing these bureaus, but knowledge of the paper and the ability to write for all four of its sections—the front, money, life, and sports—are important. Correspondents generate most of the story ideas, but messages constantly flow between the home office and the field with suggestions and modifications. What the correspondents file are not snippets of news, as in the early days of the paper, but substantial pieces on politics and society. And with the USA in mind, almost all have an American angle. That this angle isn't wholly parochial is borne out by the fact that in recent years, the international and domestic editions of the paper have come much closer together, with the international, which goes to press early in the afternoon, serving as a bulldog, or early edition, of the larger domestic version. What interests the home office in McLean, Virginia, interests Singapore—perhaps because the reader in Singapore is likely to be an American or someone with strong business or other interests in America.

The small number of foreign correspondents, even when counting the stringers, means closer teamwork from McLean. In Tingley, USA Today has a world editor who has lived and worked in Moscow and knows what it's like to cover a difficult foreign country while trying to please distant editors. Not everyone succeeds in this attempt, but most of the corps have been in place for a while. "You can't give them a USA Today handbook before they go abroad," Tingley observed. "They have to know the paper's needs." One of the main needs, for national as well as foreign correspondents, is a loose formula that says readers must know in the first few paragraphs what the story is about and why they should care.

In contrast to its old reputation of small bites of news, foreign correspondents file stories of five hundred to one thousand words and see much of that printed in the paper. *USA Today* splashed on the market with page after page of bright colors in its maps, charts and graphs, setting the gaudy tone of smaller dailies across the country. But now, staff members say, staid publications like the *New York Times* have overtaken it in the information provided by these story explainers—if not in gaudiness—and *USA Today* is devising new ways to present nuggets of information. Moves are also under way to break up the dense blocks of text that its major stories present to readers, including the thousand-word foreign dispatches.

Correspondents tend to favor the traditional inverted-pyramid story structure, with straightforward leads and quotes and not too much description or storytelling. But other approaches are welcome. Pentagon correspondent Andrea Stone sent an informative no-frills dispatch from Cairo after the al-Qaeda attacks, for example, that included quotes from official sources and analysts about Arab reaction to the U.S. war in Afghanistan as well as the necessary background. But another of her stories brought in the flavor of the Khan al-Khalili marketplace, where Egyptians observing Ramadan broke their daily fast at "God's table," a spread of food for the poor. Stone's Arab specialty was also used at home when she covered the presidential campaign for the large Arab American vote in Michigan.[14]

Star correspondent Jack Kelley is best known for his front-page accounts heavy with hard news, but he also uses narrative techniques when a story calls for them. He devoted one Middle East dispatch in 2000 to listening to Palestine radio and contrasting its news with what he found on the ground. "The Israeli criminals have fired missiles into the homes of innocent Palestinians," he said the radio reported. He checked the West Bank location and found no evidence of an attack. Another broadcast reported Hebron under siege. A visit to Hebron found calm and quiet, he said. A third broadcast reported that "our brother and liberator in Iraq, President Saddam Hussein, has just reported that hundreds of jets and helicopters are taking off from the aircraft carrier of the criminal occupation force. They are heading this way to destroy our people." "Suddenly, the report came to an end," Kelley wrote. "Perhaps the commentator realized that Israel doesn't have an aircraft carrier."[15]

USA Today staffers bristle when told that fellow journalists at the *Washington Post* now say their paper has become a good paper, even a very good paper. That isn't news, they respond, we've been a good paper for at least six years, since the editorship of David Mazzarella and his successor, current editor Karen

Jurgensen, although they also praise their predecessors, Peter Prichard and John Quinn, for beginning to eliminate chatter and stress hard news. *USA Today* also does more with less, as its staff numbers under four hundred.

USA Today bled Gannett money in its first decade, running up $800 million in losses, but by 1993 it made a profit of $5 million, which doubled the following year and has continued at a respectable figure since then, Gannett executives say.

Allen Neuharth, the former Gannett CEO who invented *USA Today*, doesn't discuss foreign bureaus or correspondents in his immodest memoirs. But he does show how concerns for turning a profit after month after month of losses weighed heavily on managers charged with cutting staff and other savings. *USA Today* proved its detractors wrong by achieving a circulation of a million in its first year of operation (in part by bulk deliveries to hotels and airlines). But the advertisers that should have followed such a circulation burst stayed away, concerned about the paper's long-term survival and put off by its apparent strategy of appealing to the Sunday comics reader rather than the more serious (and wealthy) audience of its competitors for national advertising, the *Wall Street Journal* and *New York Times.*

In a bizarre meeting of his top executives in his Florida home in 1984, Neuharth staged a replica of the Last Supper, putting on a crown of thorns to suggest what would happen to him if *USA Today* continued to lose money. The paper, a little more than two years old, was draining $10 million a month from Gannett. "We can no longer afford to run *USA Today* the way we've been running it," he told his executives. "We must produce and present even more news, with fewer people, in less space, at lower cost." With a strategy like that, foreign coverage rated very, very low.[16]

It was only many years later that *USA Today*'s managers discovered what their counterparts at the *Times* and *Journal* had long known: even though many readers want only to be entertained, enough want to be informed about the world to create a substantial, and lucrative, national circulation base and advertising market.

CABLE NEWS

If *USA Today* got into the coverage of foreign news late in its two-decade history, the Cable News Network (CNN) was international from the start. Founded in 1980, two years before *USA Today*, with $34.5 million of Ted Turner's money, it started with a mission to cover the news differently from the way the three networks had been doing it. It hired crews that were everything the networks' staffs were not: not old, not experienced, not union. Its studios, first housed in a ramshackle former country club near Georgia Tech in Atlanta, were not movie-set glossy, were not even well lighted, and, except for one, were not in New York. Its bureaus were furnished sparsely and its salaries were modest.

CNN's most important differences from the traditional networks became its greatest strengths. It was always on, not just at scheduled times for limited periods. And it was everywhere, at a time when its competitors were beginning to limit their coverage of the world.

These elements converged in the Gulf War, when anchor Bernard Shaw and reporter Peter Arnett used their presence in Baghdad and their twenty-four-hour news hole to draw millions of viewers away from the other networks. The war will be remembered as one fought in ghostly green light, with blurry images of troops and tanks and the bright lines across the sky tracing their shells and missiles, with the CNN correspondents on the scene to explain what was happening. Nighttime combat in distant time zones made the war a twenty-four-hour affair that the traditional networks found hard to fit into the regular slots. Eleven years after its founding, the war gave CNN a second launching as the place to turn to, particularly in times of crisis.

When CNN began operating in 1980, the networks called it the "chicken noodle network" because it filled its twenty-four hours of airtime with much that was amateurish and repetitive. Turner responded by labeling his rivals the entertainment networks because they weren't wholly dedicated to news. It took more than a decade, until the Gulf War, for viewers to understand his point. When they clicked to CNN, they got the battlefields and the briefings. Switching to see what the traditional networks had more often than not brought sitcoms and game shows. CNN was able to continue its round-the-clock news because it paid its journalists far less than CBS and its peers did and because it went farther afield for the news that this lean and hungry staff, often men and women fresh from their campus newspapers or broadcast stations, covered.

Reese Schonfeld, cofounder of CNN, called these recruits "video journalists," or VJs, a term he invented both to show their versatility and to demonstrate their freedom from union constraints. "For six months, they rotated through the newsroom, spent time on the studio cameras and in the editing room, loaded tape in the control rooms, fetched for the graphics department, ran copy for the writers, and answered phones on the desk," he wrote in his history of the network. "They mastered the basics of a network news operation."[17] Schonfeld also founded CNN College, a crash orientation course for both the young VJs and the more experienced newcomers to learn CNN procedures in a few days or weeks. With some budget constraints, the world was open to this new kind of correspondent, whose ranks also included network veterans seeking more challenge or just a job after the layoff cycles began in the 1980s. Derwin

Johnson was the star of CNN College. Three weeks after being hired, he was covering riots in Miami; in four months he was posted to London as a cameraman; and in a year and a half, at age twenty-four, he was the Cairo bureau chief.[18]

CNN crews came up with their own ideas of what to cover and where to go more often than the traditional network staff members did. And as CNN International grew, they were able to cover the kind of story that producers in the United States would almost never approve: an important development that didn't immediately involve Americans. Enterprise was welcomed rather than discouraged, and CNN crews did most of their editing in the field, rather than having to submit to the editorial judgment of producers far from the scene.

CNN, which turned its first profit in 1985, has reinvested money in news gathering, in contrast to the main networks and many other media. Not until the 1990s did concerns about the costs of covering the world become prominent. "For years CNN did not look at ratings," producer Steve Redisch remembered. "Now the ratings are dissected, as are the ratings of CNN's competitors."[19] Such dissections led to rounds of job cuts that were somewhat counterbalanced by higher salaries for CNN's famously underpaid and nonunion staff members. CNN still has about four thousand employees worldwide and forty-two bureaus, an increase of five in the past few years. The Atlanta newsroom is staffed by one hundred producers and editors, a number that doubles with staff called in from days off and other shifts when a big story breaks. Its world resources range from a twenty-four-hour-news-in-Spanish operation in Madrid, a fifty-member Asian bureau in Hong Kong producing for Asia-Pacific audiences, and Web sites in Swedish, Japanese, and several other languages.

CNN's foreign audience is, in fact, many times larger than its American one. It counts 151 million households as viewers around the world, compared with about 3 million in the United States at times of peak interest. Its worldwide reach makes it a factor in international politics. "Just bringing the news is a huge, huge gift to the world," maintains chief correspondent Christiane Amanpour. "It has democratized information" for people living in dictatorships or countries with only government media.[20]

During the Gulf War, the United States used CNN to respond to Saddam Hussein's offer of peace and to inform its allies that it was rejecting it. President George H. W. Bush's press secretary, Marlin Fitzwater, said that using CNN was the quickest and most effective way to get out the message because Washington could be sure that all countries in the world would be watching. Fitzwater recalled that CNN instantly transmitted his rejection of the peace offer and thus the allies as well as the enemy learned immediately that the war was continuing.

CNN correspondents have experienced the good and bad sides of the network's prominence. Charles Jaco, broadcasting charges of electoral fraud in Panama in 1989, was tracked to his hotel room by the vigilantes of President Manuel Noriega, who had been watching his broadcasts, and had to escape the country with the help of the U.S. military. World affairs correspondent Ralph Begleiter said that in the early years of the network, he was laughed off the plane when he tried to get a seat for a trip with Secretary of State George Shultz. But after a few years, he said, the State Department began routinely including CNN on diplomatic missions and even begged for it to be on board.[21]

Washington's change of heart was caused in part by the work of correspondents like Begleiter, who reported exclusively on the Reagan administration's willingness to negotiate with the Palestinians, and in part by the growth of the network. When it started, CNN was available in only twenty million homes in the United States. "Much of Washington had not been wired for cable, and many of the people we were dealing with did not even see our work," CNN veteran Charles Bierbauer said. "I remember having to explain constantly what CNN was."[22]

CNN's growing prominence and financial success began to inspire imitators. The most important is MSNBC, a complex hybrid of ownership and programming. A joint venture of the software power Microsoft and NBC News, MSNBC has a television identity of brash talk shows and domestically oriented news and an Internet presence that provides comprehensive world coverage from a variety of sources, organized by region and served by its own Web correspondents.

"My London bureau chief just got back from two weeks in Afghanistan," Michael Moran, a producer at *MSNBC.com*, told a media conference a few months before the 2001 terrorist attacks. With his miniature digital camera, "he can really go to town on a series that really profiles what's going on there." The footage, taken at a time when reports on the Taliban in U.S. media were rare, probably would not have been available without the remarkable division of labor that NBC undertook in the 1990s to disseminate the work of its correspondents by a variety of means: the original network, CNBC, MSNBC, and MSNBC's Internet counterpart. Moran said the Afghanistan footage was aimed mostly at *MSNBC.com*, which assigned the story, but that other NBC news outlets shared in the expenses of the trip and could use its video on Tom Brokaw's *Evening News* or Brian Williams's cable newscast on MSNBC.

NBC calls these outlets *platforms* and the process that serves them *convergence*. Correspondents at home and abroad give their stories and footage to the headquarters at Rockefeller Center (or Redmont, Washington, for the

Microsoft-Internet alliance), and the managers decide which programs the news will serve. The choices cover the twenty-four-hour spectrum: from the *Today Show* of morning news and chat to the evening news and the endless cycle of MSNBC or CNBC on cable or Internet. These many opportunities keep the correspondents busy and fulfill the criterion of one network executive who asked that his offerings be compared not only with the front page of the *New York Times* but also with the paper's style, financial, and other news sites.

NBC and Microsoft joined forces in 1996 to launch MSNBC because Microsoft wanted a presence on cable television and NBC didn't want to lose the audiences that were turning from their TV sets to their computer screens. Microsoft paid NBC close to $500 million to start the partnership and continues to share costs with NBC for content, meaning the work of its correspondents, producers, and anchors. Such an arrangement helps balance sheets in an era when network news audiences and thus advertising revenues are flat or declining but the costs of putting programs on the air are not.

Although MSNBC's cable television image has been characterized as talk radio with pictures, *MSNBC.com*, edited at Microsoft's headquarters in Redmond, makes up for its shortcomings in international coverage. Carrying on the tradition of some West Coast newspapers from Canada to the Mexican border, it provides a daily Pacific Rim front page, with stories from its own resources, *Newsweek* and the *Washington Post*, MSN Japan (in Japanese), and MSNBC's sister site in Sydney, Australia, NineMSN. Most stories are short and more geared to breaking news than the newspaper rim sections are, but there is also a good assortment of longer pieces. MSNBC, whose Web site carried some of the best Internet coverage of foreign news before and after the September 11 events, does well in the costly business of news gathering in distant places for three main reasons, all having to do with its corporate links. The first is money, provided by Microsoft, the MS in the logo. The second is the NBC corps of foreign correspondents and stringers, whose numbers were greatly reduced before the terror attacks and just as greatly expanded after them. The third is its alliance with *Newsweek*, which has no Web site of its own but does have a similar worldwide network of reporters.

MSNBC has stepped into a niche in international coverage pioneered by newspapers like the *Seattle Times* and *New Orleans Times-Picayune* in the 1980s. This niche is "rim" reporting: the Pacific for the *Times*, and the Gulf of Mexico for its main American port of New Orleans.

More important, *MSNBC.com* covers all the United States' rims: Europe, across the Atlantic, Latin America, beyond the Gulf of Mexico, and Africa, the Middle East, and South Asia for good measure. Its "Reporters' Notebooks" feature gives space to NBC as well as Web correspondents who contribute situation pieces or respond to questions. NBC's Martin Fletcher, a Middle East veteran, provides frequent assessments of the Israeli-Palestinian conflict. *MSNBC.com* accompanies them with useful sidebars like a list of potential successors to Yasir Arafat.

Fox, the second cable news network that started competition with CNN about the same time that MSNBC did, is a serious contender for ratings victories from month to month, largely on the basis of its focus on talk and celebrities. It is hardly a presence in international news, despite considerable effort in assembling an emergency squad to cover the Afghan war. The effort attracted more attention to the missteps of Fox recruit Geraldo Rivera than to the coverage it provided.

REGIONAL CABLE

Regional cable news stations were born a decade after CNN, with New England Cable News, and have since spread across the country, from Northwest in Seattle, Texas in Dallas, and Midway in Chicago.

New England Cable News (NECN) and its counterparts elsewhere in the country fit between the networks and local stations, covering a region. But unlike regional cable operations such as the Belo Company's in Texas, NECN has no ties to a larger entity. Belo's Texas Cable trades news with WFAA in Dallas and KHOU in Houston as well the company's main newspaper, the *Dallas Morning News*. NECN, which is jointly owned by the Hearst Corporation and AT&T Broadband, stands alone, not only in its lack of affiliations, but also in the international scope of its coverage.

NECN's founder, Philip Balboni, says that being independent gives the station the power to set its own agenda. Executive editor Iris Adler pointed out that no lines are drawn between what happens in New England and what New Englanders are interested in, which gives the station a reason to cover international affairs. Because NECN covers a region from Connecticut to Maine that includes some of the nation's top universities and an electronics research and development corridor along Boston's Route 128 second only to Silicon Valley, foreign news is a natural fit.

NECN's commitment grew from two sources: the discovery by its producers and reporters of the many international connections in Boston, Hartford, and the other cities of the region, and the interests and background of a key anchor, R. D. Sahl.

Covering the community well, not just its crime and conflagrations, "means that you learn about interesting stories with international tie-ins," Adler explained, "and that's part of what NECN has become known for." One project involved a specialist at Harvard who founded an AIDS clinic in Haiti to try to deal with the epidemic there. NECN's reporting on slavery in Sudan was an earlier international effort. "It grew out of our covering the antislavery group in Boston and led to reporting in Sudan," Adler said. "I don't think the other stations even know there's an anti-slavery society."[23]

The program, "Freedom for Sale," chronicled a slave redemption trip, during which people from the West bought the freedom of Sudanese slaves who had been abducted by the militia in the north of the country during the long-running civil war between the fundamentalist northern Muslims and the mostly black, Christian, and animist people of the south. NECN's Lorne Matalon took viewers to the actual purchase of the slaves, told the stories of their forced servitude, and reported the views of advocates on how the practice could be stopped.

Sahl, who has a master's degree in international relations, reports and produces stories from Europe and Asia in breaks from his nightly anchor duties. He researches and organizes his trips and arranges support for them from foundations. "Boston has a large foreign and a large Catholic population, and the networks simply aren't doing these things." But NECN's international outlook transcends these two factors. "We trust our audience," Sahl says. "We think they're capable of appreciating our foreign reports. There are probably thirty regional cable news operation in the United States now. But none of them do what we do."[24]

Sahl doesn't parachute in for quick looks at foreign crises. He studies his situations, does a lot of background reading, and sketches out four or five stories that will be used individually on his 9 P.M. newscast and then reused in their entirety at another time on the station's spacious schedule. With repeats, twenty-four hours a day doesn't mean twenty-four hours of original news, but it does mean a generous allotment of eleven hours.

Sahl reported on the problems of the Japanese economy and the controversial governor of Tokyo prefecture, Shintarô Ishihara, novelist and coauthor of the book *The Japan That Can Say No*, who called on his readers to be more independent and critical of the United States. Turned down for a formal interview with Ishihara, Sahl ambushed him after a press conference with a quick Q and A in which Ishihara defended his nationalism and criticism of the United States and China. "I'm a nationalist, not an ultranationalist," he insisted. "I'm proud of our identity. Is there any prominent politician who is not a nationalist?" Foreign Ministry officials maintain that Ishihara's demands, which include shutting down a large American air base near Tokyo, don't represent the national government's views. But Sahl concluded: "This is a face and name to watch in Japanese politics. He's essentially saying that Japan is an economic power and it's time that it stood up on its own."[25]

Sahl's reporting in Tokyo also showed some of the negative aspects of that economic power. He interviewed homeless laborers and restaurant workers who had lost their lodging after being laid off in the recession. A case worker who accompanied Sahl estimated the number of Tokyo's homeless at five thousand and disclosed that Ishihara's Tokyo city government provides shelter for only three hundred, and then only in winter.[26]

In Cuba for the visit of Pope John Paul II, Sahl sought out human rights activists who had staged hunger strikes in attempts to free political prisoners. Lazaro Garcia Cornuda, one of the leaders, told him that the collapse of Soviet Communism had made the return of democracy to Cuba inevitable, but a long fight was still needed: "All the governments we've ever had have taken power by armed force."[27]

According to Charles Kravetz, the station manager, after ten years, NECN has been expanding in two stages: from local to regional, establishing more bureaus in other New England states, and then, particularly in the news and discussion show at 8 P.M. and Sahl's program at 9, taking on more of the nation and the world and making use of the wealth of commentators in Boston "but being a little less elitist than PBS."[28]

NECN, which reaches 2.3 million homes in New England, outdraws CNN in its evening news audience and became profitable a few years after its founding. Such results seem to validate Kravetz's idea that stations should be as ambitious as good newspapers in bringing their audience the whole spectrum of news, from local to national to international.

Innovations in information technology made possible small cable outlets like NECN as well as huge ones like CNN. They created a new electronic audience for the *Christian Science Monitor*, and they provided resources for distributing and printing *USA Today* across the nation and the world. But as the work of the editors, producers, and correspondents of these media shows, technology alone doesn't do it. The same satellites, Internet connections, and cable links can be used for either trivia or substance. The men and women who use the technology make the difference, as Edward R. Murrow noted about television, an earlier technical marvel: "This instrument can teach, it can illuminate; yes, it can even inspire. But it can do so only to the extent that humans are determined to use it to those ends."

International journalism should no longer be thought of as something that only foreign correspondents do. — *John Maxwell Hamilton, dean of the Manship School of Communication at Louisiana State University*

It's the greatest compliment you can get if somebody puts your clippings on the refrigerator or bulletin board. —*Chris Waddle, executive editor, Anniston (Alabama) Star*

6

ABROAD AT HOME

The long trains of the Burlington Northern Santa Fe rattle across viaducts on the edge of downtown in Spokane, Washington, carrying grain and raw materials to the ports around Seattle for export across the Pacific. The *Spokane Spokesman-Review*'s reporter Hannelore Sudermann and photographer Torsten Kjellstrand traveled to Pakistan, Egypt, and China to produce "Far Afield, How Northwest Wheat Feeds the World" in 1999. "Wheat farming is our Boeing, generating more than $500 million in export sales in a good year," Chris Peck, then the paper's editor, wrote in an editorial introducing the series. Every Sunday, the paper focuses on another foreign or national issue in "Connections," a page that shows the links between Spokane and the world.

The 147,000-circulation *Spokesman-Review* is one of the many newspapers in the nation, which, along with a few broadcast or cable outlets like New England Cable News, are taking new approaches to the way that foreign news is reported and presented. One part of the trend is to make local connections to events and issues abroad, to think both locally and globally. Another is to make better use of the wealth of international material already available to newspapers and broadcasters.

The first approach started in the mid-1980s, when John Maxwell Hamilton, a former foreign correspondent who had moved to writing and generating ideas at the World Bank, began advising newspaper and broadcast editors and reporters where to find local stories that showed their communities' connections to foreign countries. Since then, subjects ranging from world trade and investment to the impact of the destruction of the rain forest have filled local news pages and, less frequently, broadcasts. "International journalism should no longer be thought of as something that only foreign correspondents do," Hamilton, now dean of the Manship School of Communication at Louisiana State University, advised. In workshops around the country, he has urged local reporters to get out and find the international links with their businesses, schools, governments, industries, service organizations, and immigrants. Continuing coverage of such foreign connections does more than fill the paper with interesting news; it puts international issues on the public agenda, helping people form opinions on problems that transcend borders, including protectionism, low-wage competition, and environmental damage.[1]

A readership survey by Northwestern University of one hundred American newspapers underscored the value of this kind of reporting. "You can make national and international stories feel like local, if you show how they play out in the lives of somebody in your community," asserted the survey's director, John Lavine.[2]

More and more American editors are starting to pay attention to surveys like Lavine's and to reexamine the way that their newspapers handle news from abroad. The American Society of Newspaper Editors (ASNE) has pressed for new ways of interesting readers in international news, and the Associated Press, owned by American newspapers, is cooperating by changing some of its old practices of foreign news reporting and editing.

"Americans don't have a clear understanding of why what happens in developing countries has any relevance to their lives," according to Hamilton. "Reporters are going to have to find creative ways of telling Americans what they need to know to live in the world." Hamilton met with editors and, in one case, local news producers to help locate local sources with foreign connections. He provided a few himself in articles included in his book, *Main Street America and the Third World*, which is used in classes and professional seminars. Many of the local-international connections he helped establish in the 1980s are still producing good and interesting news. The response to Hamilton's project showed that heartland newspapers (and one television station in Huntington, West Virginia, WSAZ) will print or broadcast foreign news of a special kind: that linked to their own communities. It also showed that far from being remote from the everyday concerns of Americans, foreign nations are partners in everything from soy bean purchases to letters of credit issued by local banks to finance trade. "Americans are becoming more mindful of their global role," Hamilton observed.[3]

Long before Hamilton's projects showed an organized way for reporters to use the news value of global interdependence, localizing foreign stories was a regular practice in some newspaper and television newsrooms. "The news is local," a producer at Chicago's WGN explained. "If the day's top story isn't local, but national or foreign, the first thing we do is try to localize it. We use world news resources to bring foreign news in, and then we put our local staff to work on it."[4] This includes contacting local ethnic communities, the Chicago Council on Foreign Relations, and the specialists at Northwestern and the University of Chicago.

"It makes sense to cover the Pacific Rim from an economic standpoint," an editor at the San Jose Mercury News pointed out. The editor, who gets to travel and report abroad, but not as much as he would like, uses wire copy from the Pacific countries, above all Japan, and then ties it in with local interests. Because Silicon Valley is not only an American powerhouse but also an expanding international business place, it makes sense to cover the links between events in Japan and the Valley from an economic news standpoint. "Foreign news equals economic news," he says, "and there are plenty of local angles" to make sure it gets in the paper.[5]

A stringer who contributes to the same paper with occasional forays abroad has her own formula, which is to write about something in Asia that interests her but to "try to have a second paragraph that has a regional business or economic angle."[6]

Although localizing is an effective way of bringing back readers to the foreign news pages, it cannot be applied as an iron rule to deciding whether to use or delete a dispatch. For one thing, a situation abroad may have no local connections now but may have a good many in the future if, for example, it is a simmering ethnic conflict that might one day require U.S. aid or even troops to help resolve. It should be the job of correspondents and wire editors to point out the situation and the potential for connections of the unwanted kind.

Another kind of story that is important to run is a human tragedy of such scale that it touches every reader, thus providing a human, if not a local, link. "You have to recognize that there may be no discrete link between Louisville, Kentucky, and Rwanda," David Hawpe, the Louisville Courier Journal's executive editor for editorials, explained. "And yet, you have to be concerned about genocide in Rwanda, as an act of world citizenship. That may not appear on any priority list that is structured out of local connections; it's important because it's important."[7]

A USER-FRIENDLY AP

In addition to establishing the local-international connections, many of the efforts to improve the play of foreign news have concentrated on making the Associated Press more user friendly for both the editors who process its copy and the audiences who consume it. The idea is that more of the many thousands of words a day the AP files as the nation's main news source for both print and broadcast should be arranged in ways more conducive to making an impact on readers: not as a revolution but only as some newsroom tinkering to make better use of the material already available.

AP editors say there's now a concerted effort on two levels to entice newspapers to print the kinds of stories that go into the background of events and explain them and, in the process, bring in ordinary people through well-written narratives. The first level is to identify the stories that need retelling and explaining, often by using several bureaus in different regions. Short, routine dispatches can turn into careful examinations of cause and effect, as when refugees or migrants die while crossing a desert or are killed while hiding in an aircraft's wheel well. Reporters in Europe or the United States can describe the attraction of jobs and a better life; those in the developing world can write about the poverty or repression that cause mass migrations. The ingredients for these constructed stories are readily available; papers like the *Dallas Morning News* have been using the survey approach for years to produce vivid and comprehensive accounts of issues like the world's dozens of little wars or the worldwide violence against women, for which the *News* won a Pulitzer Prize in 1994.

The AP and Reuters, with many times the bureau and staff, are better situated than any single paper to do this synthesis and analysis. But the approaches they take depend on management and money decisions. Someone must decide to detach an editor or an editorial group from the pressures of minute-by-minute coverage of the world. These reporters and editors must then be given adequate time and responsibility for thinking about and collecting information so that a short dispatch about a new illness or invention can be explained, backgrounded, and projected onto the world screen.

The second level is to carefully edit these specials or series; to support them with sidebars, charts, graphs, pictures, and maps; and to call attention to them with digest notices that they are coming, releasing them a week or more in advance of publication and then releasing them again on the day before in case the wire editors have missed them.

When all this comes together, the result is quite a high level of use by member newspapers, according to the clippings the state bureaus send back to New York to post on bulletin boards. These long takeouts, in fact, get a level of play second only to the very popular travel pieces that the AP files from around the world.

The agency is also working on simplifying the handling of the daily breaking news that flows to AP members around the clock. A redesigned news digest has headlines on the top to draw attention to important stories so that editors don't have to read all two thousand words to pick them out. At the bottom of the digest is a list of other featured stories selected for their writing quality or human interest, "the kind of people stories that wire editors say they want but can never find on the digest," an AP editor pointed out. "Too often, these good stories just get lost," he added.

> There are probably fifty important foreign stories on any given day. There are about fifteen slots on the digest. Washington is going to dominate that, with probably ten. That leaves five slots. We go into the editorial meeting with five stories and they will take three or four at most, with the others going to some other domestic issue. The rest of the fifty good stories are also-rans and many end up as briefs.[8]

The new system calls attention to stories about daily life or interesting people abroad that normally could not compete with the important political or economic news from the world's capitals. As a wire note to AP editors put it,

> under "Highlights," we can also push stories that editors might not necessarily notice farther down in the digest. This could be an especially well-written feature, a "letter from . . ." that points up the latest fad here or there, a piece that adds understanding to an ongoing news story. We can lead these items off with a short phrase that will catch an editor's attention: "A good read," "European Life."[9]

Northwestern University's readership survey, conducted before the AP changed its digest format, showed how infrequently these good reads from international datelines made their way from the wires to the printed page. Referring to its examination of more than one hundred newspapers, researcher Stacy Lynch remarked, "We found that stories about ordinary people account for 0.6 percent —that's zero point six percent—of the total foreign coverage, compared to 32 percent for politics and government and 13.3 percent for war and international conflict."[10]

THE FOREIGN CORRESPONDENT IN THE NEWSROOM

Strong regional papers like those in Boston, Dallas, Atlanta, Houston, Kansas City, San Antonio, San Diego, Des Moines, St. Louis, and Louisville do much of this kind of work in their newsrooms, sometimes using only their own resources but usually helped by the backgrounding and graphics they can get from the agencies and syndicates. "This is our 60 *Minutes*," is how a *Portland Oregonian* wire editor described the regular page 2 international packages he works on.

An editorial team committed to making foreign news more accessible might be as valuable as a foreign correspondent or two and is certainly a great deal less expensive. Having a team or single editors acting as foreign correspondents in the newsroom is a realistic choice for most newspapers that would never consider sending someone to Paris or Tokyo. One or two extra staff positions can make all the difference in the world, enabling someone to do careful selection and editing, some original reporting to draw on local experts, and judicious use of explanatory material that might tie the story in to local concerns.

The "World," "Insights," "Connections," and "Perspectives" pages that the best-edited newspapers run require such staffing, commitment, and experience. In monopoly towns—which mean most of the newspaper landscape—there's no direct profit incentive to provide them, although many editors argue that in the long run, quality equals profits.

It's a matter of interest, on the part of management as well as editorial staff, and time. Wire editors can use the hundreds of disparate stories that come along on the wires as raw material for multifaceted pieces that stitch together events in a region or project trends for the future. If the stories involve complex economic or political factors, the editors can provide explanatory boxes or sidebars from agencies and supplemental services or the Internet. Experts at universities or nonprofits in the area can add both local angles and new insights. The result is a better job of telling readers what happened in the Middle East or Latin America or Europe, what it means, and why they should care. Readers of the *New York Times*, *Los Angeles Times*, *Wall Street Journal*, and *Washington Post* expect this kind of editorial effort. But in most of the nation's newspapers, even very profitable ones with large circulations, this work of synthesis and explanation is undertaken only rarely.

Knight Ridder Tribune (KRT), the third largest supplemental service, has begun creating entire pages of production-ready copy for newspapers unable or unwilling to commit their own staff to such projects. KRT uses the work of its thirty-two foreign bureaus in packages of backgrounding in the form of full-page layouts with text, pictures, maps, and graphs. An example is "Countries in Conflict," a page put together by Debra Leithauser of the *Kansas City Star*, a Knight Ridder paper, which explains the conflict in Kashmir through reports from correspondents on the scene, the history and accounts of the costs of the long-running war, and current photographs from the region. The page, already made up and sized for the newsprint Web dimensions of the paper using it, can be downloaded by KRT subscribers. What's missing here is the local connection: the political scientist with experience in the region, the role of regional military bases, and the ethnic communities served by the paper. The in-house versions of takeouts like "Countries in Conflict" have far more interest to readers because of their local flavor.

The *Des Moines Register* frequently uses opinion pieces written by local academics or experts. Its "Update" section, a regular feature, links a foreign story in the news with the background in a full-page spread. One example is coupling current events—Israeli forces razing buildings in Palestinian neighborhoods—with a thorough "History of Mideast Violence," drawn from a range of sources. The readily accessible AP is there, but so is information from Web sites, including those of the government of Israel, the *Encyclopedia of the Mideast*, Macmillan, and McGraw-Hill.

The *Louisville Courier-Journal's* "A Closer Look," which runs in the weekday as well as the Sunday paper, does a good job of living up to the promise in the rest of its title: ". . . at People, Places and Issues in the Nation and the World." The special section is supplemented by other foreign news run in the traditional way. An inside front page, page 2, gathers together the most important stories in a regular nation and world section.

One example of an issue looked at closely was the water shortage in the Middle East and its effect on the conflict and politics there. Pictures, maps, and charts helped explain the one-thousand-word story written by the AP's star foreign reporter, Mort Rosenblum. Readers were led into the story with a succinct explanation of why it was important: "With the worst drought in a century, the water supply is common ground for Israel and Palestine to seek peace or another reason for war." Well before September 11, *Courier-Journal* editors introduced "A Closer Look" in the Sunday paper to restore the place that international news had once held on its pages. It proved so popular with readers that it was extended to the daily paper and given more space on Sunday. "It's an attempt to give our readers an extra dimension, depth, more explanation," a *Courier-Journal* editor said. "We wanted to raise the profile of international news in the newspaper. We were uncomfortable with the amount of international news." The readers' reactions proved that the editors were on the right track: "They indicated there was a thirst for more."[11]

Both the *Courier Journal* and the *Register* are former family-owned newspapers that are now part of the ninety-nine-paper Gannett Company, Inc., the nation's largest chain in terms of circulation. But the "Closer Look" and "Update" sections the two newspapers carry are exceptions rather than the rule with Gannett. The company is known for extreme cost cutting that has drastically reduced local and state coverage in the newspapers it has acquired while pushing profit margins beyond 20 percent in most years. The *Register* and *Courier Journal* were well regarded for their international coverage before Gannett took them over and are maintaining or restoring those reputations.

Other Gannett papers, like the *Jackson Clarion Ledger* of Mississippi, which were never prominent in foreign coverage, remain that way. On weekdays, the *Clarion*, like most American newspapers, scatters foreign stories through its "A" section, as few as one and as many as five. On weekends, when other papers use special Sunday sections to draw attention to foreign issues and explain them, it sticks to state and local news in its "Perspectives" pages. Although the *Clarion* prints as many as 160 square inches of international copy on Sundays, it makes no attempt to draw it together with boxes and sidebars. On some weekdays, the total is less than a quarter of that. In Louisville, "A Closer Look" can run to 320 square inches, ten times the international space in Jackson's paper on some days.

The *St. Louis Post-Dispatch*, an independent newspaper published by the company founded in the nineteenth century by Joseph Pulitzer, who also established the journalism prizes, uses a variety of in-house methods to make foreign news more accessible. Although it no longer has regular foreign correspondents, it is the best example in the nation for a paper of its size of using editors as foreign correspondents in the newsroom. Its Sunday "NewsWatch" section was launched in 2001, adding to an already impressive daily effort called "Nation and World." The *Post-Dispatch* uses a variety of sources—supplemental news services like Knight Ridder Tribune, Los Angeles Times-Washington Post, and Cox—to pack the "Nation and World" section with information and explanation. The section starts with a synopsis of the material to follow, designed to lead the reader into the story. A typical introduction was "In the News: Convictions in China. Just before a visit by Secretary of State Colin Powell, China convicts two U.S. based scholars of spying. The convictions add new strain to the relations between the United States and China, which had appeared to be improving." The story was supplemented by background, including a list of the scholars arrested and the accusations against them.[12]

"NewsWatch" combines information from the wires and syndicates with material written or commissioned by the *Post-Dispatch* staff, above all senior writer Harry Levins. One "NewsWatch" contained a "Letter from Shanghai" written by Richard Foristel, director of the local Webster University's MBA program in Shanghai. Besides commenting on the boost China would get from being awarded the 2008 Olympics, Foristel wrote about everyday life, including the bureaucratic troubles that foreigners must endure to get residence permits. The P-D's Washington bureau provided political context for the letter.[13]

Levins contributed his own analysis of the dispute over slavery in African cocoa-producing nations in another "NewsWatch," explaining how a consumer boycott might not be as effective a weapon as other boycotts were against apartheid. The story was buttressed with boxes and sidebars explaining the boycotts, the role of the Internet in organizing public opinion, and the response of the chocolate industry.

After the massacre of the Nepalese royal family, Levins contacted a Washington University student in Nepal by e-mail and got an on-the-spot story of tensions in Kathmandu. A *Post-Dispatch* editor says new sections enable the paper to have "a big blowout on a story of international importance," such as the Middle East, "zooming in, zooming out" with wire copy and supplementary services that provide background.

Levins is a cheerful man who writes without touch-typing skills, in the old newspaper tradition, and likes to go to the St. Louis public library, six blocks away, to do the research for the long pieces on foreign and national issues that have become a legend among *Post-Dispatch* readers. He is interested in history and in news, and where the two come together, he excels. His background series began in 1989, with a fiftieth-anniversary story on the beginning of World War II and its effects on today's world. Iraq, the Middle East, D-Day, Northern Ireland, Korea, Enron, the origins of the cold war, and many other topics have been covered since then, some on anniversaries, some because they were in the headlines, and some because the situations just needed explanation. Levins uses books, documents from the State Department, and many other government sources, U.S. and foreign.

He consults experts, some of them contacts from trips abroad with St. Louis area military units, but prefers to write in his own voice without too many quotations. There's always a bibliography for readers who want to look further. "The wires do this sometimes, and if we like the way they handled it, we'll use them," he said, "But more often, we do it here." One account he wrote at the time of the Gulf War—about how the military is organized, in regiments, battalions and logistical services, and how it mobilizes its forces when it has to go to war—brought a letter from a reader who said she'd never understood the military but had been afraid to ask dumb questions. When she read Levins's story, she put it up on the refrigerator. "The refrigerator prize is as good as the Pulitzer Prize," Levins said. "People *appreciate* what we do."[14]

The *Post-Dispatch*, in short, sounds as though its staff members have just emerged from a conference held to improve the play of foreign news: special sections, locally written background pieces, stories or letters from abroad by experts from the St. Louis area, well-crafted lead-ins to interest readers, and the wide use of supplemental services in addition to the special long-look pieces provided by the AP.

Harry Levins is a rarity in American newsrooms. But he ought to be a regular.

Every newsroom in the country could use an in-house foreign and national correspondent, someone skilled at pulling together the background that is so essential to readers' and viewers' understanding of the transient events of the day. Even the smallest newspapers and broadcasters lay out money for person-nel or services that explain the weather, business, and sports. The news of the world deserves no less.

Portland's *Oregonian*, a member of Newhouse's Advance group, has taken its foreign coverage a step further by sending its international business reporter, Richard Read, on assignments at home and abroad that contributed to two Pulitzer Prizes in three years. In 2001, Read was part of a team that won the Pulitzer Public Service Award for its exposure of abuses at the Portland office of the Immigration and Naturalization Service. He wrote about Kong Hee-joon, a South Korean technician with a scant knowledge of English who was stopped at the airport on his way to work in a Korean plant in Oregon, hand-cuffed, chained to other prisoners, and sent to jail. Although he had a visa, "just because one document was missing, they treated me as a serious criminal," he told Read.[15]

In 1999, Read explained the impact of the Asian economic crisis on the Pacific Northwest, a series of events he called "a new domino effect, more wide-spread and damaging than the imagined syndrome of old" that was supposed to describe the spread of Communism in Asia. As Asian economies tottered or collapsed, Oregon's agricultural prices and exports dropped; foreign investment faltered to one-fifteenth of its former rate, and thousands of people were laid off. Read used the simple device of tracing the route of locally produced frozen french fries—a product that earns $2 billion a year in the Northwest—from potato field and processing plant to McDonald's in Indonesia and Japan. But there was nothing simple about his use of statistics and analysis of worldwide trends that affect the Oregonian's 330,000 subscribers. "The global economy is so new, so unchecked and so crudely understood that the world's leading econ-omists can't agree on how to douse the flames," Read wrote. "The example of the Northwest french fry illustrates one sure truth: The global economy is ubiqui-tous to the point that there's no going back. Countries and regions can no more shut it out than rebuild the Berlin Wall or resurrect the Soviet Union."[16]

Read provided all the economic and statistical backing that an International Monetary Fund briefing paper would, but he mixed it in with accounts of a truck driver carrying twenty tons of potatoes to the docks at Tacoma, a Mus-lim cleric examining Indonesia-bound potatoes for Halal certification, and American Hutterite farmers who use neutron probes to measure soil moisture, infrared photographs to check on fertilization, and tractors "packed with more modern technology than the lunar rover." In this and other examples of the new kind of writing on foreign affairs, readers want to read on, not only because they think they should, but because they're enjoying the story.[17]

Read worked for the paper before going abroad to freelance and then become its first Tokyo bureau chief in the halcyon days of the 1980s, when regional papers like the *Oregonian* and *Atlanta Journal Constitution* were opening bureaus there. He says he thought his job was mostly to cover business, and so he did. In addition to the easy and obvious ones with direct Portland links to Japan, Read said, he did a lot of long takeouts on the trade balance with the United States and the relative strengths of the yen and dollar.

After about a year, on home leave, he went around the newsroom in Portland and asked people what they liked or remembered best about his work. The trade balance stories mostly drew blanks, but people did recall the relatively few stories he'd written about how ordinary Japanese live, what the place is like. "It was a time of great U.S. and world concern about the selling of America to Japan, Japan the almighty, and there was great curiosity about just who these people were and how they thought," Read said. That was the start of his letter from Japan, which became a letter from Bangkok or Beijing as he traveled around Asia. Someone got the idea for him to do a short audio piece on the same theme and to append a note to readers at the bottom of his letter to call in, listen to it, and leave comments if they wished. "The response was terrific," he said. "There were about a thousand calls a week, and some good suggestions for more letter topics." About a year after Read returned to the United States to begin working out of Portland, the paper decided to cut costs and closed the bureau. "When I went there," Read said, " I was told the cost of the bureau was about that of two reporters' salaries. By the time I left, it was nearly the equivalent of three, and that was too much for management to sustain."[18]

Read became a home-based foreign correspondent, mixing in local and regional interests with the news from abroad. The paper decided to devote page 2 to a single important issue, much of the time foreign. The *Oregonian* took a three-pronged approach to foreign news. First, it set aside the page, putting some of its best editors on it, even though as Read agrees, a lot of people don't see that kind of work as particularly advancing their careers. Second, it decided to hit some issues big: not huge, "with doubletruck introductions," but of reasonable full-page size so that people can really understand a subject. Space can always be found for such an enterprise, as he found on his Pulitzer Prize–winning Asian economy story. Third, the paper concentrated on this kind of reporting of foreign issues to the relative neglect of a repeated story about routine Middle East violence or NATO matters. Readers remember the big hit. If they don't follow every development in long-running stories, perhaps that's the necessary price of limited space (30 percent less, Read estimated, for foreign news than was the case a few years ago).

One of the keys to this big-picture treatment is a reporter like Read, who knows both sides of the Pacific and can generate story ideas and ways of carrying them out so that readers will be interested. These are keys to Pulitzers, too. Was Read's background as a correspondent in Asia a necessary ingredient for the success of the Asian economic series that won the prize? "Absolutely," he says. "I couldn't have done what I did without having worked there and been able to understand those societies—understanding what the role of the french fry and McDonald's was in a whole generation of Asians making it to the middle class, and choosing that as a step-up food past their street-food snacks, and what the [economic] collapse meant to them. It couldn't have been done without that understanding."[19]

In Spokane, Chris Peck, the *Spokesman-Review's* editor for nineteen years, sent reporters abroad to write about Spokane's international connections and established the Sunday page of the same name to show them on a weekly basis. In "Connections," readers know they can find a related story or even just a paragraph that ties the news from abroad to the local community.

The environmental controversy over Canada's plans to use weapons-grade plutonium from Russia and the United States to produce electricity in its nuclear plants headed one "Connections" page. Woven into the story was a separate piece on how the local Hanford plant was dealing differently and more safely with the issue. A story from Mexico on the compensation claims of the millions of Mexicans who worked as *braceros* on American farms also was coupled with a local story. "Without the *braceros*, many Northwest farmers would have gone broke in the 1940s and watched their crops rot in the fields and orchards," "Connections" reporter Jim Camden wrote.[20] Peck said reader response has been gratifying: "We had just dozens and dozens of people who wrote, called, and said, 'Thank you, I finally understand why I should be caring about this international news.'"

The *Spokesman-Review's* readership surveys show that foreign news is a fifth—a weak fifth, as Camden tells it—in readership preferences. Local is, of course, first, with a 70- to 80-percent rating, and foreign is probably around 30. Peck decided that unless something was done to make foreign news a topic to which readers could relate more easily, it might disappear from many papers, or at least be so insignificant as to be of little value. A "Connections" kind of foreign news, he thinks, is the only one that will survive in papers like the *Spokesman-Review*.

At a "Connections" editorial meeting, this line of reasoning emerged: Most people watch television and get at least the headlines of major foreign stories early in the day and, if it's a major one, are with the story all day, and so the *Spokesman-Review* doesn't always have too much to tell them the next morning.

This argument doesn't even consider those who get their news from the Internet. A small elite in places like Spokane—grain exporters or those active in other international businesses—read the national edition of the *New York Times*, but they number only about fifteen hundred or two thousand. "That leaves a lot of people who could be served by foreign news in the *Spokesman-Review*, if it's well presented," Peck remarked.

And not only those with business interests. The people who never left Spokane, who never earned more than $30,000 a year, they too need or ought to know about the world around them and how it affects them, whether they have kids in the military at the big base here or what changes in their personal economies will be brought about by the world economy. So we decided to fix foreign news, not get rid of it, to make it (and national news) something that goes directly to the interests and concerns of the readers, and to really put some effort into it, with a special staff, a section open every week in the same place on Sunday, so they'd know where to find it.[21]

The section is taken seriously and written with special effort; it's not a slapdash afterthought on deadline. Planning starts Tuesday afternoon, when the stories are selected and assignments given to find the local links.

Spokane has some great built-in connections. They include the regular air force and National Guard personnel at its air base, where KC 130 tanker planes are stationed to fly wherever there is military action, from the Balkans to the Gulf and Afghanistan. One college specializes in teaching English to Japanese students. And Washington State University has a corps of academic experts who travel the world on conservation and water resources projects.

Camden does some of the reporting and plans the section with news editor Kevin Gramann. They set aside wire copy and buy pieces as needed from *The Economist* and other sources. They go through about two hundred stories a day to pick the ten that make the final cut. The reporters are helped by a database called World Link, which contains information provided by reporters and editors about sources they had previously contacted. As they develop new contacts, they are added to World Link. The system lets anyone on the newsroom computer choose countries, get a quick paragraph or two on the links, and then call the source appended. "You can search your computer, hit a button, and when it says Japan, what pops up is 'Washington State exports apples to Japan,' or you can hit Pakistan, and it says 'the largest wheat buyer in eastern Washington is Pakistan,'" Peck explained. But the software is more finely calibrated than that. For Malawi, for example, the database easily finds the professor at

Washington State University who is an expert on its agriculture. The professor is interviewed by Camden or other reporters for a story accompanying the main piece, which could be about famine and war and why it concerns local readers.

Peck started "Connections" as part of his paper's contribution to the community, to explain in a clearer form how foreign news in Asia becomes local news in Spokane. Although the project is an outgrowth of the traditional localizing process long practiced by some papers and stations, it adds the important ingredient of explaining, not merely telling. Explanation is at the top of the list of the qualities that editors believe their newspapers should have, according to a survey taken for three journalism organizations in 2001. Nearly a third of editors of newspapers of all sizes stated that providing knowledge and explaining the news were their paper's most important services, ranked ahead of breaking the news, investigative reporting, and other categories, including "disseminator of just the facts." The study concluded that "the explanatory role of newspapers was considered by more editors as the most important role they have to play in their communities. Among the six roles suggested, that of just disseminating facts brought up the rear."[22]

The AP's new policy is intended to serve papers like the *Spokesman-Review* and *Courier-Journal* with the explanatory copy needed to fill up the new sections. It may also have an effect on other papers considering whether to experiment along the same lines. The AP's Tom Kent, who spent a decade as international editor, asserted that the old response to requests for more backgrounding might have been "well, you should have been listening." Now, he said, "we're realizing that points of entry to stories are important."[23]

Many other papers responded to the two-year program of discussion, education, and example set by newspapers belonging the American Society of Newspaper Editors (ASNE). "We believe U.S. editors should focus on pragmatic solutions, policies, and real-life models rather than always being led by the White House and the State Department," Edward Seaton, a former president of ASNE, explained. "They should help people cope with the globalized flow of money, jobs, technology, arms, culture, travel, communications, consumer goods, health care, medicine, illegal drugs—in a word, localize."[24]

ASNE's committees and seminars have found three ways of getting more readers interested in foreign news. One is to make better use of the resources already at hand, the millions of words of wire service and syndicate information on international issues that flow automatically into their computers but are not used or are underused. Newspaper staffs are urged to call on local or regional AP offices to find coverage or angles that would attract their readers' interest. A second recommendation is to follow John Maxwell Hamilton's ideas and localize international events and trends through links that reporters can cover at home. "The third area is cost-effective coverage abroad," says George Krimsky, the former AP foreign correspondent who now works as a news consultant.

The assumption is, if you haven't got a big bureau and you haven't got the resources of the *New York Times*, or the Knight Ridder group, you might as well forget about it. We say, take another look at the possibilities of stringers, using travelers, all kinds of creative possibilities with websites you can go to.[25] It's not always easy to find qualified stringers and free-lancers, but it's worth the effort. Assume the copy will need extra editing attention. Don't expect letter-perfect copy or the needed local context. Because most stringers tend to be less experienced or reliable than full-time staffers, some editors use them only for explanatory copy, not break-ing news.[26]

A decade ago, the *Orange County Register* had two reporters assigned to the Vietnamese community around Santa Ana, California, the largest concentra-tion of Vietnamese outside Vietnam. Jeff Brody and Kim Christensen wrote about the Amerasian children from Vietnam who came to California to search for their fathers, the federal government's neglect of Vietnamese refugees, gang conflicts, and the many successes of Vietnamese business and professional peo-ple. Cost cutting ended the special coverage, but it has now been revived in a different and broader form to reflect the growing diversity of Orange County's 2.7 million people. Thirty percent of the county's residents are Latino ("soon to be 50 percent by 2010," according to a *Register* editor); 15 percent are Asian, including Vietnamese, Koreans, and Japanese; and there are large communities of Iranians.

To serve this population as well as its traditional readership, the *Register* developed "World Report." Readers wanted news from all around the world, not just from Europe, and they wanted it every day, in the same place, consistently. Editors chose five regions to concentrate on in daily newsletters, often with ref-erences to longer stories elsewhere in the paper. Visual stories, designed to attract new readers, link into the feature.

The *Anniston Star* of Alabama, a paper with a tenth of the *Register*'s circula-tion of 350,000, presents a weekly briefing, "Your World," with graphics, color, a map, and explanatory stories culled from the wires and edited. "Your World" covers the top half of a Sunday-section page. A recent example was made up of datelines from the United Nations, Cuba, Argentina, Ivory Coast, Germany, Israel, Armenia, and East Timor.

"People are very glad that we keep track of world events and explain them," executive editor Chris Waddle explained. "Teachers are cutting out that map and putting it on bulletin boards, using it to teach history, social studies, and current events. It's the greatest compliment you can get if somebody puts your clippings on the refrigerator or the bulletin board."[27]

"Your World" is only one of the *Star*'s many contributions to better international coverage. Presiding over a family-owned newspaper with a strong commitment to public service, publisher Brandt Ayers devotes more of the *Star*'s pages to news (52 percent) and fewer to advertising than the 40- to 60-percent news-advertising ratios toward which corporate group newspapers aim. His editorial budget, too, is considerably higher than that of a group-owned paper of the same size.

As a result, reporters go abroad to follow the tracks of the Anniston area's two main businesses: chicken and chemical weapons disposal. The chickens, divided into three parts like Caesar's Gaul, as Waddle noted, are sold to China and Russia along with Colonel Sanders. The Chinese buy the feet, the Colonel the white meat, and, Waddle said, "the dark hindquarters go to Mother Russia, where they're called Bush Legs, for [the first] President Bush, who negotiated this very valuable trade relationship between Alabama and Russia." A reporter sent to Russia to find what happened to the Bush Legs did such a good job of explaining the story that ASNE named him a finalist in an international affairs writing competition. "But these are local stories," Waddle said.[28]

Another link between Russia and Anniston is their vast stocks of chemical weapons, which, under international treaty provisions, must be destroyed by 2007. *Star* reporter Jonathan Lifland traveled to Russia and Belgium, which also has the dangerous stockpiles, and to the neighborhoods around the Anniston Army Depot's chemical weapons incinerator to report that "across the miles and the cultures, life is surprisingly normal. Where the weapons are stored in Anniston, two Russian towns, and Belgium, mothers and fathers are alike in matters of the heart. They are worried, but they trust." In an eight-page special Sunday section, Lifland found that the mayor of Anniston, Gene Stedham, and the mayor of Pochep, Russia, Nicholai Kazulin, shared concerns about the safety of their citizens and the need to have the weapons destroyed as quickly as possible without political interference. "To me, it's the sooner, the better," the Anniston mayor said. "The weapons stockpile and its destruction [are] the main concern of our population," Kazulin added. A map of chemical weapon danger zones across the world and pictures and interviews with ordinary Russians, Belgians, and Alabamans helped explain the story, as did details of the international agreements and descriptions of the threat the still-existing weapons cause.[29]

"In the tribes of southern Sudan, a man's family may pay 25 cows and five bulls to a teen-age girl's family to arrange their marriage," Stephen Buttry wrote in one of a series of stories in the *Omaha World-Herald.* "In the Sudanese refugee community in Omaha, arranged marriages of teen-age girls continue, with payments in cash rather than cattle." Buttry found that many of Omaha's four thousand refugees from Sudan's civil war got married without licenses or went out of state to circumvent Nebraska's nineteen-years-old age limit. Chol Tut, a seventeen-year-old girl, told Buttry that her family first tried to arrange a marriage when she was eleven. "If you don't follow their rule, they just turn their back," she said. "They called me a whore." Chol left her relatives to live with an American family. Buttry's coverage of the Sudanese community was coupled with information on how Omaha residents could help the Sudanese cope with American culture, as well as provide rooms or apartments so the refugees could move out of their crowded temporary shelters.[30]

Some other samplings of the new approaches to foreign news include the *Sarasota* (Florida) *Herald Tribune*'s coverage of a Yugoslav-American retirement community, for which residents were interviewed during the Kosovo war to help explain the conflict's roots to the paper's other readers. Attitudes changed from defiance and denial to rationalization and hurt during the war, an editor noted: "Rationalization that there was a background here that the Americans simply didn't understand, and hurt that the country for which many of these men fought would be actually harming their families back in Serbia."[31]

Matt Storin, former editor of the *Boston Globe,* sent two additional reporters to cover the peace process in Northern Ireland. The *Globe* has long had a permanent correspondent in Ireland because, as Storin said, with a 150-year history of Irish immigration, "Boston is the first parish west of Shannon." The *Globe* produced a special section on the conflict and the conferences. "They told the history and the issues, and then told the story through various individuals and families that represented every point of view," Storin recalled. The special section ran in the *Globe* in Boston, and the paper also distributed ten thousand copies in both the Republic of Ireland and Northern Ireland on the day of the peace referendum.[32]

In Keene, New Hampshire, the *Sentinel,* with a circulation of sixteen thousand, makes up for not having a foreign coverage budget by assigning articles to traveling business people, academics, and others who specialize in regions or countries abroad, including the report of an aid worker sent to alleviate hunger in Africa. The *Sentinel* uses its Web site to carry the long Associated Press specials on world issues that it can't fit into its limited news hole, including the No Gun Ri Korean civilian massacre exposé and a series on Afghanistan's growing poppy production and the heroin trade.

Savannah Morning News editor Rexanna Lester directed a series on how the downturn in world trade not only affected the 2,600 workers at International

Paper, the Georgia city's main exporter, but also, through its ripple effect, hurt the rest of the economy, including shops with as few as nine employees.

A California paper, the *Star-Free Press* of Ventura, found a new group of readers in its Philippine American community while pursuing a story on sex tours to the Philippines. "We talked to the Philippine Americans who live in our community," editor Tim Gallagher said. "They made a complaint that probably all of us have heard—'great, you never cover our community, and when you do, it's about something sordid.'" Gallagher's reporters were sent to learn the other side: Philippine Americans active in county civic and business affairs. The paper printed both stories.[33]

The budget of the *Beaver County Times* in western Pennsylvania, with fifty thousand subscribers, could never support foreign correspondents. But so many of those readers are of Serbian, Croatian, and other eastern European origin that the paper was deluged with letters asking for better coverage of the war in Bosnia. The *Times* decided to send reporters to the scene to put together a series of articles which were praised for illuminating what was happening in Bosnia and connecting those events to people back in Pennsylvania.

THE NEWS FROM YAKIMA

The locally written foreign story was not a wholly welcomed phenomenon in the Yakima valley of central Washington. The mostly Anglo farmers of the 125-mile-long valley had long employed migrant laborers from Mexico to work in its orchards and asparagus fields and help maintain the irrigation systems that keep the valley a spectacularly bright green against a background of dry hills. As more and more of the workers decided to stay north and sent for their families, the Latino population boomed to 30 percent in Yakima, the valley's main city, and to even greater percentages in some of the surrounding farm towns.

In 1995, the *Yakima Herald-Republic* decided to take a look at its new neighbors and the state in Mexico, Michoacán, that most of them had come from. It was conceived as a big project for a traditional small-city paper known more for routine political and crime coverage than for examining trends, but the editors then in charge assigned lots of reporters, ran a great deal of promotion, and started the series on the front page.

Three reporters and a photographer spent a week in Mexico, and six others in Yakima contributed to the project. "Like the Yakima Valley, much of Michoacán is rural, arid, and sprinkled with farms," the *Herald's* Jane Gargas wrote. But "a day picking corn in Pajacuaran, Michoacán, earns $6," about the same as farm laborers earn in an hour in Washington State. The sections contained boxes of statistics, quotes from people on the street, and photographs showing both ancient architectural beauty and poverty. In Yakima, reporters tracked down statistics on crime figures (Mexicans' involvement was about equal to their percentage of the population) and local immigrant histories, usually about successful people.[34]

The editors also made a point of soliciting readers' reactions, to both the series and the relations between Yakima's Anglo majority and the newcomers. The result was a disaster. The switchboard was flooded; the phone mail system set up to take calls was, too; and most of the reactions were negative, a response made easy by the announced policy of requiring no signatures or identification on the letters or comments.

Publishing two full pages of the responses, the editors warned that some might be considered offensive, and they certainly were. "A few years ago we were worried about the Communists taking us over but with our help the Mexicans have done what the Communists couldn't," one reader said. "I do not like the Mexican series," another anonymous comment said,. "You're trying to force us, shove it down our throats. You're not telling about the drugs and the sickness and the filth they bring in here. You might just as well start printing the paper in Spanish because sooner or later that's all you're going to have is Mexican readers." A third response stated, "If the thousands of Mexicans living here and still call Michoaco-an or whatever the hell the name is, home, tell 'em to go home."

In midstream, the editors decided to put the eight-part series inside the paper: "No one had seen so many brown faces on the front page of the *Herald*," Bob Crider, the managing editor who joined the paper later, remembered. But the controversy was long and bitter and was assuaged only in 2000 when, under Crider and editor Sarah Jenkins, the paper ran another series on race, including African Americans and the Yakima Indians as well as Hispanics.[35]

Jenkins, referring to the vitriolic responses the earlier series drew, wrote in the new section that "rather than address those who wanted to shout down any discussion of race, the newspaper chose to ignore them" and the issue. "Talking about race is not easy, but it's a discourse that can't be ignored." This time, readers were polled on their attitudes, and instead of letting off steam in anonymous calls, they were interviewed by reporters, who put some of their remarks in context. An interview with a white woman who claimed she was the only one in a supermarket line who didn't pay with food stamps was bracketed with statistics that 42 percent of food stamp users in the county were white. "Ninety-five percent of the people in jail here are Hispanic," one interviewee insisted. The reporter noted that the real figure of 37 percent was only slightly above the Hispanic share of the population.

Making the complainers part of the story was one tactic. Another was for all departments to prepare better for the reaction. Advertising was warned to expect ads to be pulled; circulation staff was warned that subscriptions would be canceled. Everyone in a position to pick up a phone was given a form to record complaints and coached on explaining the series. Nothing, or practically nothing, happened. Forty to sixty unfavorable responses were received, out of a circulation of forty thousand.

"The series was far more balanced," Crider said. "It gave those opposing tolerance a forum to air their views." In addition, a gang crime wave during the time of the earlier series had abated. People might not want all their Mexican neighbors to go back to Mexico, a reporter pointed out, but they do want to them to obey the law when they're here, and that's what's happened. Also, the economy had improved in the intervening five years, and people were less fearful of losing their jobs to the Mexicans. But some people on the paper think the earlier series was better, told more, and had a harder edge. If a series is so controversial that you have to prepare staff and know you'll antagonize a lot of readers, why do it? "It's our job," Crider said. "We're part of this community. We owe it to our readers to understand their community."[36]

As both series showed, that community stretches down many thousands of miles to Michoacán state and Morelia, its capital. Yakima has great interests there, not only in trying to get along, but also in keeping the valley's economy prosperous. A delegation from the city, about half of it Latino, children of or natives of the region, went to Morelia on a mission that combined making business contacts, hiring teachers, and learning. *Herald* reporter Jessica Luce, whose proposal to cover the Mexican elections had been turned down, got to go along. Luce, who speaks fluent Spanish, stayed on after the delegation left and wrote about Morelia in ways surprising to both herself and her readers. She expected a desert and poverty but she found great cultural riches, lovely green neighborhoods, and graceful homes.

"This city of nearly 1 million people in the heart of Mexico is a jewel of colonial glory amid the farms or campos of the surrounding state of Michoacan," she wrote. "This may be Yakima's sister city, but it is definitely the elder, the more sophisticated and worldly sister," with its universities, museums, and cathedral. "People leave it mostly because of the economic malaise affecting all of Mexico."[37]

It wasn't a travel story, like, go to Mexico, it's great, she said, but according to some letters, it was an eye-opener to readers. Mexico isn't just a poor place, and Mexicans aren't just impoverished people trying to beg from us, but they have a lot to offer and to teach us.

The thing that attracted most readers' attention, however, was a quotation from a teacher about to come to Yakima: "Now I can afford a better car." Luce said she used it just to provide specifics to the story of his living standards, but many readers took it as "Yeah, they just want to come up here and rip us off," even though getting a better car is also a common aspiration of people north of the border. More teachers, from Mexico or elsewhere, are a critical need for Yakima's schools. Half the fourteen thousand schoolchildren are Latino and many need bilingual help. The teachers' union agrees that it can't find enough qualified bilingual teachers and must even hire some from Spain. But to some of Luce's readers, that didn't seem to be the point.[38]

Coverage of Mexico continues. When editors examine the run of foreign stories, with all other things being equal, they look for one from or about Mexico. An example was a story on the meeting of the Mexican and U.S. southwestern state governors, which a wire editor agreed would not have been used by a paper in Connecticut.

When Lazaro Cardenas was elected the governor of Michoacán, a detailed AP account of what the victory meant for the province was one of six foreign stories in the *Yakima Herald-Republic* on a day heavy with news about the fighting in Afghanistan. The paper interviewed migrant worker representatives who went to Mexico to complain about working conditions under the rules of the North American Free Trade Agreement. The migrants, represented by the United Farm Workers, contended that living and working conditions in the Yakima valley fell far short of the standards written into the NAFTA agreement and were able to use an arbitration panel in Mexico City to make their grievances known. Yakima's vigilant letter writers protested to the *Herald* that the workers should return to Mexico if they didn't like it in Washington State.

Luce says that her coverage of both sides of the border gives her hope that the end of the seventy-year rule of Mexico's Institutional Revolutionary Party will improve conditions there but thinks that it will be a long process. In the meantime, the immigration stream, now totaling more than half a million to Washington State, will continue as long as the great disparity in the two nations' economies remains. And that means that the *Herald* will continue its level of coverage.

Edward Seaton has countless stories like those of Yakima, Keene, Savannah, and Sarasota, illustrating his point that progress can be found in many newsrooms, not just the big and well-financed ones. A lot of smaller newspapers, he said, are finding the resources to write stories connecting their readers to the rest of the world, and some not so small have made some remarkable strides in bringing more and better-edited foreign news to their readers.

But the turnaround has barely begun, and Seaton stressed that much more work remains to be done: "Our readers are more engaged with the world than ever, yet our news columns seldom help them understand that world. The situation cries out for better ideas, information, and explanation" so that readers can figure out how international forces are affecting their lives. "If newspapers don't do it, who will?" Seaton asked, noting the dearth of international coverage in newsmagazines and on the networks.[39]

Houston is what America is going to look like. Houston is a model
for the United States as a whole with its racial and ethnic composition.
—*Michael Devlin, news director, KHOU-TV Houston*

7

NEWS FROM ABROAD
FOR THOSE FROM ABROAD

Every winter for nearly four decades, Theodore Andrica would sit at his dining
room table with stacks of coupons sent him by readers of the *Cleveland Press*,
sorting them out by country, city, and village. Readers clipped the coupons from
the paper in response to an annual appeal: "Teddy Andrica will visit your home
town in Europe." For many readers in Cleveland, where immigrants from eastern Europe formed a large part of the population, Europe meant Hungary, Slo-
vakia, Yugoslavia, Poland, and other points east. Shifts of borders through war
and diplomacy had left many of his respondents unsure of what country to
send him to, Andrica recalled in a conversation many years ago, although they
were always right about the name of their village and what roads and rivers led
to it. His own birthplace at the turn of the nineteenth century was Romania, in
a region he once described as where four national borders meet. No such place
existed, but cultures in eastern Europe do overlap in a way that makes his
description plausible. Andrica was fluent in at least six European languages and
deeply knowledgeable about the prejudices, fears, and hopes of the people of
the region. With his maps and his coupons, he planned trips and reporting that
satisfied both his ethnic constituents and the general public, readers who knew
they could turn to the *Press* for detailed information about a region important
for them to understand. Andrica interviewed relatives and village mayors (often
sitting down to three or four festive dinners every day), but he also analyzed
national and regional politics, producing some of the best-informed reporting
on Eastern Europe at the height of the cold war.

After the Soviet invasion of Czechoslovakia in 1968, Andrica's analysis was
one of the first to point out that using troops and tanks to defeat ideas was a

sign of weakness, not of strength. Thirty years ahead of the pack, he foresaw the decline and collapse of the Soviet Union: "The Communist dream for world domination ended with their invasion of Czechoslovakia, even though they may have won a temporary victory. No matter what the Soviets do in Czechoslovakia, the Soviet empire is lost."[1]

At home, Andrica was equally well informed about U.S. domestic politics and the effects of ethnicity and race. In 1972, he wrote that

> in the old days, the word "ethnic" hardly was known and seldom used. The polite collective name was simply "foreigners." The impolite but often used expression ranged from dago to hunky. It was thought that by depriving the newcomers of the century-old cultures and customs they would become "real Americans." Now the melting pot idea has practically disappeared. Politicians claim that in Cleveland the ethnic and black votes are the determining factors in local elections.[2]

Before television and the Internet, Andrica saw the advantage of using other media for his reporting. His still photograph of Adolf Hitler reviewing troops after the German march into Austria in 1938 was widely reprinted. He carried a movie camera on most assignments, taking shots to illustrate his lectures when back home in Cleveland. He once estimated that over four decades his audiences totaled 400,000 people.[3]

Andrica had counterparts on other newspapers, most notably Ruben Salazar of the *Los Angeles Times*, who served as a foreign correspondent in Vietnam and Mexico City and covered the barrios of East Los Angeles. Salazar was the first Mexican American journalist to report for mainstream English-language newspapers, beginning with the *El Paso Herald-Post* and moving to the *Los Angeles Times* in 1959. In both foreign and domestic assignments, his reporting produced insights and information new to the generally conservative *Times* editors but increasingly welcomed by the paper's readers, as excerpts from his dispatches to the *Times* show.

"A student anti-government movement seems to be spreading throughout Mexico," he wrote in August 1968 from Mexico City. "In taking their cause directly to President Gustavo Diaz Ortaz, the students were breaking a tradition long held sacred in this 'one-party democracy.' A Mexican, it is understood, can criticize anything except the president, leader of the almost monolithic Institutional Revolutionary Party (PRI)."[4] Two months later, Salazar witnessed the bloodiest clash between students and government troops and went beyond the official count of six dead to check out doctors and hospitals. "One doctor said three floors of the Red Cross hospital were filled with wounded and dead from the battle," he reported. "Sources said as many as 30 people may have been killed," a figure that proved to be correct.[5]

"When *la migra* calls, the Mexican trembles," Salazar wrote in 1970 in a report on immigration based on his coverage of Los Angeles's barrios. "*La migra* is Chicano slang for the U.S. Immigration service." Using the derogatory term for illegal border crossers, he wrote:

> A wetback lives in constant fear. Fear that he will be discovered. Fear of what might happen to him once *la migra* finds him. . . . The wetback employer knows no such fear. There is no law against hiring wetbacks. There is only a law against being a wetback. When the wetback is caught he is jailed and deported. Nothing, however, happens to the employer.[6]

Salazar wrote in support of a proposed law to impose fines on American employers for hiring illegal border crossers but noted that

> anyone who has seen the fetid shacks in which potential wetbacks live on the Mexican side of the border can better understand why these people become wetbacks. It is obvious that the United States and Mexico must talk and plan on the highest level to forestall an even more serious wetback explosion in the future.[7]

David Shub, a Russian émigré writer, first made his name in the *Jewish Daily Forward* of New York when early in the twentieth century it began printing dispatches from correspondents in Russia, Palestine, and other countries. The *Forward* was the first to report the man-made famine in Russia accompanying Stalin's collectivization drive, in which some six million peasants died of starvation, Jacob C. Rich wrote in his history of the paper. *Forward* staff members Harry Lang and M. Osherowich visited Russia at the time and brought back eyewitness accounts. Rich remembered that the *Forward* was also the first to analyze the purges on which Stalin based his power and the Soviet system of forced labor. "Well before the Hitler-Stalin pact, the *Forward* received information that Stalin was making secret approaches to the Nazi regime," Rich wrote. "It was also the first to report Soviet anti-Semitism."[8]

The *Forward* was published in Yiddish, however, and it was up to the writers themselves to make the crossover to the English-language reading public. Shub, who had known many of Russia's revolutionary leaders, did this in the *New York Times Magazine* in 1930 with one of the first articles to focus attention on the

Soviet Union's totalitarian direction. "Four years ago less than a name to the outside world, unknown even among the masses, today the dictator over the destinies of 150 million people—that has been the phenomenal rise of Josef Stalin," he wrote. "No emperor has ever commanded such authority as this son of a Georgian shoemaker."9

Shub went on to become a leading authority on the Soviet Union. Salazar was killed in a police attack on a demonstration he was covering in a Los Angeles barrio in 1970. Laguna Park, where the demonstration took place, is now named after him. Andrica retired in 1973 from the *Cleveland Press*, which ceased publication in 1982. In the intervening years, the foreign and ethnic media in the United States have burgeoned to keep pace with the increases in immigrant populations, and Americans who don't speak foreign languages are gaining more access to them.

Many students of American immigration patterns say that these foreign media developments are likely to be only temporary, citing example after example in which Finnish-only readers become bilingual and then English-only. But the world has changed since large numbers of Finns set sail for New York. Latino and Asian families are much more in contact and in flux, with e-mail, cut-rate international calls, and cheap air fares making it easier to maintain residence and family links between the United States and Latin America and Asia. Patterns of immigrant assimilation are already different from those in which immigrants got off boats and stayed in place until they or their children learned English. As the migration streams continue and the technology of communications and travel advances, these patterns are likely to diverge even more from those of the past.

Salazar and Andrica aimed at both ethnic and general audiences. The general audience included many whose interest in foreign and local ethnic community affairs was stimulated by living among large numbers of neighbors from abroad. Angelenos who had never been to Mexico needed to know more about the place if only because more and more of their neighbors came from there. Salazar gave them that information and also news of some of the barrios in their own city. Clevelanders who were uninterested in the old animosities between Pole and German or Hungarian and Slovak were vitally interested in the cold war and Andrica's detailed knowledge of life and prospects under Communism.

Since their time, this kind of international news has taken two paths. The first, a continuation of this tradition, uses the mainstream media to cover foreign events and their impact on local communities. This makes these stories accessible to everyone, both ethnic audiences and the general public. The second informs Americans with a foreign background through foreign-language television, radio, and newspapers, as networks like the Spanish-language Univision gain market share in American cities and foreign newspapers cater to big-city ethnic communities through electronically transmitted editions from their homelands.

Reports on politics in northern Mexico and the border economy are followed by Anglos and Latinos alike in the *San Diego Union-Tribune*, as are the cross-border stories in the *Houston Chronicle* and the *Dallas Morning News*. The *Los Angeles Times*, which like the other papers in the region has long had correspondents in Latin America, started a Latino initiative to put young bilingual journalists on new beats in Los Angeles's Latino community. San Jose's *Mercury News* covers the California Vietnamese community's interests and those of its wider readership with a bureau in Hanoi and many local stories. It publishes a Vietnamese-language weekly as well as *Nuevo Mundo*, its Spanish supplement. When the main paper's Spanish-speaking reporters produced a long investigative series on fraud and theft in the transfer of dollars to Mexico by immigrant and other Latino families, the series ran in *Nuevo Mundo* in Spanish before appearing in the English-language *Mercury News*. The *Mercury News* was the first U.S. paper to establish a bureau in postwar Vietnam, in 1994, and five years later became the first to publish a separate Vietnamese-language paper, *Viet Mercury*. In 2000, to mark the twenty-fifth anniversary of the fall of Saigon, both papers ran special sections. They included stories by Mark McDonald, chief of the Vietnam bureau, and *Viet Mercury* editor De Tran, an émigré who wrote about the lives of the San Jose area's Vietnamese community, which, has about 100,000 people.

A New York ethnic paper, the *Irish Echo*, broke the 2001 story of the historic decision by the Irish Republican Army (IRA) to disarm. Jack Holland, an *Irish Echo* editor who has written extensively about the IRA in a book and in the newspaper, had the story a week before the rest of the world. Although it was couched in escape clauses because of the volatile history of the IRA's infighting and broken promises, Holland's report said clearly that a "gesture of good faith" would be undertaken by the IRA within the month. The *Echo* story was widely reported by wire services and daily papers; Holland's reporting was confirmed when the IRA made its announcement two weeks later.

This kind of ethnic-to-mainstream reporting, however, has been greatly overshadowed by the surge of foreign news written in foreign languages aimed at American audiences. Across the nation, Spanish, Chinese, Greek, and Urdu newspapers and broadcasts report about events abroad and at home. Some of the news they carry is of interest only to their narrow ethnic audiences, but a great deal offers insights into issues and events that affect the larger public, like the coverage and analysis of the Tiananmen Square massacre on San Francisco's Chinese-language television station KSFT.

Spanish-language newspapers and television networks have transformed the way that the nation's Latino citizens and residents get the news. Los Angeles's *La Opinion* is one of the country's one hundred largest-circulation newspapers. The daily Nielsen ratings of Univision's Spanish-language television station in New York have surpassed those of WCBS and challenged those of its other English-language competitors, following audience patterns already recorded in Miami, Houston, and Los Angeles. Univision's rival Telemundo now belongs to NBC, which sees it as a way of tapping the expanding Latino advertising market. There about five hundred foreign-language newspapers across the country, some produced locally and some sent electronically from the home nation. All are rich sources of international news for Americans from those countries and hence a growing force in those sectors of public opinion. In New York City, where half a million new immigrants became residents in the 1990s, the immigrant affairs office has contacts with 177 foreign-media outlets that publish or broadcast in more than thirty languages.

A United Nations of different foreign-language papers or broadcasts, however, does not itself guarantee more foreign news for the public as a whole. Few Americans who are not of Polish or Arab background can read the Polish-language *Nowy Dziennek* or understand al-Jazeera's broadcasts in Arabic. To reach the mainstream with news of immigrants at home or their countries abroad, stories must be published or broadcast in mainstream media.

There are two ways of doing this. Foreign-language news can be made accessible to larger audiences by being translated into English or by providing bilingual material. Newspapers like the *Forward* switched from their original language to English as their readership changed. In Texas, Laredo's *Morning Times* has been bilingual for eighty years, publishing news from Mexico and the border region in both its English-language columns and *El Tiempo*, its Spanish-language section.

Now, two offshoots of those traditional methods are emerging, with a potential for far larger audiences. In San Francisco, New California Media is a project of translators and editors who tap the expertise and insights of a range of small foreign-language media and provide them to English-language news media and Internet audiences. In Miami and Los Angeles, the managers of Telemundo and Univision are beginning bilingual programs that could someday open their news and public affairs coverage to English-speaking viewers.

New California Media's program is driven by journalists who think the ethnic media are a neglected source of information for American audiences.

They and the reporters who use their news service or visit their Web site find good foreign stories in their ethnic communities. One that made national news was the disclosure in *India West* that McDonald's was using animal fats in its french fries, to the consternation of Indian and other vegetarians. Such reaching out to new sources is simply good journalism. Univision and Telemundo think more of advertising revenue, seeking to attract the millions of Latinos who prefer watching English-language to Spanish-language programs or like to switch between them.

Both the terrorist attacks and the 2000 census focused more interest in news from the world outside the United States' borders. The census gain of more than 59 percent for Latinos (which was accompanied by smaller but impressive increases in other foreign-born residents) made Latinos the nation's largest minority, with a slightly larger population than African Americans. More than half the Latinos counted by the census bureau are from Mexico.

In Miami, *El Nuevo Herald* editor and publisher Carlos Castaneda thinks the new makeup of the nation's population will bring about a realignment of its international priorities. *El Nuevo Herald*, an offshoot of Knight Ridder's *Miami Herald*, will be there to serve the needs, not only of the city but also of the region, he says. In both papers, the weather map stretches all the way to Bogotá, and this city with a Latin majority shows its status as the capital of the region in many ways, from neighborhood to international.

"This region will become a new European Union," Castaneda says, "with Miami as its capital, its Brussels," when Presidents George Bush and Vicente Fox complete their plans to extend the North American Free Trade Area from Mexico southward. "Our readers are Spanish-speaking Americans and Latin Americans from West Palm Beach to South America, and not a few bilingual business people who need to know in detail what political and economic events affect them." Cuba isn't foreign news in Miami, it's local news, Castaneda points out, and more and more, news from Colombia and Venezuela is becoming local news, too, as political crises push immigrants from those countries to Florida. *El Nuevo Herald* has a correspondent in Bogotá who also covers Caracas and many reporters who cover the growing South American populations in and around Miami in Broward and Dade Counties.

Because the *Herald* has a larger and more diverse readership to serve, and one that includes African Americans, Haitians, and Jews, *El Nuevo Herald* can concentrate on Latin America. It focuses on Spanish literature and the arts, for which Miami is the hemisphere's capital, instead of serving disparate tastes. Whatever their native language, the export bankers, lawyers, manufacturers, and traders follow the economic, political, and social issues of the region in *El Nuevo Herald*. "If they have a need to know about events and trends in the region, it's on their desks every day," Castaneda says. So is the *Herald*, but they'll find far more coverage of the region in the Spanish-language paper, he says. And because of cost cutting by Knight Ridder, there is considerably less coverage than in the *Herald* a few years ago, according to Miami journalists. *El Nuevo Herald* staff members say their paper has become a conduit for news from Latin America to the English-language *Herald*. "First it's reported here, and then they pick it up," an editor of the Spanish-language paper said. When dissidents in Cuba demanded a referendum on human rights, for example, the first Miami coverage was in *El Nuevo Herald*.[10]

But this crossover effect is more limited than his description would indicate, according to a bilingual reporter on the other side of the building who works for the English-language paper. He estimates that two to four stories a month make it from Spanish to English. Still, that's a net gain in knowledge of the region for English-speaking readers.

One undisputed sharing is the "Oppenheimer Report / El Informe Oppenheimer," the international column that appears in both *Herald*s. Andres Oppenheimer, a member of the *Herald* team that won the 1987 Pulitzer Prize for its investigation of the Iran-*contra* scandal, stresses the links between the region and issues in the United States. An example is his analysis that U.S. legislation to counter the al-Qaeda terror network contains measures against money laundering that will help in the fight against political corruption in the hemisphere and elsewhere in the world. The reporting in Oppenheimer's columns resulted in a book on illicit cash flows and politics, *Eyes Blindfolded*, which made the bestseller list in his native Argentina.

Miami's radio links with the Caribbean are another main source of news for the city's Cuban and Haitian communities. Some of this news gets into the two *Herald*s, but most is circulated only in the communities. Cuban American radio stations in Miami keep close contact with the Coast Guard and Immigration Service concerning the constant landings of refugees in rafts or boats on Florida's coast to find out the names of those who have made it safely. In broadcasts heard in Cuba as well as Miami, they deliver the news of their arrival and, through their omissions, those who didn't make it.

Haitian Americans read the *Herald*, but many also get their news from local radio programs. Small stations deal with entrepreneurs who pay a few hundred dollars for an hour of airtime and then attract audiences by providing news and earn money by selling ads. The news comes from telephone calls to and from the island, visits, and the thick currents of rumor and gossip in Miami's Haitian community. Of course, the programs are political and slanted, but some of the best ones are quite informative, according to *Herald* reporter Yves Colon, who covers Haiti and Miami's Haitian community. "You have to listen to a lot of stations and then read between the lines," a Haitian American artist commented about local Haitian radio. "A lot of it is opinion, but if you cross-reference enough, you can get the facts."[11]

The *Orlando Sentinel* serves its English-language and Spanish-language readers differently than the *Herald* does with a bilingual paper, *El Sentinel*, supplementing the main one once a week. The Orlando area's Latino population has grown to 300,000 and is expected to add another 100,000 in a few years. *El Sentinel*, a free paper, started with a circulation of sixty thousand, distributed to "selected residences," meaning Latino neighborhoods, and also available in stores frequented by Latinos. Its companion Web site exemplifies the intertwining of foreign and local news for the Latino community. Connect with your compatriots, it says in Spanish, offering links to seventeen Spanish-speaking countries in Central and South America as well as to Puerto Rico and Brazil. The front page is already connected with their compatriots: stories from Venezuela, Colombia, Argentina, and Puerto Rico—all in Spanish, with English summaries.

Maria Padilla, Hispanic affairs editor of the *Sentinel*, is *El Sentinel's* editor, and the paper uses reporters from the parent paper as well. The *Sentinel's* bureau in Puerto Rico and the Havana bureau of the *Chicago Tribune*, which owns the *Sentinel*, are other resources. The *Sentinel* chose a bilingual approach, according to publisher Kathleen Waltz, because the Orlando area is "a truly bilingual marketplace," where advertising is aimed at readers in both English and Spanish. Spanish-only papers sometimes have trouble attracting ads from large retail stores unwilling to translate their copy.

Public editor Manning Pynn, whose job is to answer readers' complaints, found that some objected to the *Sentinel's* giving away the new paper when they had to pay for their English-language edition and also to publishing a paper in Spanish. "People who don't have to learn the language of the land they have come to are now more special than the rest of us," one reader wrote. Pynn explained that the bilingual paper means "people who speak Spanish and want to learn English will have the translation right at hand, as will those who speak English and want to learn Spanish." But why learn Spanish? "Because those people are our neighbors—our coworkers, our customers, our employees, our employers. And there are 181,300 more of them—a 163 percent increase—in Central Florida than there were just 10 years ago," Pynn wrote in his *Sentinel* column.[12]

"We're bilingual because our demographics show that our Hispanics are much more bilingual," Padilla says. Most of the Latinos in central Florida have migrated from other parts of the United States rather than from their home countries and thus want a paper in both languages. Miami, on the other hand, is a port of entry from Cuba and South and Central America, and it makes sense for El Nuevo Herald to be only in Spanish. Padilla notes that the growing number of Latinos among the Sentinel's readership means that the English-language paper prints more news about the homelands of its readers than it used to. The controversy over U.S. Navy's bombardment of Puerto Rico's Vieques Island is an example. Since many of the Orlando area's Latinos are of Puerto Rican background, the story gets far more play than the Sentinel would otherwise give it.[13]

An Arkansas publisher has used his English- and Spanish-language weeklies to provide two viewpoints on the problems of the small town of Danville, where an influx of Mexican and Salvadoran chicken plant workers reduced a nearly all-Anglo population to only about half. Reporter Lisa Broadwater, interviewing long-time residents for the Arkansas Times, found a great gap between their opinions and those expressed by the migrants in the Spanish-language paper El Latino. "You have a certain amount of prejudice," Mayor Steve Pfeifer told her. "But overall, most of the people have been as receptive as they could be to the Hispanics." Moving to Danville from California was horrible, Veronica Hernandez recalled. "In California, we have other nationalities. Here it was kind of crude at first. There was a lot of discrimination."[14]

Publisher Alan Leveritt started the Times as an alternative voice when the state's two main dailies, the Arkansas Gazette and Democrat, merged. El Latino is following the Times's pattern. One of its first stories dealt with the Catholic Church's criticism of working conditions for the Latino immigrants. With an editorial staff of only two, El Latino doesn't do much outside reporting, although it prints a lot of foreign news that its editor, former Argentine journalist Michael Leidermann, gets off the Internet for the Mexicans and Central Americans who are the bulk of El Latino's readers. The Times, whose focus is the state, leaves this foreign news to El Latino.[15]

The telephone book in Laredo, Texas, is like a two-language dictionary, with Yellow Pages in its front half and turned upside down, Las Paginas amarillas in its back half. The Laredo Morning Times has been putting out at least two pages of news in Spanish every day since 1923.

"After the Mexican Revolution, Mexican priests, accountants, lawyers, and other professionals came to this side of the border," longtime editor Odie Arambula explained.

They didn't speak English, so they were given jobs in production. There was tremendous hunger for news from Mexico, so they convinced the editors to let them write an article or two from the backshop in Spanish. Since then the Times has always had editors and reporters who write in English and Spanish.[16]

Laredo, founded in 1755 as a Spanish colonial town, was briefly the capital of a tiny republic that included parts of present-day Texas and northern Mexico and proclaimed independence from both. After the Mexican War it joined the rest of Texas as part of the United States. Without the Mexican border, the Rio Grande, and the Mexican city of Nuevo Laredo across the river, Laredo would likely be just another of the spare small towns spaced out along the plains of West Texas. The border gives it business, life, and news. Forty percent of the overland trade between the United States and Mexico goes through Laredo and Nuevo Laredo. Arambula says that Laredo and its surrounding county grew by 45 percent between the last two censuses, twice the figure for the state. In fact, he's seen nothing but growth since starting on the paper more than thirty years ago. Another census statistic that defines Laredo and his readers' interests in news from across the border is its Latino population of 94 percent, three times the statewide figure.[17]

Arambula provides a four-way flow of foreign news in the twenty-thousand-circulation Hearst paper, if news of the immediate transborder area is considered foreign instead of local. The first two flows are the foreign news that both the Spanish- and the English-language papers print from abroad, more than the usual amount for other papers their size. The emphasis is on Latin America, with Mexico predominating. But the *Times* also pays attention to the rest of the world, with a good selection of opinion columns, and *El Tiempo*, its Spanish-language section, does the same in its use of wire copy.[18]

What is different is the work of Miguel Ramirez, the *Times/Tiempo*'s man in Nuevo Laredo. Ramirez covers the day-to-day happenings across the river, filing four or five stories a day for *El Tiempo*, many of which are translated by bilingual staff members for the *Times*. "This means that both our English- and Spanish-speaking readers have a regular source of news from across the border," an *El Tiempo* editor noted.[19]

The two Laredos have always been close, but Ramirez's bylined stories give readers on the U.S. side a reliable source of information, something that wasn't always available in the past. Crime and trade are the two basics. Although the rise in cross-border trade since NAFTA was passed has led to enormous economic growth, particularly in Laredo and the highways and truck depots that sprawl around it, it also has created many problems. Mayor Betty Flores has complained personally to President Bush about the environmental and traffic impact of the nearly twenty thousand trucks crossing the border each day. The *El Tiempo* editor noted that one of Ramirez's most important functions is to make sure the paper also gives the views of Nuevo Laredo's political leaders and citizens on such issues.

In Granger, Washington, in a rickety brick building on the edge of town, a former railroad hotel called the Highline, KDNA has been broadcasting for more than twenty years. It is the only Spanish-language public radio station in the United States and has music, call-ins, news, and numerous services for its 28,000 listeners. The station, which Latinos call Cadena, the "chain" or "link," in a reference to its similar-sounding call letters, has won awards and Benton Foundation support for the health programs it broadcasts for the Mexican Americans and Mexican and Central American migrant workers in the Yakima valley.

But as the program director, Gregorio Martinez, points out, what the station does with links to the homeland is nearly as important as its considerable community service. Now the station has three foreign correspondents to tie Granger to the places from which most of its population came: Morelia, Sierra Nahua, and Mexico City. Once a week for about ten to fifteen minutes, a link is established between these places and Granger. The Mexico City segment is a traditional correspondent's report of what's happening in national news; the other two are an open forum for callers who want to get their thoughts and point of view back to the folks in the Yakima valley. They talk about a range of subjects, but not about Tia Maria's leg pains, station manager Antonio Balderas says. It has to be of general interest, and there is plenty that ties the valley to the Old Country, with politics and the economy heading the list and immigration news from both sides of the border a strong and steady feature. NAFTA and Vicente Fox's administration in Mexico dominate the talk these days. Morelia residents get on the radio with far-reaching assessments of the president's performance, and despite general approval, Balderas said, plenty of people have plenty to criticize.

Michoacán, like agricultural areas elsewhere in Mexico, has been losing population since the 1960s, first to Mexico City and then to the United States. About fifty thousand people leave the state each year for work north of the border; half of them stay. As Balderas's call-in correspondents from Morelia and Sierra Nahua report, the flow of money from the United States continues, helping residents restore houses, improve farms and villages, and maintain roads and other services. There are also more and more unoccupied houses and half-filled school classrooms as the migrants send south for relatives to join them in leaving Mexico for good. This is why KDNA's news coverage places so much emphasis on Fox's policies: at home, improving the economy and reducing corruption so that talented people will want to stay, and abroad, loosening U.S. border restrictions so that Mexican workers can come and go freely.

In addition to the call-ins and the links, news of Mexico and Latin America dominates the generous news hole of Radio Cadena, with the sources a variety of newspapers and services that Balderas pulls off the Internet: EFE, the Spanish news agency; *La Opinion* of Los Angeles, and *El Nuevo Herald* of Miami.

Balderas is a one-person foreign desk, but he also keeps an eye on local events. He's a familiar figure alongside the farm fields around Granger, in his baseball cap and pickup truck, checking on working conditions and chatting with laborers and sometimes using their complaints and observations on the air. One summer morning, after he'd been watching crop spraying in a field adjacent to one in which pregnant women were working, he warned the owner to stop. Balderas used to work in such fields. He emigrated from Mexico as a twenty-two-year old in 1973 and cut asparagus, picked fruit, and worked on a dairy farm before joining the station as a volunteer when it started in 1979. His first job was to wake up listeners with *musica rancheras*, Mexican country music, and now, as station manager, he still starts the day that way until his news broadcasts begin.

Radio Cadena's bootstrap news operation is highly successful in terms of its core audience, but its appeal to the valley's majority population is limited to the relative few who are bilingual. Thus none of the concerns in Morelia about migration or education are reported to the emigrants' new neighbors around Yakima. One narrow window of information comes from the reports by the bilingual journalists working for the *Yakima Herald* and other papers. Those trying to thoroughly cover the neighborhoods, majority and minority, sometimes turn to Cadena's broadcasts or talk to Balderas and others at the station. But this is usually done in times when the Hispanic community is in the news because of crime or charges of discrimination. The full story of the human, social, and economic relations between Michoacán state and the Yakima valley is reserved for Cadena's regular listeners.

SPANISH-LANGUAGE TELEVISION

In Miami, Telemundo's dozen huge satellite dishes rise above the neat single-story houses of Hialeah, a mostly Cuban American community where motorboats on trailers are crowded into driveways and a fruit-and-vegetable truck still makes the rounds. The network's warehouse headquarters is in a district of auto glass and furniture shops, but its reach is international. It competes for the largest and fastest-growing ethnic television audience in the United States, and it broadcasts abroad to reach millions of other Spanish-speaking viewers. Long a distant second to the dominant Univision, Telemundo gained enormous potential strength when it was acquired by NBC in 2001.

Across the city at Univision's national newsroom, anchors Jorge Ramos and Maria Elena Salinas broadcast a nightly news program that reaches ten times more viewers than CNN does in its 6:30 P.M. time slot. Ramos drove for twenty-one hours from Miami to New York after the attack on the World

Trade Center to report on the tragedy, including the toll of the undocumented aliens, most of them Mexican, who worked in the buildings.

Ramos came to the United States in 1983 as an undocumented immigrant himself, crossing the border with other Mexicans. Unlike most of them, he left for political reasons, the censorship and political pressures on his work as a journalist under the long rule of the monopoly Institutional Revolutionary Party. His first job was waiting tables in Los Angeles, where he decided to go to a language school to improve his English. "'You need it,' they told me," he said. "'There's no future in Spanish-language journalism here. Your accent will keep you from finding a job on English-language stations.'"

Now there are signs that Univision's news program, *Noticieros*, with a hard news and international emphasis reminiscent of the best days of the American network news, may begin to reach audiences beyond the Spanish speakers in this country. Univision is going bilingual, not in news at first, but according to sources in the network, eventually, perhaps first in the form of a newsmagazine program designed to attract both Spanish- and English-speaking audiences.

With its purchase of the USA Network's television stations, Univision, which is owned by Venezuelan investor Gustavo Cisneros, has more than doubled the number of its twelve stations, gaining access to Atlanta, Boston, and Philadelphia, and has acquired second stations in seven of the eight top Latino markets.

Since those acquisitions and NBC's purchase of Telemundo, bilingual programming has been much discussed by both networks. The aim is to attract the many hundreds of thousands of potential Latino viewers who share the culture but not the Spanish language, as well as the millions of others who are bilingual. The target is the young, the favorite of advertisers in any language, and this means that sports and music will predominate in the new programming. People at the networks think that news is a definite possibility not too far down the road. Will it be tailored to the generation that isn't supposed to be interested in serious matters like news from abroad? Not if the record of Ramos and Salinas's nightly news program has any weight in network news policies and not if September 11 has any meaning, Ramos says.

The new programming got its start with Telefutura, a second network launched by Univision on its newly acquired stations. From Univision's point of view, capturing this audience of Latinos who want their programs in English or both languages is very important. Part of the thinking is to provide them with links to their or their parents' homelands with regular news of political and cultural developments there. Members of this potential new audience are considered a bit more removed from the homelands than their parents, since they were born or raised in the United States, but they have many of the same interests.

Both networks hope to attract yet another audience, whose size they can't estimate: Anglos with an interest in the culture of and information about Latin America. The U.S. networks, Ramos observed, learned after September 11 the consequences of their emphasis on scandal and celebrity: "When you ignore issues around the world, they do affect you nevertheless. Hopefully, this will make Americans more interested in what's going on in the world." Before the terrorist attacks, Ramos explained, Univision had been under a little pressure to lighten up its news selection after Telemundo began to gain some ground among viewers. But it wasn't the news, Univision producers decided, it was *Betty the Ugly One*, a phenomenally successful *telenovela*, or serial drama, imported from Colombia, which proved so popular with its Cinderella theme that Univision bought it out from under Telemundo. "Then came September 11 and we proved we'd been right" about keeping the focus on world events, Ramos concluded.[20]

Ramos says his audiences turn on *Noticieros* every night for several reasons: to find out what CBS and the other networks are saying in English, particularly when a big story breaks; confirmation of important stories that everyone's talking about; explanation of what the U.S. government might be doing or planning; and finally, because of the authority they've established, the experience of and trust in the Ramos and Salinas names and the Univision brand.

Univision's margin of popularity over Telemundo is so huge that when poll takers call Latino homes to ask which network they're watching, they say "Univision" even when their television sets are broken, a Miami producer says. What's notable about this story is that he works for Telemundo.

Telemundo, with about 20 percent of Univision's audience, is highly competitive and will become more so as the changes brought about by NBC ownership move forward. It owns and operates television stations in the seven largest Latino markets—New York, Los Angeles, Miami, San Francisco, Chicago, Houston, and San Antonio—in addition to a station in Puerto Rico.

As they offer more choices in English, both networks are likely to attract some English-speaking viewers with no Spanish roots but an interest in Latino culture and issues. Ramos maintains that there are ways to reach audiences beyond the million who watch his news in Spanish. "We try to broaden the field, taking in all of Latino culture, those without Spanish language included, and in the process attract some Anglos who are interested in the Latino world around them."[21]

Bilingual broadcasting is beginning to grow on television and cable, too, although not yet in news reporting. *Dora the Explorer*, a children's program on Nickelodeon and CBS, which has an animated little girl character who switches between English and Spanish, is commercial television's top show for children two to five years old. Information and entertainment programs for older view-ers are next on the list for bilingual treatment. Univision's new network, Tele-futura, and Telemundo's counterpart, Mun2 or Mundos, are aimed at the Lati-nos, most of them young and born in the United States, who now mostly watch English-language programming. Sprinkling a little English into music and sports programs is one way of starting this bilingual approach, since the footage of bands and soccer teams tells most of the story anyway, in pictures and sound.

Each night both networks present a fat package of foreign and national news, the former slanted to Latin America and the latter to issues like immi-gration. Local stations across the nation pick up with programs on the same themes. And if the news you can use concerns the exorbitant costs of wiring money home or the unfair procedures of immigration bureaucrats, that's more of a service to the audience that Ramos and Salinas attract than the latest obesity cure.

This cross-fertilization is growing with the sale to NBC of Telemundo in a $2.7 billion stock, cash, and debt deal. The purchase, from Sony and Liberty Media, means that NBC may be producing Spanish-language versions of some of its most popular English-language shows, programs that are likely to be refocused as well as translated for the new audiences. Along with entertain-ment programs, news or magazine shows like *Dateline NBC* may be translated from English to Spanish. "There are so many things we can do together," declared NBC's president, Andrew Lack. Telemundo's chief, Jim McNamara, added that "with the resources offered by our new owners, we're going to have an even greater opportunity to improve the quality of our network and local newscasts."[22]

These opportunities will translate into more sales of advertising, executives of both networks hope. The 35 million Latinos in the United States constitute 13 percent of the population and equal the population of Canada. Their con-sumer spending is estimated at $500 billion a year. And although the advertis-ing revenues of NBC and other mainstream networks have been falling, those of Telemundo and Univision have been expanding along with the Latino pop-ulation, at 15 percent a year. This means a greater need for quality content to attract higher-level sponsors, as the Latino population inches up into the mid-dle class. As the producers say, often news and documentary programs fit those needs well, particularly those of an audience with an interest in events and trends in their homelands.

The purchase gave NBC ten more television stations and forty affiliates, with access to eighty-six markets. It also gained highly regarded news and sports operations that cover the world, particularly Latin America, in Spanish. These journalists are likely to find themselves on NBC's other networks when a big story breaks in their region or an investigation they have initiated is broadcast. NBC already is adept in using its different "platforms"—MSNBC, CNBC, and the traditional network—to spread the same news coverage to a wider audience.[23]

For foreign news, this is good news. Television stations want larger audiences. Immigrants and their descendants want more news from their homeland and their home region. Paying attention to this interest should raise ratings and revenues and thus do well by doing good.

Although Univision is attracting more viewers than are many English-language news programs in many large cities, its competitors aren't ready to cede the field. Immigration from Mexico and Latin America seems likely to continue at a high rate, but no one can predict whether in the long run these new residents of the United States will look for the news, and pay for the ads, in Spanish or English.

Houston's KHOU-TV is famous for hiring a young Dan Rather as a local correspondent and, more recently, of investigating and exposing the link among a series of fatal accidents, Ford Explorers, and Firestone tires. It's also known in Houston's Latino and Anglo communities as the place to find news from Mexico from a correspondent stationed in Mexico City. Until New York's WCBS sent a permanent correspondent to Israel in 2002, KHOU's news director and vice president Michael Devlin pointed out, KHOU was the nation's only television station with a foreign bureau. "Houston is what America is going to look like," Devlin says. "Houston is a model for the United States as a whole with its racial and ethnic composition." Or perhaps a little ahead of the rest of the country: Houston's Latino population, about a third of the city's more than three million inhabitants, increased by 72 percent between the 1990 and 2000 censuses, compared with 59 percent for the nation.[24]

Houston television managers recognize Spanish-language broadcasting as a force they must reckon with, even though as a laboratory of immigration and assimilation, Houston can't tell them accurately what the outcome will be. "No one knows where assimilation is going," Devlin says. "Among the Latinos who live in this country are those who live in two languages, with one or the other predominating, and also those who live in only one." Well-educated residents of Miami's Little Havana can conduct their entire professional lives and consumer existence in Spanish, at the workplace, the doctor and lawyer, the dry cleaner, and the supermarket. Gardeners and construction workers in Houston, fresh from Mexico or Central America, have to be able to speak English to get jobs and get along. Univision and Telemundo program for both kinds of audience. In Houston, two outlets, the Fox and ABC local stations, try to hedge with Spanish translations of their English-language news.[25]

Devlin said that KHOU "wanted some way of covering this growing population" (and growing consumer sector). An opportunity came along when the Belo Corporation, KHOU's owner, bought a station in the state capital, Austin, eliminating the need for a separate KHOU bureau there. KHOU's management decided to use the savings from Austin to open its Mexico City bureau. It chose Angela Kocherga, a bilingual reporter of mixed Latina and European descent who is on good terms with Mexican president Vicente Fox, and hired a driver and cameraman at a total cost that was far less than Austin's had been.[26]

"Her instructions were to cover everything but drugs/crime and immigration, although she does do that sometimes," Devlin said.

Everything that tells the story of Mexico and its relationships to Houston. There is more to the relationship than those constantly repeated stories We wanted to add another dimension to the news about this large part of Houston's population, not only for that population but for those who live alongside it.

Who watches? "Part of our local news audience. Our job is to cover local news. We don't do foreign—local is our brief. Mexico City is local news in Houston."[27]

Among Kocherga's topics are living conditions, issues in the Roman Catholic Church, cross-border labor flows, and police torture. Her stories focus less on government officials and more on ordinary Mexicans, including retired textile worker Manuel Jimenez, whose $130 a month pension doesn't stretch far enough for all his needs. "With two weeks before the next payment, he has about $5 left," Kocherga reported. "So Jiminez collects cardboard to get by, earning about $10 a week." In another story, she traced the African slave roots of communities of Mexicans who live on the Pacific Coast south of Acapulco. "Perceptions of race are evolving, but some Americans believe there is much to be learned from the Afro-Mexican experience," she said, quoting a local Catholic priest who asked: "How is it in these villages people seem to get along and live together at a level of harmony that is very hard to find in the United States?" The camera work on Kocherga's reports—old shots of *bracero* laborers, scenes of Mexico City's architectural grandeur, footage of boys and young men fleeing Guatemala on rafts on their way to the United States—attracts viewers who might not otherwise be interested in the issues.[28]

Houston's Spanish-language stations have large audiences that score high on ratings scales because their members do less channel switching, typically choosing the same station twice as often in a week than English audiences do. Devlin notes that KHOU has to appeal to a broader audience, African Americans, whites, and Asians, including many who don't care about Latino affairs or coverage of Mexico. Are Houston's Latinos switching to or finding KHOU because of its Mexico City coverage? "Perhaps not in great numbers," Devlin says. "But some will, and some of their neighbors who can't understand Spanish will, too."[29]

Ramos of Univision takes up the question of assimilation in his book *The Other Face of America*:

What will Hispanics of the future speak? Responding to that question is of vital importance for the development of the Spanish language media in the United States. Radio and television executives would like to have a magic ball in order to find out if in two or three decades Hispanics will speak more English than Spanish, if they will adapt or if they will remain more independent than other ethnic groups in their cultural customs, like the Italians or the Poles. There are more than 35 million Latinos in the United States today, half of whom prefer to communicate in Spanish, 35 per cent in English, and 15 per cent of whom are bilingual.[30]

Ramos says that most Latino parents try to have their children learn to speak both Spanish and English well. Those who try to exclude English usually fail: "No matter how hard they try, English tends to prevail among the new generation. The need to speak English in order to succeed in this country, the influence of schools, and the bombardment of English from TV and the Internet are winning the war against Spanish, word by word."[31]

If this English juggernaut is at work in Latino families, there would seem to be no long-term future for Spanish-language media. Ramos explains why he thinks otherwise:

For the time being there is no need to worry. The continuous immigration to the United States (estimated at 1.3 million a year by the Census Bureau), as well as the high birthrate among Latinos, assures a captive audience that will speak—or at least understand—Spanish for years to come.

Nine out of every ten Hispanics speak Spanish at home, and this has allowed Spanish language radio, television, newspapers, and magazines to flourish. Italians and Poles never had national television networks in their own languages in the United States. Hispanics, however, do, and they are very successful. Univision is the fifth largest television network in the United States.[32]

Ten years from now, will more people in Houston be watching Ramos or KHOU? "All of the above," says Rice University sociology professor Steven Klineberg, who has studied immigration in the city for more than two decades. "Most of the audience is going to move around. Spanish is here to stay, but the Anglos will be paying more and more attention to the news from the regions where Spanish is spoken, because in the new international system, that affects their lives." Latinos are both assimilating and keeping their Spanish, Klineberg has found. "A powerful assimilation process is continuing," he said, "even as people are realizing the value of their Spanish and bilingual ability in a changing international world."[33]

Traditional flows of immigration from Europe stopped for the most part after World War I broke out, and thus immigrants had no choice but to learn English. They were here, and they needed to assimilate, Klineberg explained.

But we now live in a different kind of world, in which it is an enormous advantage to be bilingual in order to succeed in the world economy. All these global cities like Houston are linked into a single global economy. So, unlike the Germans and the Italians, there is a great advantage to maintaining communications with the old country. In the old immigrant world, you became more American by becoming less Italian. That's an old concept now.

Anglos are trying to improve their Spanish. Third-generation Latinos are trying to regenerate their Spanish. Everybody's learning English. Every Latino kid knows it's a tremendous barrier not to know English. But Anglo parents also complain if their kids aren't learning enough Spanish.[34]

A study by the Tomàs Rivera Policy Institute at the Claremont Colleges in California supports Klineberg's findings that Latinos move around between English and Spanish when choosing what television programs to watch. Three of four respondents watch in both languages; with half of them equally divided between the two and the other quarter favoring either Spanish or English but still viewing both.

The switching takes a different pattern when news is involved. Most Latinos revert to their native language because of their identification with Latino anchors and reporters and perhaps to make sure they understand every detail and nuance. "The most widely watched Spanish-language TV program was news," the study said. "Even many respondents who characterized themselves as regular English-language watchers said they often switched channels to watch the news in Spanish."[35] More than two-thirds of the one thousand Latinos polled across the country reported that having a Latino anchor or newscaster improved coverage of the Latino community.

With a vast audience both interested in foreign news and attractive to advertisers, it would seem to be good business to cater to that interest and reap the advertising income. But does this help the general public?

The crossover is happening all the time, as the studies by the Rivera Institute and Klineberg show. It is helped in many parts of the United States by the gradual creation of a multicultural society that bridges language gaps because neighbors of differing backgrounds in these communities are simply more interested in one another's business than they would be if they were more isolated.

As an executive producer at Telemundo explained, "We broadcast lots of foreign news, most of it from our region, and far more than any of the Anglo outlets do." But what good does that do for the general viewership?

They don't watch us if they can't understand Spanish, that's true. But they do talk to someone who does. Miami is a city where the population really mixes, where Anglos take Cuban coffee breaks and where neighbors switch effortlessly from Spanish to English and back as needed. If there is an important story that impacts Miamians as a whole, it quickly gets around from community to community. This produces a common outlook and interest. *Everyone* in Miami is more interested in the world outside than *anyone* in Iowa City—it's just a part of our lives.[36]

Another Telemundo producer who works on breaking news agreed.

The [news] soon is repeated in the Anglo media, or vice versa. When there is a big story about Cuban refugees in boats or rafts, as contrasted to the daily one of routine safe landings, everybody knows about it. Immigration scandals are news to both Latinos and Anglos, and they pass it along.

Univision and Telemundo are also a part of those lives, more so in the more integrated cities like Miami and Houston and less so in New York, Chicago, and Los Angeles, according to this Telemundo producer. "Even for those who don't watch, word gets around" when they carry a major story on issues that concern all of a city's communities.[37]

Just the fact that 35 million people in the United States—immigrant, documented, citizen, or simply resident—have access to and a personal interest in a good supply of foreign news (even in Spanish) is a huge leap forward for the nation's understanding of international issues. When the opinions of those viewers who are citizens are expressed in votes, their understanding of the outside world is a factor. It used to be that liberal opinion leaders, most of them Anglo, were the driving force behind criticism of U.S. policies in Latin America. The criticism of the twenty-first century is likely to come more and more from Latinos who read *La Opinion* or watch the evening news in Spanish.

The expansion of Hispanic television has created professional opportunities for Latino journalists, who, since the days of Ruben Salazar, have worked for both English- and Spanish- (plus a few Portuguese-) language media. As Ramos's experience with English lessons shows, it's far easier for Latino journalists to find a place in Spanish-language broadcasting. But many go to Univision or Telemundo from English networks or stations because of the career opportunities there. "My co-workers include former staffers who left NBC, ABC, CBS, and CNN for better jobs at Univision," Ramos's coanchor Salinas wrote. "Even though we still attract some journalists with limited English skills, our newsrooms are no longer seen as just steppingstones for those who want to make it in mainstream media."[38]

Latino journalists' contributions to the mainstream media include the work of reporters like Juan Forero, later a *New York Times* correspondent in Latin America, who wrote in the *Newark Star-Ledger* about the life and death of a fourteen-year-old immigrant, Juan Manuel, and the return of his body for burial in Mexico. Guillermo Contreras of the *Albuquerque Journal* exposed the failure of aid efforts for the victims of Hurricane Mitch in Nicaragua. Many Latino journalists, including Maria Hinojosa, who reports both for National Public Radio and CNN, wrote or broadcast background stories on the rapid growth of the Hispanic population measured in the 2000 census. Hinojosa's CNN series was careful to avoid stereotypes. She included new immigrants having difficulty with jobs and housing but then moved to an established middle-class family to show that neither of these categories of income or social status is typical of the immigrant population.

Like Latinos, Asian American journalists have followed the tradition of every other immigrant group in informing their audiences about news from abroad and in their communities at home. They started with Chinese-, Thai-, or Japanese-language newspapers; expanded into radio and then television; and added English to make up for the diminishing knowledge of the homeland's language. Many journalists have gone from this point to the mainstream media, as either Asian American reporters covering general news or ethnic reporters covering ethnic news.

"Asia" refers to the huge area that's home to the world's two largest populations, in China and India, and hundreds of languages, and so there is far more diversity in this community or communities than the Latino community, where despite national differences, the major division is between Spanish and Portuguese speakers. There are about three hundred Asian newspapers, a third of them dailies, in the United States, along with fifty radio and seventy-five television programs. In each category, some of the media originate in the United States, and some come from abroad.

All these media outlets except the satellite-transmitted editions of Japanese or Korean dailies provide a mixture of news from the old home country and the new one. Each one's readers, listeners, and viewers are overwhelmingly of the same ethnicity, although many political analysts, business people, and academics who are not still are glad to benefit from this instant access to the foreign press.

Asians have a larger impact in their work for mainstream media, in which they can inform both the ethnic and the general audience about events abroad and at home. Evelyn Iritani's *Los Angeles Times* report on how Chinese nationals are helping shape the U.S. economy and Susan Han's television reporting for KCTS Seattle on how China's one-child policy is affecting early-childhood education there are examples of this kind of journalism.

Local coverage of ethnic affairs is hard to separate from the more traditional foreign news that is reported from other countries. In the most effective of these local/foreign stories, the narrative usually features a strong international connection, whether it is an account of an undocumented worker in Chicago and his family in Mexico or the impact of bilingual education disputes on California's Vietnamese population.

Well-written or -produced (in English) accounts of trouble or progress among Indians or Poles at home or abroad attract audiences that are not exclusively Indian or Polish. Conversely, soap operas and comedies produced in Spanish in Venezuela and Mexico, which account for 90 percent of the leading U.S. Spanish network's programming, attract few viewers outside the Hispanic community.

What is not apparent so immediately is the impact of the foreign-language outlets on the general public. Ethnic news comes in two models, one new and one traditional. New California Media represents the former and makes a conscious effort to bridge the gap, to make foreign news available in English to the general audience. The editors at Orlando's *Sentinel* and *El Sentinel*, San Jose's *Mercury News* and *Nuevo Mundo*, Miami's *Herald* and *El Nuevo Herald*, and their counterparts elsewhere do this more or less unconsciously, with news judgment the principal criterion. English-language editors choose news for its relevance to their readers, and Spanish-language editors do the same, leaving the cross-fertilization up to individual readers.

NEW CALIFORNIA MEDIA (NCM)

Franz Schurmann, professor emeritus at the University of California at Berkeley, likes to take visitors to San Francisco's Chinatown to an intersection that once marked the shoreline of Oakland Bay. Above are the nineteenth-century buildings of the old Chinese immigrant associations, and below on landfill are the office towers of the financial district. The Chinese kept their links to their homeland across the Pacific from the time they arrived in the United States, Schurmann says, and this bridge over the ocean still connects China to their communities in this country: "They may go back to their homelands rarely or not at all, or they may be dot.com entrepreneurs who commute weekly, but they still have the bridge as part of their consciousness."[39]

Schurmann and Sandy Close are using these bridges in a project called New California Media (NCM), a news service aimed at bringing the news and insights of the ethnic media in the Bay Area and beyond to a general audience that doesn't speak Chinese or the dozens of other languages that Schurmann and Close pick up and translate on the service. Schurmann and Close started Pacific News Service during the Vietnam War as an alternative source of news. With its NCM offshoot, they're tapping into more than 350 newspapers, Internet sites, and broadcast stations, ranging from *Iran Today* to *India West* and including five Chinese dailies and a twenty-four-hour Chinese television station. "They tell the daily stories of people in their communities in California as well as in the countries they come from," Close says. "The ethnic media really are producing something the mainstream media can't duplicate, and that is this incredible new virtual geography, the neighborhood and homeland all in one."[40]

NCM's stories are sold to newspaper subscribers and are available on the Internet and weekly public radio and PBS television programs, connecting ethnic papers and broadcasters to one another and the mainstream media. Although Close and Schurmann consider both kinds of linkages to have equal value, others at NCM argue that the project's main role should be to bring its diverse range of minority viewpoints to the majority who seldom get to hear them, including the readers of the *San Francisco Chronicle* and other newspapers.

Many of those viewpoints come from China. *Sing Tao Daily*, a newspaper based in Hong Kong with editorial operations in six U.S. cities, has a reputation for independence that balances the more opinionated *World Journal*, an offshoot of a Taiwanese publisher, and the pro-Beijing *China Press*.

Sing Tao's largest U.S. editorial operation is in south San Francisco, in an area of Asian airfreight warehouses not far from the airport. Every night *Sing Tao's* staff produces a sixty-four-page paper with transmissions from Asia and local news of interest to its sixty thousand subscribers in the Bay Area, about half its total circulation in the United States. For more than four decades, *Sing Tao* has reported on one of the world's most important stories—and for its readers, *the most important*—mainland China, in a way that its editor, Wellington Cheng, describes as neutral and other staff members contrast with the pro-Beijing or pro-Taiwan stances of their local rivals. A good example of that neutrality was how the top stories were played in the three papers on one day in June 2001. The visit of Taiwan's president, Chen Shui-bian, to Houston was on the front page of both *Sing Tao* and *World Journal* with the usual cowboy hat pictures, but *Sing Tao's* account was more straightforward and the *World Journal's* was more favorable to Chen. *China Press* stressed the demonstrators protesting the visit as a violation of Beijing's one-China policy. *Sing Tao* also carried a story on Wen Ho Lee and the violation of his rights, as well as a straightforward account of leaked Chinese government documents on the Tiananmen massacre.

Cheng says the English newspapers in the Bay Area seldom pick up anything from his columns, local or international, but on an important story, *Chronicle* reporters sometimes interview *Sing Tao* editors. Cheng got a chance to show off his calligraphy and explain linguistic nuances to local journalists during the 2001 Hainan Island spy plane incident, when Americans were trying to figure out the different gradations of apology in Chinese. Editors at *Sing Tao* agree that Americans are underinformed about China, but they don't have any quick solutions. They tried an English-language page for a time a few years ago but discovered that it attracted only a few non-Chinese readers. Those Chinese who read it belonged to a small in-between group: not the old, who never learned English, or the new, who haven't learned it yet and feel quite comfortable with a full account of news in a language whose red banner headlines they can read easily.

About half the content of *Sing Tao*, with bright colors throughout in its photographs, headlines, and ads, is about China and the rest of Asia, stories transmitted from Hong Kong. The other half is American news, with sports and a vibrant business section competing with a big news hole for national, foreign, local, and regional issues of interest to Chinese. *Sing Tao's* Larry Li, a diplomatic reporter who works in both Washington and San Francisco, won a local World Affairs Council Award for a ten-year anniversary analysis, translated and carried by NCM, of the effects of the Tiananmen massacre. Li's reporting also is picked up by NCM in the stories Schurmann writes on what the Chinese press is saying. Early in the Bush administration, Li quoted mainland Chinese diplomats as saying that "the most important issues that can make or break

U.S.-China relations revolve around Taiwan." NCM readers got the story soon after *Sing Tao* ran it.[41]

When Chinese troops massacred demonstrators in Beijing's Tiananmen Square, KTSF-TV of San Francisco broadcast half-hour special reports in Cantonese and Mandarin, the two most widely spoken Chinese languages. The station had gone on the air a few months earlier with the United States' first live Chinese television news, *Chinese News at Nine*. The program on Tiananmen carried exclusive reports like an interview with a former army officer whose unit had been blamed for much of the bloodshed.

Since then KTSF-TV has grown into a twenty-four-hour station that reaches the entire Bay Area, where 1.6 million Asian Americans live, with regular news programs in Vietnamese, Japanese, Laotian, Korean, and Tagalog, the language of the Philippines, as well as Cantonese and Mandarin. In addition, it has links with home-country broadcasters NHK in Japan, ATV in Hong Kong, and ABS-CBN in the Philippines. Eight other languages are represented in its other broadcasts. Today, San Francisco's population is 33 percent Asian-Pacific, but in fifteen years, with the influx of other races, it is the white population that will be 33 percent.

KTSF-TV covers both community news and foreign news, with the usual blending of those two categories found in ethnic news operations. A remarkable 82 percent of Cantonese speakers in the Bay Area watch the 8 P.M. *Cantonese News*, an hour-long program that covers local, national, and international news, preceded by a half-hour of the same format in Mandarin.

New California Media has its own television program, a weekly half-hour with subjects that cover the spectrum of the ethnic media, from Asian and Asian American film to the Kashmir dispute and Muslim women's voices. Mexico is a common topic because of the border and the large number of Mexican immigrants. NCM-TV's host, Emil Guillermo, anchored a program about the Mexican elections that showed how these issues are intertwined for all Californians, whatever their ethnic background. "Immigration, the economy, jobs—how the candidates tackle these issues is a concern for the new California," he explained. After footage was shown on the campaign that Vicente Fox was waging against Institutional Revolutionary Party (PRI) candidate Francisco Labastida, Guillermo moderated a panel that included Jose Luis Sierra of Los Angeles's *La Opinion*, who had been to Mexico to talk to voters. Their comments came close to predicting Fox's victory over the seventy-year rule of the PRI.

"The PRI had been buying election after election," Sierra said. "There's real change now—some sense of democracy, something they haven't had for decades. What we found was a more outspoken country, more willing to talk, even though they were afraid of the police, the narcos, and the government—still, they're willing to talk."[42]

NCM's most prominent showcase is in a section every Sunday, appropriately named "Bay Area Bridges," in the *San Francisco Chronicle*. The stories in "Bridges" are a mixture of both local and foreign news, stories such as that of a Vietnamese American soldier of fortune imprisoned in Thailand, job offers in Shanghai for Americans laid off in Silicon Valley, and emergency water supplies left in the desert to save the lives of Mexican immigrants crossing borders.

In addition to this weekly multiethnic news, NCM and the Pacific News Service have begun to place longer pieces in the *Chronicle*'s "Insight" section. In one, Andrew Lam, a Vietnamese American, wrote about the ghosts of the past that haunt the older members of the Vietnamese immigrant community in the United States, using his father, a former South Vietnamese army general, as his focus. Despite the bitterness of defeat, Lam wrote, his father thinks globalization and pressures from within Vietnam will restore democracy there.[43]

Mary Jo McConahay, a veteran Latin America correspondent, described the newest of the waves of immigrants to California, the Indians of the central Mexican highlands and Guatemala. They are arriving at a rate of up to forty thousand a year for unskilled jobs that pay as little as $6 an hour. Few know English, and some don't even speak Spanish well, McConahay wrote, which makes it difficult for activists and local governments to deal with their problems with worker rights, health care, and education. Some organizations are turning out trilingual case workers, those who know Spanish, English, and a pre-Columbian indigenous language like Mixteco. "Some words can't be explained well in Mixteco, for instance X-rays," a case worker told McConahay.[44]

NCM has been providing this kind of news since 1996 on its Web site and public radio and television programs, translating the best of what Close calls the explosion of ethnic media that serve California's new majority. She credits the Chinese- and English-language Asian media for leading the fight to free scientist Wen Ho Lee from espionage charges.

NCM does more than translate. Schurmann and other specialists also analyze and compare. Schurmann, who taught history and sociology at Berkeley, reads Chinese, Farsi, and Arabic, among many other languages, and uses these skills to keep English-only readers up on trends and news in the Middle East, China, and the rest of Asia. His Middle East analyses are based on a broad reading of the press in Arab nations, moderate as well as confrontational. Schurmann moves from translation to comparison, using a range of newspaper viewpoints to support his conclusions. He quotes from both pro-Beijing and pro-Taiwan Chinese newspapers as well as *Sing Tao*. In 2002, mainstream journalists began noticing the rise of the apparent new leader of China, Hu Jintao, whom they described as a man no one in the West had ever heard of. Readers of Schurmann's NCM stories would have known about him in 2001.

"Aren't we close to the brink of war with China, as the American media keep harping on?" is how Schurmann began one analysis at the height of tensions over the downed reconnaissance plane and Beijing's criticism of the U.S. visit of Taiwanese president Chen Shui-bian. Then, analyzing comments by officials in both Beijing and Taipei, he described the situation in much calmer terms. He used the term "hot peace" rather than hot or cold war to describe U.S.-Chinese relations, noting that its cause was business: "The U.S., China, and Taiwan are bound together by strong economic ties that are getting stronger every day."[45]

On the Middle East, Schurmann quoted a range of Arab and Iranian voices in a similar departure from most mainstream American analysis of the value of former Senator George Mitchell's peace plan. "Finally, America is doing something for the Arabs," announced a headline in an Arab newspaper quoted by Schurmann. The Arabic press, he said, " writes of hope for some sort of peace settlement if Bush uses the Mitchell proposals to check Sharon."[46]

Jon Funabiki of the Ford Foundation, which supports NCM, calls the alliance "an exciting experiment in ways to strengthen the ethnic news media."[47] Can the NCM idea spread? New York would be the logical next step, with nearly two hundred ethnic publications, a threefold increase from the number ten years ago. Miami, Houston, Los Angeles, Boston, and Chicago are other cities with a rich fabric of ethnic populations and density of ethnic media. Establishing a nationwide New American Media would be more difficult because of the ethnic media's strong community orientation.

As an outgrowth of the Pacific News Service, New California Media anticipated the changes in California's ethnic composition long before the 2000 census figures were released. Pacific had long worked with the state's diverse communities and had journalists of many ethnic backgrounds on its staff. But it was the surge in immigration and births by immigrant populations that put NCM in the spotlight, attracting the attention and endorsement of San Francisco's mayor, Willy Brown, Governor Gray Davis, and other politicians who know the power of the ethnic vote.

The new census figures confirmed California as the second minority-majority state in the nation, after Hawaii, which has never had an Anglo majority. Hispanics led the increase, making up 33 percent of California's population in 2000, compared with 25 percent in 1990, or three-fourths of the 4.1 million people California gained during the decade. More than two million of this larger Hispanic population represented births, not immigration. Asians added about a million in the decade between the two censuses, giving them an 11- or 12-percent share of the population instead of 9. In 1990 the number of majority-minority counties stood at three: Los Angeles, San Francisco, and the agricultural Imperial County. By 2000, fifteen others had been added.

NCM's coverage of local ethnic stories, like one about a wealthy Asian who kept indentured servants, Close explained, can't be told without referring to the background outside the United States. "They are private stories," she adds, "but have a public sense in which they interest us all—not the prurient way that snappy little shorts in papers about foreign foibles do, but as real chronicles of people like us. This is for the New California Majority," Close says, using the same initials as her project's. "The ethnic part of the California population was always neglected in the mainstream media, but with the immigrant growth continuing, it's more important than ever that these voices be heard." Unlike the European immigrants on the East Coast and Midwest, Schurmann observed, San Francisco's Chinese and many other ethnic groups distinguished by their skin color or features, "never melted into the general American population, are never going to, and are going to maintain, as logically and easily as they have always done, a dual cultural identity."[48]

NCM's partners include twenty-one Asian media outlets, reflecting the preponderance of Asians in the region. All together, the partners have a combined circulation of more than a million for their publications, Web sites, and news services. If they are written in another language, NCM's staff translates the partners' contributions and sends them to about fifty-five subscribers, including the Washington Post, as well as posting them on the NCM Web site. "We know that there are about a thousand hits a day—that's modest now, but we're working on a marketing campaign to get more information about it out," a Web editor said. "The typical site visitor will click on the home page and look for a single story. The average visitor is probably someone looking for a specific story or for a specific ethnic newspaper."[49] If NCM's Web site visitors want to sample the ethnic press, many links are provided to the newspapers and online outlets that constitute its contributor network, in their original languages, bilingual, or in English.

Close says she wants to promote more contact between ethnic communities. "We're trying to encourage Indian papers to print news about China and vice versa," she said. "It's already happening in some ways like sports stories and big elections." Schurmann said that NCM should be looked at as a wheel with hub and spokes. The hub of the wheel is the English language, and the rim is all the languages represented in the ethnic media. The spokes lead to the common hub. But there are no cross connections, nothing to link the spokes with one another. "That's a function of NCM, and it's a job we've only begun," he says.[50]

Many of NCM's Web stories are written by Pacific News Service (PNS) editors, who have a better understanding of mainstream media preferences than many ethnic journalists do. But the ethnic contributions enrich these dispatches with description, detail, opinion, and unusual points of view. PNS editors are careful to screen out advocates who write for political parties or interest groups, although NCM does encourage open debates, like those it sponsored between Indian and Pakistani journalists on the issue of nuclear weapons. A chat room serves as a forum for ethnic differences, with some fairly loose supervision by an NCM moderator, who asks only if the opinions are fairly and accurately expressed and add to the other participants' knowledge.

Because of this partisanship, editing is a central part of the process at NCM. The Bay Area's Philippine community, for example, has papers representing many political positions. The Filipino who goes to an ethnic grocery for fish and condiments also has a rack of newspapers to choose from: some free, some for sale, some political tracts, and some objective. "This is habit for newcomers and those here for thirty years," an editor of Filipino descent said. "To simply translate them would be to risk passing on bias to the larger readership. To use them as source material by specialists who know the reefs and rocks is the method chosen."[51]

NCM proved its worth in the aftermath of the World Trade Center and Pentagon attacks, presenting a broad spectrum of the foreign media's reaction to the disasters and the hate crimes against foreigners and Americans of foreign background that followed them. Some articles condemned the superpatriotic headlines like "Bastards" in the *San Francisco Examiner*.

All provided a more nuanced view of the attacks and their consequences than did most of the mainstream U.S. media. "Japanese Americans, who were forced out of their homes on the West Coast after the bombing of Pearl Harbor and incarcerated in concentration camps are likely to relate to the fear and anxiety burdening those of Arab, Muslim, Sikh and South Asian descent," *Nichi Bei*, the Japanese-language newspaper wrote.[52]

Iran Today urged intelligence operations against the terrorists rather than massive military attacks that would alienate the Muslim world;[53] the AllAfrica Web site criticized U.S. arrogance and bullying.[54] The leftist *Confidencial* of Nicaragua warned against all extremist forms of religion, whether Islamic or American fundamentalist.[55] The Chinese-language *World Journal*, which supports Taiwan, took the unusual step of criticizing the Bush administration's foreign policy as an explanation for the terror attack. The administration's core principles, the paper said, "are to dominate Asia, contain China, and on the Middle East to ask no questions."[56]

Both the London-based Arabic newspaper *Al-Sharq al Ausat* and the Chinese-language *Sing Tao*, in translations by Schurmann carried on NCM's site, criticized the tightening of U.S. detention laws designed to fight terrorism.

Al-Sharq described the case of a Saudi student in Santa Monica detained without recourse to lawyers. *Sing Tao's* front page reported fears in the Chinese community about the new antiterrorism law. "For some," Schurmann wrote, "the bill conjures up historical discrimination measures such as the Chinese exclusion act which banned immigration of Chinese laborers and banned citizenship" until it was revoked in 1943.[57]

A look at an average week of NCM's offerings shows that it doesn't take a crisis to produce a broad palette of interesting news. The top stories from the ethnic press include a British election preview, a story speculating that President Arnoldo Aleman of Nicaragua may be brought down on corruption charges, an account of civil war among Colombia's paramilitary forces, a report based on 2000 census figures showing that Indians are the fastest-growing Asian group in the United States, and a European roundup on the dispute between California and the federal government on how to solve the state's energy crisis.

The sources of the stories describe NCM's work as much as the topics. The British election and California energy stories were the work of Paolo Pontoniere, a one-man *World Press Review* who scours the British, French, German, Italian, and German press for important themes that can be linked in a single English-language roundup. The Nicaraguan story was a translation from the Nicaraguan weekly *Tiempos del Mundo*, and the Colombian story came from *Semana*, another newsweekly published in Bogotá. The story on Indian immigrant growth was written for NCM by Raj Jayadev, using his own reporting and information from the *New India Times* and *rediff.com*, an Indian online news source.[58]

New California Media is an idea with a future in the rest of the United States, impelled by the same forces that caused it to take hold in California: the changing composition of the U.S. population. As minorities grow in number and influence, the majority will need more information, more insights, more understanding about them. It's fortunate that the minorities are producing their own talent—media entrepreneurs, editors, producers, and reporters—to do this informing and explaining, and that majority journalists are making use of the news they provide to reach a broader public. After NCM, New New York Media may be next, with New Texas, New Illinois, and New Florida not far behind.

Washingtonpost.com has taken the Washington Post brand and made it a national, no, an international medium. —*Doug Feaver, the online edition's executive editor*

When they know their names and quotes might be on the Internet within the next couple of hours, politicians return your calls a lot faster. —*Randall Palmer, Reuters correspondent in Canada*

8

THE ELECTRONIC NEWSPAPER

Every morning, when the daily papers arrive at mailboxes, newsstands, and front porches across the United States, another delivery takes place in the computer systems of millions of Americans. The images on their screens are most likely to be *washingtonpost.com* or the Web sites of the other major newspapers, but they might also be the local daily or even the digital versions of the *Tonga Chronicle* or *Slovak Spectator*.

The information revolution of the last decades of the twentieth century profoundly changed the way journalists do their jobs in their three main functions of reporting, transmitting, and disseminating news. The advent of satellites, computers, and the Internet gave reporters a wider range of information, a wider audience, and speedier means of linking the two. The implications of this change are enormous for the spread of foreign news. Technology has already begun to contribute to a reversal of the trends of diminishing foreign news coverag. But, wires or fiber-optic cables can't do it alone. There has to be a way to make the coverage interesting, compelling, or perhaps just more accessible. For this task, humans are required.

Foreign news aficionados have always had the option of shortwave radio (and, of late, satellite television broadcast from abroad). But it was a question of getting out the set, finding the station, fixing the antenna, and often staying up late at night. The Internet has finally reached the point at which it is a better shortwave radio.

The electronic newspapers have blinking and flashing ads on their front pages and color splashed on their headlines and pictures. Instead of long columns of news, they feature short summaries with headlines, and parts of the texts are underlined to show that a mouse click will provide more information. Other sections draw attention to live events coming to your computer screen: talk, video, and analysis.

In its first decade of existence, the World Wide Web is beginning to transform the way in which Americans get their news, providing greater access and flexibility and particularly benefiting those interested in foreign news. *Beginning* is the operative word here. Determining Internet usage is still a developing science, but by any measurement the pulp paper version that hits the porch is still far ahead in readership, and radio and television outdraw the Internet by twenty to one. But the figures for the traditional newspaper distribution systems—electronic transmission from editor to production process, and then truck, mail, foot, bicycle, or red wagon delivery—keep stagnating or declining, and those for the direct electronic transmission from Web site to home or office desktop keep increasing. The traditional newspapers, unable to fight the trend, long ago decided to join it. They are responding by competing with themselves as well as with their rivals, the Internet news sites of the networks and search engines like Yahoo and AOL. Some papers, including the *New York Times* and *Christian Science Monitor*, publish three versions: the regular paper, a facsimile of the regular paper transmitted to computer screens, and a Web edition generally based on the same content but with far more flexible presentation.

The *Washington Post* is the leader in this trend to use the resources of its print edition, both the work of its worldwide correspondents and its capital reporters, in innovative ways made possible by computer technology. The printed *Washington Post* is a finished document made up of stories, ads, pictures, headlines, editorials, and columns, but *washingtonpost.com* is a news medium constantly in motion. All day, developments change the focus of stories, and *washingtonpost.com*'s stories stay fluid as editors add or remove details, rewrite headlines, add or subtract sidebars, and substitute newer or better pictures to illustrate them. In sideshows to the main tent are ten or more audio talks or chat sessions on media criticism, terrorism, travel, the workplace, technology, and astrology.

"*Washingtonpost.com* has taken the *Washington Post* brand and made it a national, no, an international medium," Doug Feaver, the online edition's executive editor, said. Feaver pointed out that the *Post* is international in both its reporting—it has twenty foreign bureaus and twenty-six foreign correspondents—and the new audience the Internet has brought it. A twenty-nine-year veteran of the *Post*, Feaver was present during the *Washington Post*'s first transformation from an undistinguished small-city paper to one much quoted but little read outside Washington and a few other eastern cities. Now, nearly three out of four of its Internet users come from outside its paper circulation area.

"Washington Post" is an attractive brand name in an era when the world watches the capital of its only superpower with interest and concern. But *washingtonpost.com* also earns its high user ratings by making optimal use of both traditional journalism and the capacities of the new technology.

These two elements combine throughout the day and evening as the site changes with developments in the news. In old newspaper parlance, it's a replate, a replacement of the earlier printing plates with new ones containing later information. Current technology, however, doesn't require plates, ink, or delivery people. Stories can be added, subtracted, or deleted on the terminals of *washingtonpost.com* editors and then sent on, just in time for the lunch hour users on the East Coast, for the first main electronic replate, or, three hours later, for those lunching and viewing on the West Coast.

The main color photograph on the front page also changes frequently, with better or more dramatic pictures of the same subject sometimes changing several times. What comes on screen on the Web site is the electronic equivalent of a newspaper's display on a busy urban newsstand: the more often it changes, the more customers think they're getting a new product. But newsstands no longer offer many successive editions of newspapers, if they do so at all. Traditional replates are expensive, whereas electronic ones require only staff time on computer keyboards.

The *Washington Post* print edition has a daily circulation of about 785,000 on weekdays and a little more than a million on Sundays. Its monthly Internet audience exceeds three million unique visitors, with huge spikes after the World Trade Center and Pentagon attacks in September. About 70 percent of the Web audience are what Feaver calls "out of market" and about 20 percent of those are international, the government officials, business people, scholars, and ordinary citizens around the world who want a clearer picture of the plans and actions of the U.S. government and see the *Post* as the best place to find it. "If that's all the online version of the paper achieved, it would have been enough," Feaver said. "But the Web version is far more."[1] The *Post*'s electronic edition and those of other quality newspapers and the television networks provide many functions beyond those of accessibility and constant updating. They offer unlimited space, a great news hole in the sky for material that can't be crowded into the print edition or the short time period of the evening news, including the texts of statements and speeches, question and answer interviews, and maps, graphs, and drawings.

The Web is particularly welcomed by editors concerned about the scaling down of foreign news in their papers, although they concede that the development of online editions is not a wholly satisfactory substitute. When the American spy plane was forced down on China's Hainan Island, the *Chicago Tribune*'s

Web site supplied sketches and descriptions of all the aircraft involved. On *latimes.com*, there are links to the Web version of *La Opinion*, the *Times's* partner, with its extensive Latin American and local Latino coverage. The *Christian Science Monitor's* Tom Regan roams the Internet for a daily Web site feature on the day's most important news with comments from a wide range of sources, including *Slate*, the BBC, China's *People's Daily*, and Russia's *Izvestia*. Those who want to do their own tailoring find it easy on many Web sites with links to others. Log on to El Nuevo Herald Digital in Miami, for example, and find not only current issues and background about the city's politically active Cuban community but also a direct pipeline into the Cuban media, long Castro speeches, propaganda, and all. Cuban Americans who may hate Castro but still like to know what he's saying are joined by other viewers interested in developments in Colombia, Venezuela, Mexico, and the other nations of the region covered by both *Herald* correspondents and the Internet links to newspapers there. Raleigh's *News and Observer*, a pioneer in Internet use, puts three or four columns of foreign news—five thousand words—in its paper edition but at the same time gives Internet users the option of accessing twenty thousand or more words from the links, the archives, and the supplementary material it posts on the venerable Nandonet. The Associated Press has supplemented its daily listings of foreign stories with longer pieces backgrounding important issues, presented as attractive packages on Web sites and particularly welcomed by small papers with limited space for such offerings in their newsprint versions.

As one editor says, if Web sites are well designed and managed, they "are not just dumping newspaper content onto the Net." One main difference is their immediacy: "They are constantly in motion, like a wire service [in fact, most are based on the AP or Reuters wires for all but local news] they're filing all the time." Another advantage is space. In the view of a *Chicago Tribune* staff member, "it doesn't matter what our news hole is in terms of space limitation. On the Net there is no news hole limitation. So stories can run long; on the Net you can have all kinds of neat sidebars and graphics and chronologies."[2] For foreign correspondents, the extension of their paper's reach through the Internet provides an opportunity to be read by the sources they interview in other countries. There was some initial grumbling from the *Washington Post's* foreign correspondents about filing their stories earlier for the Web site, but the experience of instant recognition in foreign offices and chancelleries (and instant criticism) made the foreign staff realize what the benefits were.

Washingtonpost.com provides a place for "Web-exclusive" copy, like Marcela Sanchez's political column, which reaches audiences across the United States and abroad in English and Spanish. Sanchez writes on Washington from an international perspective and thus is widely read in Latin America as well as by

U.S. Latinos. The column covers subjects like the drug war, discrimination against American diplomats of Hispanic background, the hidden costs of foreign debt relief, and the downside of free-trade agreements. The site also carries a reference to Sanchez's daily Spanish-language reports from Washington on Univision. Other Web sites, such as *MSNBC.com*, in which *Newsweek* is a partner, and *Time.com*, offer space to newsmagazine correspondents abroad with a single main deadline every week whose notebooks are usually bursting with other information they can now use in daily spots on MSNBC or *Time's* Web site.

Newspaper's and other Internet sites provide a whole new audience for the wire services, the mainstays of international news. Most newspaper Web sites rely on the AP wire to keep their foreign and national news up-to-date through the long cycle between print editions. Reuters on the Web is finding its way to many more American readers than it ever did through the relatively few newspapers that subscribed to it. "Since we've linked up with Yahoo, people finally know who we are," Randall Palmer, a Reuters veteran in Canada, noted. "When they know their names and quotes might be on the Internet within the next couple of hours, politicians return your calls a lot faster."[3]

Web sites also serve as a record, an archive, a treasure of background material. Like good print newspapers, they provide maps of conflict areas, pie charts to illustrate votes or ethnic compositions, diagrams of sunken submarines or volcano eruptions. But what newspapers can't provide every day is hundreds of pictures and videos, multiple thousands of words of text, or searches of their printed columns, new and old, with key words.

Producers of *Frontline's* PBS series on the Gulf War used their exhaustive research and interviews in a Web depository for viewers seeking additional background. *Frontline's* executive producer, David Fanning, calls the system "a new form that permits the ephemeral documentary to survive." In addition to the clips of the video shown in the original documentary, the archive contains an oral history of the conflict: long transcripts of the interviews the *Frontline* producers conducted in tandem with the BBC, including those with General Colin L. Powell, former British prime minister Margaret Thatcher, military analysts, battlefield commanders, and Iraqi officials. Such use of Web sites, Fanning says, "is opening up the possibilities of what lies beneath the visible part of the documentary." At a basic level, viewers can make sure that quotations in the documentary are accurate and in context, but he thinks the technique goes much further than that. "It's reinventing a kind of journalism. It gives us a chance to explain ourselves and what we do. You become the guardian of a piece of intellectual history."[4]

The *Philadelphia Inquirer* used the Web to present the investigative work by Mark Bowden on the disastrous U.S. military involvement in Somalia. Bowden's "Blackhawk Down" saga was printed every day for a month in the paper before it became the basis for a best-selling book and movie. The twenty-nine-part newspaper series also was expanded on the Web with video and still pictures, audiotaped interviews with veterans of the conflict, and more than a thousand pages of government documents. Carrying multimedia a step further, Bowden and his colleagues also made a television documentary for Philadelphia's public station.

American RadioWorks, a subsidiary of Minnesota Public Radio, considers the Web a coequal partner. "When we do radio programs, what we do online is as important as what we do on the air," producer Stephen Smith says. "We go into these things with almost a dual purpose. We're a dual-medium institution. Even though we're called RadioWorks, we should probably be called Media-Works, because we do a very extensive Web site where there is additional information, primary documents, all the photographs, all of the audio."[5]

Washingtonpost.com's own video images play a major part in the makeup and impact of its Web site. Some stand alone, as in the series shot in Serbia by a staff member with a small digital video camera who showed how the survivors of Yugoslavia's civil wars were making ends meet under conditions of scarcity and inflation. Others are tied in with the print paper. A series on Siberia appeared first online and then, with pictures and a long text summary, in print. "The one form of the story creates interest in the other," Tom Kennedy, *washingtonpost.com*'s managing editor for multimedia, explained. "A Web visitor might want to read a text version after seeing the clip, or it could be the other way around." Kennedy says the site attracts viewers who "really enjoy seeing strong visual coverage" as part of the news. "It enables them to connect emotionally with events and information and come to an understanding of the implications of those events and information for them more concretely than a pure text play would. We're trying to build a video documentary tradition where the voice of the subject comes through." But Kennedy says much is to be gained by even briefer looks at some of the world's problems: "It brings it home; it makes it real to people. It gives them a sense of how their lives here differ so dramatically from the other parts of the world." On *washingtonpost.com* and elsewhere, still photographers who compete for the limited space in printed papers for a single shot can offer a whole series of pictures in the Web version.[6]

Another *washingtonpost.com* feature increasingly found on other sites is tailoring the news to the viewer's own interests through *mywashingtonpost.com*. Editors say the personalization is a good thing for both their viewers and themselves.

Instead of six clicks, a regular user can find the day's news on Rwanda with one click if he or she has signed on to the "my" button. The company also can sell ads based on a steady guaranteed audience. Building a steady viewership extends to a system for getting regular bulletins on a PalmPilot or cellphone.

Journalists as well as users are constantly experimenting with new software and new technology. Teams or individual journalists who go out to do what Kennedy calls "very short form" documentaries are equipped with compact digital cameras. In the early days, the technology limited video clips to three minutes at most, but now as much as eight minutes is possible, and, as high-definition screens and broadband connections become more common, the resulting improvements in quality will eliminate time limits for viewer patience or interest.

In *washingtonpost.com*'s newsroom in Arlington, Virginia, across the Potomac from the newspaper's offices, staff members and editors take both sides of the position of whether *washingtonpost.com* is or isn't the *Washington Post*. The consensus is that the Web site wouldn't work without the brand name of the *Post* and the stories, editing, pictures, and analyses the *Post* sends out every day, whether on pulp paper for its readers or into the under-Potomac cable as material for the site.

Industry analysts say that in the first five years, the *Post* poured at least $230 million into its dot.com and that advertising revenue, at roughly $2 million a month, falls short of what is needed to make the site profitable any time in the near future. The editorial costs of the constant electronic replates is one reason that the site lost more than $100 million in its first years of operation.

But editors at *washingtonpost.com* insist that those figures aren't the only ones to watch, that the Web site was established in part as a bridgehead against the loss of classified advertising to dot.com companies like Monster that offered nationwide Web classifieds without the expense of news, pictures, or columnists. The percentage of classifieds available online is expected to double, to 20 percent, in the next five years, and the *Post* and other newspaper sites are willing to spend and lose money to make sure they are positioned to compete for that.

The editors maintain that the advertising challenge was only one reason for the *Post*'s investing a great deal in the site's staff of more than fifty members and its newsroom atop what passes for a skyscraper around Washington. Just as important was a chance to make the paper truly national. The days after the terrorist attacks showed how successful this national and international acceptance has become. *Washingtonpost.com* readership doubled in September 2001. About two-thirds of the viewers are from outside the Washington area, meaning that their interest is Washington and foreign news and analysis, not restaurant reviews. *Washingtonpost.com* is always listed in the top few news sites whose visitors are measured by ratings services, along with the sites of the *New York Times*, *Los Angeles Times*, and *USA Today*, and the broadcast Web sites of ABC, CNN, and MSNBC.

Depending on what's in the news on a given day, the *Los Angeles Times* Web site has as many or more viewers than the *Washington Post* site, but, *Post* staffers say, doesn't have the worldwide audience. "People all over the world want to know what Washington is thinking, what the Washington line is, and so they check in with us," a mid-level editor at *washingtonpost.com* explained. "The same isn't true for the *L.A. Times*." Few at *washingtonpost.com* dispute the preeminent position of the *New York Times*, on paper or on the Web, but some editors say it can't match their special combination of world and Washington news and their reporting of the interaction between the two.

Another difference in the importance of the Web to the nation's leading newspapers is the circulation and distribution of the printed version that each can offer. The *Wall Street Journal* and *USA Today* are in a class by themselves, with no home-city readership or news and a network of printing and distribution centers across the country. This means that their combined circulation of close to four million is entirely national. The *New York Times* has a huge home base but gets at least a third of the million-plus readership for its daily edition through national distribution. In other words, if someone pulled the plug on the Internet tomorrow, these three papers would still be read widely from coast to coast.

The *Washington Post* has a smaller home base to start with: the Washington area and East Coast cities. Its weekly edition, which contains a great deal of foreign reporting, has not attracted a large readership. The *Los Angeles Times* supplements its metro editions with a national version, one printed and delivered in Northern California and another on the East Coast. Total circulation is about forty thousand. Along with the *Post*, it relies on the Internet for a national audience.

Unlike some smaller Web sites, *washingtonpost.com* presents a carefully edited and vetted product, based for the most part on the reporting and editing already done for the newsprint edition. Since deadlines for the print paper are much later in the day, a couple of Web hands based at the print newsroom on M Street supply the early updates on Congress and the administration every morning. This enables the print reporters to be out covering the stories they'll be filing later for the paper (and the Internet). Most *Post* correspondents who are asked to contribute updates or different versions for the Web do so willingly, editors say, but in every case they also are given the chance to refuse. Not everyone is happy with the appearance in the newsroom of this new electronic device with a voracious appetite. "Our online edition asks me to update the story I wrote for today's paper throughout the day," a *New York Times* political reporter recounted. "I'm asked to go on our Webcast. I'm asked to comment on the cable outlet we have ties with. If I do all this, when do I have time to do the new reporting I have to do for the next day's paper?"[7] Many Web sites solve the problem by simply plugging in AP and letting it keep the developing stories flowing. But some organizations are pressured to have the paper's own well-known names and faces in the Internet edition all the time. In one television bureau in Europe, the Internet was received as far more an annoyance than a marvelous new means of communications. "It's something extra to do, something not appreciated, and something no one wanted to get their teeth into," a producer said.[8]

In cases of conflict, the editors of the various media must decide, according to the *Chicago Tribune*'s David Underhill.

> The first priority is to the medium you're assigned to. Reporters can be tugged in all directions, but it's their editor's job to keep track. A reporter can also say he doesn't have time to do radio or TV at all—because if we allow this, it will hurt the person's ability to *get* the news.[9]

On the positive side, Underhill said, if the big names are overcommitted, "people beyond the marquee players in the bureaus" get a chance to show what they can do.

Underhill is proud of the Tribune Company's multimedia presence and told a journalists' conference that reporters must be expected to work for all the media under the Tribune's logo: traditional television at WGN, the print version, and interactive. This, he said, is a way to "create new value for our journalism and our business across those group lines." Underhill showed the conference video footage as evidence for his premise that there were untapped ways of getting international news from *Tribune* bureaus abroad. The footage, taken at the time of the spy plane crisis in China, showed the *Tribune*'s Beijing correspondent Michael Lev being questioned in a telephone link by WGN's local anchors.

> ANCHOR: Good morning, Michael, or good afternoon or evening, whatever it is to you.
> LEV: Well, good evening to me and good morning to you.
> ANCHOR: What's the very latest? What have you heard in the last couple of hours that can bring us up to speed with the latest developments? Is anything breaking, or is it still kind of quiet?
> LEV: It was a fairly quiet day today.

A second telephone interview was little more productive.

ANCHOR: Michael, is the situation getting more tense or are things getting better?
LEV: Well, I think we're somewhere in the middle. We're definitely short of a crisis.
ANCHOR: Now, why the holdup in getting these servicemen back? A lot of Americans are wondering why they just can't be released.
LEV: Well, because China isn't ready to do it. The perspective from the Chinese government is completely different from the American view of what's happened.
ANCHOR: And how do we get out of this? How does one country appear to have won this thing without losing face?[10]

Lev's response that time and diplomacy were needed, as well as his other answers, showed his grasp of the situation as much as the questions of the anchors showed their lack of information. But the real shortcoming of the footage seemed to be a hasty marriage of local and foreign, based not on journalistic values but on the business side's idea of squeezing more value out of journalists' efforts.

Gannett, also known for its attention to profit margins, is nevertheless providing a far better example of the use of multimedia techniques. Its USA Today Live uses the content of the newspaper in electronic form on both the USAToday.com Web site and Gannett's twenty-two television stations nationwide. USA Today Live, then in the planning stage, had a premature but successful debut when it covered the Concorde crash outside Paris in 2000. Since its official launch at the 2000 political conventions, it has featured both foreign and national stories. Jack Kelley sent audio reports to the USA Web site at the height of the fighting in the Tora Bora Mountains of Afghanistan. Jim Hopkins's newspaper story about the growth of Asian immigrants' businesses appeared on the Web site and television, where it was presented by a television reporter, although some USA Today journalists make their own TV appearances with their stories.

LOCAL AND NATIONAL WEB SITES

The viewer statistics of the big newspapers' Web sites show that people with a real interest in national or foreign news go where they can find it, not to their local newspaper's site. Even though the local paper probably pumps more AP foreign wire copy onto the site than onto its pulp pages, those AP dispatches are usually briefer and less detailed than those of the leading newspapers.

The Gannett Company makes the search for national and foreign news easy in its ninety-eight local papers, at the same time contributing to the user total of *USAToday.com*. Viewers of the Jackson, Mississippi, *Clarionledger.com* get a lovely picture of a magnolia; lots of sports news, local and regional; and a selection of news stories, also mostly national and local. Users have two choices to search further for national and foreign: a news button that leads to more scrolling through the *Clarion Ledger's* roster of AP headlines or, more prominently, a USA Today button that brings the flashy front page of the paper's Web site on the screen, complete with pictures, headlines, sidebars, and all. In the fuzzy world of Internet advertising, where ad rates are based on how many users click onto them, this system would seem to be a double benefit for Gannett in its efforts to capture a larger share of the $5 billion spent each year. Jackson's Web visitors first seek out *Clarionledger.com* for the local news; those interested in events farther afield make the second choice of *USAToday.com*. Both are counted in the Internet's usage measurements. Advertising aside, Gannett's Web relay system seems to be a rationale for small, locally focused papers like the *Clarion-Ledger* to print or post only a minimum of foreign wire copy. Whereas other editors say, "Let them get it from CNN," they can say, "Let them get it from our Gannett flagship Web site."

CNN.com and the BBC's news bulletin are the most concise and complete sites for viewers looking mostly for foreign news. They supply computer screens with a little world newspaper with breaking stories, pictures, and background. Their news is kept up-to-date around the clock. It is well sourced, objective, and free of hidden agendas. The BBC promises news updated every minute, twenty-four hours a day, and fulfills the promise with a ticker tape of headlines, like the Times Square zipper, that constantly flash across its home page.

There are many ways of measuring audiences in general, but two ways of measuring news audiences: those that provide their own original content and those who serve as portals for others' content. Thus the general-purpose Yahoo and AOL sites have huge numbers of visitors but cannot be described accurately as news sites: Yahoo, at the top of the list most of the time, has eleven million unique visitors a month, but its function for news is directing them to Reuters and the *New York Times* on the Web dispatches. MSNBC, which offers its own content as well as that of the wire services and *Newsweek*, does almost as well at 10.7 million unique visitors a month. As defined by the rating service Media Matrix, "unique visitors" are the actual number of total users who visited the site in a month or other measuring period. Visitors are unduplicated, meaning that they are counted only once. The rest of the top rankings of pure news sites is made up of the following, although their positions change as frequently as the weather: CNN, *New York Times*, ABC News, *USAToday, Washington Post, Time, Los Angeles Times,* Fox News, *Christian Science Monitor,* and *Wall Street Journal.*

But hits or visits don't add up to readers' penetration of a newspaper. By some measurements, a million unique visitors to a site adds up to about three million individual sessions on the Web, on the assumption that each visitor clicks on to the site three times a month. Other systems count as many as six page views for every unique visitor. Media Matrix and other services also measure how long people spend during their visits or hits. For the *New York Times* on the Web, it's about eight minutes, for MSNBC, about six. But again, others who measure Internet use say that time spent on a site is not necessarily a sign of interest. As users become more experienced in navigating the Web, they need less time to find their way to the sites they want. In any case, none of these millions being measured add up the way the millions do for newspaper readership (about 100 million daily) or the network newscasts (20 million to 30 million daily). Newspapers have lost circulation but generally have held their ground as a medium that offers far more ease of use than do their electronic competitors. Not everyone wants to consult an archive on the Gulf War over morning coffee, and many millions of readers are quite satisfied with the amount of backgrounding and explanation they've been getting for years in the columns of the well-edited print papers. They also like something they can hold in their hands, fold and read on subway or bus, take to the beach, put away for later, easily clip, tear, or circle for reference. This ease of use, however, has been counterbalanced by the difficulty of production and delivery. The paper that is so easy to handle is difficult and expensive to produce. Because of frequent price fluctuations, newsprint manufacturers keep even the biggest publishers uncertain of how their balance sheets will look. Indeed, high newsprint prices have forced many publishers to narrow the width of their pages and make further cuts in news holes.

At first, newspaper managers regarded electronic editions as a way to cut the costs of two of their largest expenses, production and distribution. What they got instead were more expenses and assorted headaches over reliability and damage to the reputations of established newspaper names. All but the smallest newspaper in the United States has a Web site. Most, however, provide only an electronic look at the printed version, or some of it, with a few embellishments like events calendars and restaurant reviews. This requires minimal staffing and no original reporting. It's a low-cost model that most sites use until they begin to receive the hoped-for profits from advertising. But other sites, like the *Post*'s, have gone much further in their imaginative use of the technology, bringing readers up-to-date on breaking stories between issues of the paper or providing extra background on events and issues.

Although the boom and then bust in dot.com ventures slowed the growth of newspaper Web sites, it did not demolish them, as it did many Internet businesses. Unlike Net merchandisers, newspapers don't have to pack and ship their offerings: they simply go out on the wire. Fifteen percent of Americans say they go to the Internet every day to get news, and a third say they do so once a week. The *Wall Street Journal* has persuaded more than 650,000 customers to pay for its service. Others, including the *New York Times*, tried that for a time but found there was too much free competition. In the meantime, more efforts are under way to make Web sites more enticing. Even small newspapers offer car, job, and home ads; entertainment listings; and a wire report that is constantly and automatically updated even on sites that don't change their own postings of news from the paper. To most, the service is local, although users from Germany tap into the *York Gazette* in Pennsylvania to find out about visiting the Harley-Davidson factory there. Honolulu's *Advertiser* and *Star-Bulletin* sites serve local users with Hawaiian political and business news and are accessed also by many thousands of the six million annual visitors to the islands for information on hotels and beaches.

The largest newspapers in paper circulation are also the largest on the Internet, with the exception of the *Wall Street Journal*, whose relatively limited Web exposure is explained by its $59 a month subscription fee.

ETHICS

What Web newspaper sites did not change for journalists is equally important. That is the need for accuracy, honesty, and fairness, the bedrock of journalism's ethics since the early days of the printed press. The new technology, with its speed and apparent effortlessness, made it even more important to maintain these ethical principles. An easily accessible Web site purporting to offer objective information about a political or economic cause can disguise advocates for or against that cause. Downloading a government statement is quick and easy but does away with the vital journalistic function of asking questions.

"Journalists should be really skeptical of everything they read online," Sreenath Sreenivasan of Columbia University warned. "They should be aware of where they are on the Web, just the way they would be if they were on the street."[11]

Lobbyists, pressure groups, and bigots, often with their real identities care-fully camouflaged, mix with professional news and information providers on the Net in a way they never could on the pages of a newspaper or on a televi-sion screen. Even shortwave provides clear labels like Beijing or Vatican radio.

Journalists who use the Internet know these pitfalls. One is Jim Anderson, a veteran foreign and State Department correspondent who writes for Germany's Deutsche Presse-Agentur. He and his colleagues seldom file a story without checking through the various sources available on the Internet. But they also understand that the Net has many counterfeit sources as well as accurate ones. "News organizations are going to have to deal with this huge gusher and how to distinguish between the true and the false," Anderson said. Journalists' choices are complicated by the decline of traditional sources of news from abroad and the proliferation of new untested sources, he adds. "Somebody has to figure out a system to deal with it."[12]

Used wisely, the Web can be a guarantor of reliability in the same way the nameplate of the *Wall Street Journal* or the peacock of NBC is. Within Web sites guaranteed by these brands, subsidiary sources of information, and even links to sources outside the site, are branded. What isn't possible for the Internet to do, however, since its hallmark is freedom of choice, is to guarantee that view-ers will choose a guaranteed site. One way to do this is to stick with brand names. In addition to the national sites, the most reliable is often the *News*, *Times*, *Observer*, or whatever the name of the local paper is. Many have been around for a century, compared with a decade for the Web, and the well-run newspaper Web sites use the same care in editing and checking the electronic version as they do the paper one.

Many newspapers, however, haven't put much effort, money, and personnel into their electronic editions. Just as they were in the beginning days of radio and then television, newspaper managers are uncertain of what role the Web sites should play. There is a temptation to shovel a few headlines from the paper onto the site and plug in the Associated Press. Until Web editions begin to make a profit from advertising, there is little incentive for change.

Public broadcasting is trying to put its brand on reliable sources of national and international news on the Web with a program that might make up for some of these local deficiencies in quality. The Corporation for Public Broad-casting and Public Radio International have invested $650,000 in Public NewsRoom, an interactive online news service that provides international, national, and local news. The service is available to public radio and public television. Launched in 2000, Public NewsRoom has about a hundred subscribers.

In order to attract the public broadcasting audience, Public NewsRoom has to present news and information that is up to the standards of the programs on PBS like the *NewsHour* and *Frontline*, programs they watch on television when they're not on the Internet. Like these programs, NewsRoom provides explanation, analysis, and different viewpoints.

Vince Winkel, NewsRoom's managing editor, and a national editor select the day's leading stories from a range of sources and keep them up-to-date in a news cycle that starts with Winkel working from home in suburban Boston at 6 A.M. and continues from Public NewsRoom's newsroom in an old building on the edge of the city's Chinatown. It's not a case of plug and play. Winkel says he doesn't want users simply to scroll down a long list as it comes in from AP or Reuters. Reuters, the *Christian Science Monitor*, the *Los Angeles Times*, and the *Washington Post* are the most frequently used sources. Public NewsRoom appears on public radio and television Web sites with the day's news and a number of special sections, such as the Middle East, Afghanistan, and terrorism at home. The sections display a fat column of developments from wire and newspaper reports and a thinner column of media links, many of them foreign, that users might want to turn to for additional information. "I want them to be aware of opinions from outside the United States," Winkel says, "not just the American take on things." For perspectives on the Middle East, he uses *The Economist*, *Financial Times*, and Palestinian, Israeli, Syrian, and Lebanese English-language newspapers.[13]

Is Public NewsRoom really needed, with the multitude of commercial packages like CNN and Yahoo already available? "The public stations want stickiness, to use an old Web term," Winkel answers. "They want you to go to their site instead of *CNN.com* so that you'll continue to identify with them and their programs, buy their coffee mugs, maybe give an extra $10 during their fundraising drives." NewsRoom wants to attract users by doing a better job than many local sites do. "We can't just plug in a wire service and let it run the way so many sites do," Winkel explained. "These sites don't have real people making decisions on what is important, relevant, and interesting, what advances their audience's knowledge about an issue." Even if the Web provides limitless space, Winkel says, "We don't ask our users to scroll down huge pages of one-line tags for stories without some editorial guidance."[14]

NewsRoom also uses contributions from public stations. About twenty stories a day are suggested to the Boston headquarters, and two or three are put on the Web. They include international commentaries like one that KERA in Dallas offered from a viewer, Maxine Shapiro, who had visited the Middle East. The new service also gives the *Monitor*, *Los Angeles Times*, and Reuters (not to mention the Middle Eastern papers) exposure in smaller cities and university towns where its foreign news offerings overshadow those of the local newspapers.

The Internet's flexibility, which makes it easy for even small news operations to participate on the Web, also creates opportunities for misuse by propagandists and advocates who want to be seen as genuine news providers. Hyperlinks, those underlined words or phrases that provide an instant connection to another site for more information, are particularly open to manipulation. Links are often provided by news sites to give all sides of an issue, but sometimes they lead to benign-sounding organizations that actually have partisan agendas, or worse. The *Miami Herald* and other Knight Ridder papers carry Web page statements welcoming links but warning that stories or headlines can't be used by other sites without permission. They also forbid "framing," displaying a newspaper's headlines or text so that it appears to be part of the outside site.

The American public is reserved in its assessment of the Internet's reliability. A 2001 poll by the Markle Foundation, which supports media research, showed that nearly three out of four respondents agreed that "you have to question most things you read on the Internet," despite a generally favorable attitude toward its advantages and potential. Sixty-three percent of all of those polled, and 83 percent of those who use the Internet, had positive feelings about it. Nearly half said they used it as a library rather than for shopping or banking. But by equally large percentages, they thought that some sort of policing was in order to address the issues of reliability, privacy, and pornography, a system that would include not only government but also industry self-regulation and participation by the public and by nonprofit organizations. According to a survey commissioned by the Online News Association, the Internet appears to be gaining acceptance as a generally reliable source of information. The survey found that the public generally considers online news credible, although only 13 percent considered it their most reliable source.

The tabloid reputation of Internet news, which came about because of the historical coincidence of exploding Internet use and the Clinton scandals, has been toned down or eliminated. Just as they do with supermarket newspapers and magazines, viewers quickly learned to click past Matt Drudge and on to a Web site with the nameplate of their local newspaper or a national brand like MSNBC. But the pressure of a deadline every minute—to use the title of a book written long ago about United Press International—is still a danger to the reputation of online journalism. This rush to get on the screen is exacerbated by Web sites run by people with too little journalistic experience or staffed so skimpily that they sometimes don't have time to check their sources.

The rumors and gossip that crowded the Internet in the wake of the attacks on New York and the Pentagon and then redoubled with the anthrax scares brought out the Web's self-policing mechanisms for those willing to use them. Some sites did more than debunk tales of Nostradamus prophecies and devil faces on the World Trade Center; they provided context and history. Many reported a tenfold increase in visitors. General-purpose search engines like Google were geared to respond to the most popular chain-letter and hoax subjects. Typing in the topic produced many pages of links to reliable sources like the Centers for Disease Control, state governments, and media Web sites.

The online product certainly gets away with practices that the parent newspaper would never permit: flashing ads on the front page, gaudy teasers pointing inside. But online editors say that's confusing presentation with content. The Web sites of news organizations are developing into a medium of their own, or perhaps a crossbreeding with television. When *Headline News* changed format and personnel, hiring a former actress and cutting up the television screen in half a dozen ways with flashing headlines and blurbs to attract younger viewers, it seemed to be copying Internet sites, where these younger viewers spend a lot of time. In time, there may be more merging and blurring, as the technological barriers to interactive television broadcasts fall and the television possibilities of the Internet mature.

Two academic studies found fault with corrections policies for both newspapers' and broadcast stations' online sites. One, commissioned by the Radio-Television News Directors Foundation (RTNDF), examined nine broadcast sites and found that none had special corrections sections to notify viewers of the often frequent changes in breaking stories. Some posted a revised story, "noting the time of revision but leav[ing] no trace of the original [erroneous] story."[15]

Janna Quitney Anderson of Elon College and M. David Arant of the University of Memphis surveyed more than two hundred editors of online editions of U.S. newspapers, with circulations from less than fifteen thousand to more than 200,000, and found that all but 2 percent of the respondents thought the online offshoots should follow their newspapers' codes of ethics. But nearly half of those surveyed believed that the speed of the Internet had eroded the standard of verifying facts before putting them before the public, and nearly one in three said that online outlets were less likely than traditional newspapers to follow ethical standards.[16]

Closely related are standards of accuracy. One editor responding to the survey wrote that although newspaper standards of accuracy should be applied to the Web, "obviously the way copy is handled must be changed—it's gotta be faster." More than half the respondents from small newspapers agreed that the ability to publish information immediately has chipped away at standards of accuracy. The standards still apply in theory, one respondent observed, but "the speed of the medium prevents a traditional copy-editing process. Every piece of copy can't be touched by a copy editor—only select content." Correcting the mistakes that slip through sometimes adds to inaccuracy. Seventeen percent of the respondents thought that their Web sites simply ran a new story when the old one was in error, with no mention of the mistake. One editor commented that this "smacks of '1984' and the wholesale revision of history." The survey authors suggest that instead of trying to conceal corrections, newspaper Web sites should have easily accessible buttons so that site visitors can find them and that corrections also should be included in archival material. The Wall Street Journal Interactive's corrections policy does just that. It has a corrections section accessible from any part of the site and includes corrections, even those made later, to its archived material.[17]

Some of the reasons disclosed by the survey for this loss of accuracy are understaffing and pressure to keep updating the news on the Web sites. Both can be related to the bottom line. In order to attract advertisers, Web site managers must keep their sites current. But since profits for most Web sites are elusive or illusory, at least in the first period of a Web startup, management tries to use as few staffers as possible. Nearly half the sites polled by Anderson and Arant were staffed by only one full-time worker or by all part-timers. These online teams "are asked to constantly remake the news stories in their Web editions to keep them fresh and to push hot-breaking-news items online quickly," the authors say. "High standards of responsibility and ethics are difficult if not impossible to uphold in this sort of environment." Arant and Anderson concluded that newspapers risk losing their reputation for accuracy and trust by the public by permitting understaffed, overworked Web sites to represent them on the Internet. If they abandon their traditional standards in the transition from newsprint to electronic transmission, they advised, "the online offspring could damage the newspaper's reputation and squander the immense value of the parent's good name."[18]

Rich Jaroslavsky, who heads the Online News Association, states that a Web journalist must go beyond merely providing information and become "a broker of information, a filter, a moderator—and sometimes even a referee." Jaroslavsky says the stakes have been raised by the new technology. "It is now infinitely easier than ever before to disseminate misinformation around the globe, [but] honesty, accuracy, and fairness didn't go out of fashion because technology has changed."[19]

In testimony before Congress, Jaroslavsky addressed the issue of those who claim that the Internet would sound a death knell for traditional journalism because each person could function as his or her own reporter and editor and there would no longer be a need for anyone to sift and interpret information.

> Instead, what we've seen is that the Net has made the role of the journalist even more important. Precisely because there is so much information out there—a good deal of it from sources of dubious reliability—people have an even more critical need for help in separating fact from fiction and for developing perspectives on events and issues.[20]

The Poynter Institute's Aly Colon thinks brand names are the best guarantee of reliability on Web sites. "If everyone is a journalist, then no one is a journalist," he told a class at New York's New School University in an online lecture. "If everyone purports to offer news, then no one offers news." Colon believes that newspapers with long reputations for accuracy and integrity are the best bets for the same qualities on the Web; newcomers have to earn their reputations. In the first category he puts the *New York Times, Wall Street Journal, Washington Post*, and good regional papers like the *Seattle Times* and *Miami Herald*. Online spin-offs from established broadcasters CNN.*com* and MSNBC pass his test as newcomers.

But brand names can be stolen. Stormfront, a white supremacist group, tinkered with the nuts and bolts of online delivery systems to post its hate messages on reputable newspaper sites. Users seeking the *Atlanta Journal-Constitution, Philadelphia Inquirer*, and seven other newspapers found themselves connected instead to racist diatribes. Restraining orders and technical measures stopped the deception, but tinkerers are unlikely to be deterred for similar attempts in the future. The Federal Trade Commission steps in to stop Internet operations that use names similar to familiar sites, as in the site that diverted children from the Cartoon Network to a barrage of ads promoting gambling and pornography. But FTC concerns are consumer fraud, not political trickery.

The credibility of the Internet is thus a two-part problem: the journalists who gather news from the Web, for online or traditional publication or broadcast, and the consumers of Web information, not all of which is provided by trustworthy journalists. The problem of Web site reliability is as great for producers of the news as for consumers. Checking the Internet for information has become as routine a practice for reporters, at home and abroad, as calling the local police station or Foreign Ministry. If a consumer is misled by a Web site, only he or she is harmed. But journalists who pick up and pass on faulty or deceptive information also are misinforming an audience that may number in the millions. Mike Wendland, a freelancer who reports on the high-tech industry for the *Detroit Free Press* and NBC, says that using Internet sources requires some extra skills beyond the traditional journalistic skepticism. His PCMike Web site lists his rules, the first of which is not to believe anything he reads online unless the person or organization behind the site is clearly identified. A real address, not a post office box or e-mail address, and a telephone number to contact a real person, must be provided. His third rule concerns sourcing:

Don't just accept the facts you find on a Web site at face value. Make sure they are attributed, the sources for information are clearly identified, and the sources are reputable and reliable. The problem is that on the Internet, many of the traditional "gatekeepers" are gone. Anyone with a modicum of computer skills can be a publisher. Hate groups, cults, and extremist organizations have designed very impressive and compelling pages to lure surfers to listen to spiels that are cleverly camouflaged as educational information.[21]

The Arant-Anderson survey's findings confirmed this view. Although 70 percent of their respondents said that their sites should not provide links to hate groups and other questionable sites, only 22 percent thought that their newspapers had a policy prohibiting such actions.

THE ELECTRONIC MISSING LINK

If only newspapers could figure out a way of reaching their customers without all the high costs of printing and delivery and without worrying about losing control of their content on the World Wide Web. They have made many efforts in the past, from video text transmissions on television screens to an electronic tablet portable enough to go on the bus and beach, even if it can't be folded up the way a newspaper can.

Now the hopes of many newspaper managers are on electronic systems that reproduce the printed version on computer screens—including laptops, for portability—or in laser-printed facsimiles sent all over the world. No extra staff is needed, and no one need worry about outsiders' use of the newspaper's good name.

The systems are NewspaperDirect, which delivers a little printed paper to your hotel room, cruise ship, or home, and NewsStand, which eliminates paper entirely in providing a replica of the New York Times and other papers on your computer screen.

In newsrooms across the nation, stories and photos are edited, headlines are written, page design is completed, and then the whole thing is sent over wires to printing plants for the cumbersome and costly transfer to newsprint and delivery to home and newsstands. NewsStand utilizes the first part of the process to ensure the integrity of the publication but steps in at the second part to divert the content of the paper to computer screens. It transmits the entire newspaper, including advertising, to subscribers' computer screens, desktop or portable. New York Times publisher Arthur Hays Sulzberger told a newspaper technology conference that NewsStand "may be the missing link of newspaper circulation."

What subscribers—and single-copy purchasers—get is, in effect, the news-paper printed on their screen, but with some improvements. Reader/viewers can zoom in to an enlarged image of stories or photos. And there's no need to turn pages to find the continuation of a story; the software does it for you.

Electronic delivery is particularly important to the *Christian Science Monitor*, which reaches its nationwide audience largely through the U.S. Postal Service. The *Monitor* began promoting free electronic reproductions of the daily print paper in 2002 and followed up with a subscription system at half the price of its paper edition.

Whether readers will find the NewsStand delivery system unwieldy remains to be seen, but if it is widely adopted, the benefits to publishers will be numer-ous. They get to sell, not give away, content, as most now do with Web sites. The online sales of a few thousand copies a day in the first few months after the *Times* introduced the system will be counted in audited circulation figures, which raise advertising rates as they increase. And there should be no worries about inexperienced or overworked online edition staffers committing errors in the paper's name, because what NewsStand sends on the Internet is the same fully edited and vetted version that goes to the printing plants.

This shortcut gives NewsStand the ability to deliver the *New York Times* any-where in the world, ads, graphics, and all, without the costly and time-consum-ing processes of producing and distributing the printed paper. Unlike the *New York Times* on the Web, access to the facsimile costs money. "NewsStand will make it possible for anyone in the world to buy the *Times*," the paper announced, although not everyone in the world can afford the $350 annual sub-scription cost, the 65-cents-a-day introductory single copy price, or the high-speed Internet connection that the electronic edition required in its introduc-tory phase. It is available at *NYTimes.com*, can be downloaded and printed out, in part or entirely, but cannot serve as an archive, since it remains in computers' memories for no more than seven days.

Readers served by the New York–based NewspaperDirect receive their world news already printed, in thirty-two-page miniature versions of papers like Russia's *Izvestia*, Spain's *El Mundo*, or the United States' *International Herald Tribune*, *Miami Herald*, and *El Nuevo Herald*. NewspaperDirect transmits the content of the newspapers electronically to printing plants around the world and delivers them on the same day to airlines, hotels, newsstands, and offices.

Some combination of this electronic reproduction and the free-form Web sites will be the basis of the newspaper's future. Just as Web sites coexist with traditional newspapers in the same home or office, it is likely that an electroni-cally delivered paper will not put the Web out of business, anymore than broad-casting did away with newspapers. Moving the printing machinery from big plants in cities to small cabinets attached to home computers is an idea that has been around for decades, since generations of schoolchildren were told that their newspaper would one day come out of their radio (or television, depending on the generation). The new entries in the field make it seem closer to realization. But the widespread adoption of PrintingPress, or whatever the new system is named—in the current fashion of squeezing together titles—will mean greater access to news of all kinds. It will be up to the editors and managers to decide what role foreign news will play under these new conditions.

What all these electronic journals lack, whether they're full-blown video-spinning Web sites or carbon copies of that day's printed pages, are methods of reading them that can compete with the ease and convenience of picking up a paper. Knight Ridder spent millions on Roger Fidler's Tablet, a hardcover book-size screen that provided both text and hyperlinks to related topics in the tablet's memory. Starting with its development in 1981, before anyone knew what Internet meant, Fidler fashioned a light pencil that would focus on electronic headlines on the tablet's screen and lead to stories and other information stored in its memory. The Tablet could be recharged, he thought, at ATM machines. But the chain gave up on the Tablet because people didn't want to lug it around.

The current entry in the field is called eBook, or "the amazing eBook," sold by RCA for about $300. It gains in portability from Fidler's Tablet by being much smaller but loses in readability. In addition to the *Wall Street Journal* and *Washington Post* interactive editions, it can store magazines and ten best-sellers (or slow-sellers) to be read on a five-and-a-half-inch (measured diagonally) screen "about the size of a paperback." A hint that eBook's portability may hamper its readability is contained in the company's promotion of a more expensive model with a screen measuring more than eight inches diagonally. But only a few thousand of the readers have been sold, most of them as gifts, despite promotions by Oprah Winfrey. One problem is that eBooks don't connect to the Internet but must be fed by a telephone line that provides their content. Such a system would make it difficult to keep current with breaking news on *Washington Post* or *Wall Street Journal* sites. "The drawbacks of reading onscreen will discourage all but the most motivated readers," concluded Daniel P. O'Brien, senior analyst at Forrester Research.[22]

Another print-electronic hybrid had a short life, only one of the nine that might have been expected. CueCat was a handheld device that looked like an elongated computer mouse. It could read bar codes printed in newspapers and connect its users with an Internet site containing more information about stories or advertisements. The Dallas-based Belo Corporation, which publishes the *Dallas Morning News*, *Providence Journal*, and *Press-Enterprise* of Riverside,

California, invested $37 million in CueCat's supplier. Belo's Dallas television station, WFAA, also used the system to connect viewers' television sets and computers. Although the papers gave away more than 200,000 CueCats and Digital Convergence made them available without charge at Radio Shack stores, Belo dropped the program after about a year because it found too few people were using it. One reason was that people don't often read their newspapers in front of their computers. Another was that readers who are computer users have become sophisticated enough to click to the Internet for information without the aid of gadgets. And users were worried about the loss of privacy because the system identified them when they connected to it, a means of keeping track of those interested in the advertisements.

But new devices continue to be introduced or adapted, some of them with real potential to become a source of news of all kinds. A number of companies have tailored services to link with the PalmPilots, cellphones, and pagers that people are already carrying, adding news or news alerts to their other services. All the top news Web sites have such services. A subscriber signs up to be notified by e-mail of breaking news. Some sites offer few such notices, but others put out alerts when they receive them, often several times a day, from their wire service news sources. The alerts that appear on their tiny screens can be pursued by going to the Web sites. None is a full-service news provider; cellphone messages are limited in most cases to one hundred words. But in an uncertain time, it's one more way to keep track of events minute by minute.

In Manila, cellphones made news instead of merely transmitting it when the opposition overthrew the corrupt president, Joseph Estrada. Activists sent hundreds of thousands of instant messages to cellphones listing demonstration times and sites and succeeded in quickly rallying the crowds that forced Estrada to quit.

Walter Bender of the Massachusetts Institute of Technology's Media Lab was the first to develop a software system to tailor the news to viewers' needs or wants, permitting them to eliminate the Middle East and concentrate on Norway or eliminate international treaties and concentrate on inflation and industrial output. In exchange for a narrower scope, the customer's computer receives much more detailed coverage. Dozens of Web sites now have variants of this service, offering Tamil news for Tamils in the United States or news likely to affect share prices, a main concern of subscribers to the *Wall Street Journal*'s Personal Journal. Smaller Web operations are joining the big operators, including the *Minneapolis Star-Tribune*'s News2Go, which sends customized news to Palms, Handsprings, and other handheld devices, and PImail, a service of the *Seattle Post-Intelligencer* that promises to deliver news breaks on topics the user selects.

Some American papers use Internet links to broaden their offerings from abroad. The *Forward*, which began with mailed dispatches from correspondents abroad, now has electronic links with the liberal newspaper *Ha'aretz* in Israel. *Forward* readers get a constantly updated supply of stories in English or Hebrew that puts them ahead of most other sources of news about Israel. The *Jerusalem Post*, which is published in Israel, counters with home delivery in the New York metropolitan area of pages sent via satellite and printed locally.

Freedom from unseen media managers or manipulators was one of the big arguments for people navigating the Web on their own in its early days. With the Internet user free to what he or she wanted, there was no opportunity for the priesthood of editors to decide what was good for the public. What this argument didn't take into consideration was that someone had to assign, cover, write, or at least release the stories that the users were selecting, which meant that somewhere along the line, a professional was indeed making a choice. In any case, data from Jupiter Media Matrix show that most people prefer to have someone else select their news. Seventy-two percent of news site users in July 2001 used the three most popular sites: MSNBC, CNN, and the *New York Times*. Although Internet usage continues to grow in numbers of users and in the time spent in front of the computer screen, there is less roaming and more concentration on a few sites each user has found reliable and useful.

ELECTRONICS IN THE FIELD

The work of the electronic gadget researchers helps journalists as well as audiences by accessing news from remote locations in the world. When Americans waited for the release of the twenty-four crew members held by China in 2001 after their spy plane was forced to land there, a CNN satellite phone linked to a video camera and powered by a car battery provided the first jerky footage of their takeoff from Hainan Island. CNN scooped the world twice in 2001, a feat increasingly difficult to manage given the plethora of satellites and far-flung news-gathering crews (most of them working for European or Asian organizations, not the U.S. networks). Weeks before the Hainan Island coverage, CNN used the same kind of satellite phone, a device that can be stored in an attaché case, to send the first video of the devastating earthquake in northwest India. It took six more days for the competition's regular satellite equipment to reach the remote scene and start transmitting.

The jumpy images sent by CNN's Lisa Rose Weaver from Hainan were not only a worldwide exclusive but also an example of how fast technology is changing news gathering. Only a few years ago, the ability to move in satellite dishes gave the world instant access to breaking news from all but the most remote locations. But as the Hainan and India stories were broadcast and widely commented on, the traditional satellite systems were being dismissed as cumbersome.

Hainan and India were short test flights for the debut of the satellite video phone as the mainstay of spot coverage in the war against Afghanistan. As the world's other networks and agencies tried to catch up with CNN and the BBC, the other major user of the technology, they turned to a little company in London called 7E which was selling its eleven-pound "Talking Head" equipment for about $16,000 a set. Its basis is a standard video-conferencing unit attached to a satellite-communication terminal, or two such terminals to double the speed of transmission. About two hundred were sold in the first weeks of the war.

The Talking Head is carried in a small suitcase, and the satellite phone in another small bag, neither likely to arouse suspicion from hostile officials. Powered by a car battery or plugged into a hotel room outlet, the system can transmit from a small antenna poked out a car or building window without the telltale satellite dish. If the images are to be broadcast quality, transmission is slow: an hour for a minute of video. Satellite phone charges are up to $8 a minute. Direct transmission that goes right on the air produces jerky movements and low-quality pictures but is prized for its immediacy. The quality appears better if the image is reduced to a half or quarter of the screen and the anchor or other footage occupies the rest.

Talking Heads connects to Inmarsat, a satellite system designed for communication with ships at sea and now serves journalists as well as relief and disaster workers, peacekeeping forces, airlines, and civil defense workers. It transmits telephone and data signals to and from more than 200,000 terminals around the world. Talking Heads engineers say they can shrink their instrument to less than half its present size and weight, but that may not be enough to stay ahead of the advances in wireless telephony, for which 3G, or third-generation, equipment is already becoming available. The first of these phones will be able to match the current transmission speeds being used by correspondents in the field, and they are likely to become even faster. As 3G equipment replaces that of the earlier generations of mobile phones, it will become cheaper and more readily available, although it can transmit only in countries that have an advanced network in place, which rules out many current trouble spots. Correspondents might soon find they can carry their video links in their pockets, although in places like Afghanistan, Talking Head or something like it will be needed for some time.

Television viewers around the world have become used to the jerky movements of the pictures that Talking Head and other such devices transmit, but they have also enjoyed the access that the devices give them to spot news by allowing television crews to work in countries where the infrastructure is inadequate or entirely missing. They also permit these journalists to evade restrictions on their activities by suspicious authorities. This combination of inadequate support systems and official intrusion is a good description of most of the world's trouble spots. Talking Head and the other gadgets of its generation have a secure future in international reporting.

THE INTERNET AND SEPTEMBER 11

The attacks on New York and Washington were either the Internet's finest hour or the Internet's failure, depending on what was being measured and the time of the assessment. Five and one-half million people told Pew Internet and American Life researchers that the Internet was their primary source of information about the attacks. But that is only 3 percent of the adult population of the United States. Eighty-one percent of Americans used television and 11 percent, radio, the Pew study found. "When there is an enormous news story, the overwhelming number of people immediately want to go to where they can get the most vivid, up-to-date information," Lee Rainie, the Pew project director, stated. Far more people used the telephone rather than e-mail to contact friends and relatives: 51 percent to 15 percent, Rainie said, because "the immediacy of hearing someone's voice and making contact that way is a powerful thing."[23]

In the first hours after the attack, the most popular sites, CNN, ABC, and the *New York Times*, were inaccessible, and other sites could accommodate only a fraction of the users trying to connect, so heavy was the traffic and so great the damage to the networks that were connected through the World Trade Center. Internet sites failed because they, along with the nation's entire communication system, quickly overloaded. But eventually they succeeded because they pushed out millions of words of information at high speed. A few hours into the emergency, Web managers tapped emergency bandwidth from other sources. They also found ways to speed access by stripping away advertisements and graphics, leaving only low-power text versions. *CNN.com* slimmed down to a tenth of the kilobytes it usually has on its home page. Its 162 million page views were far more than its previous record in the aftermath of the 2000 elections in Florida. The list of successes and failures continues: unable to deliver video images of the disasters because of overloading and still inadequate technical capability, the Internet was able to connect millions by e-mail. It attracted double the number of unique users, at least thirteen million, than the previous record set in the elections by MSNBC, with 6.5 million. Relying in large part, particularly at the start of the disaster, on the reporting of others, the Internet relayed wire service reports and hitched onto the network television accounts that most of the nation was watching.

For the first time, NBC used its three channels of information—MSNBC and CNBC on cable, in addition to the network—as separate entities. With so many stories and images from around the world to handle, NBC News stopped using its cable channels to rebroadcast the content of the network and used them for original content. MSNBC was devoted to running coverage of breaking news, much like CNN's *Headline News*, carrying, for example, full coverage of a news conference of which the NBC network was using only excerpts. CNBC concentrated on the financial aspects.

To Rich Jaroslavsky of the Online News Association, the attacks showed the world that online journalism, born in the 1990s, had come of age.

> We are no longer an experiment. In the aftermath of September 11, we've seen people come online for news in unprecedented numbers. We are now a major source of news and information for millions of people across the nation and around the world. More than that, we've begun to see where we fit in in the journalistic landscape: more timely than print, more in-depth than broadcast, more interactive than either.
>
> People expect more from us now. They aren't just intrigued by us—they *need* us. That raises the stakes enormously. People need us to have high standards, to bring them information with accuracy and integrity—with credibility.[24]

Jaroslavsky's own paper was a good example of the strengths of the Internet. Within minutes of the World Trade Center attacks, the editors of *WSJ.com*, housed in a nearby building, had to be evacuated, but not before they switched control to its Brussels bureau. As American staff members moved to continue operations from New Jersey, Hong Kong joined in picking up the slack. *WSJ.com*, the most successful pay-to-view site among newspapers, decided to offer its information without charge for the first two days of the attack and its aftermath. Users went up 30 to 50 percent, and many stayed on when charges were restored. From twenty thousand to thirty thousand new subscribers joined in the next few weeks, increasing *WSJ.com*'s count to more than 650,000. The print *Journal* got out an issue the next day, combining New Jersey editing and other makeshift devices, but its dot.com sibling showed how wires and satellites can work, sometimes, when ink and paper can't.

Users turned to sites they could identify and trust during the crisis, which meant the offshoots of newspapers and broadcasters. "People want reliable intermediaries," Rainie of the Pew Internet project observed.[25] Other Web sites were used more as bulletin boards for survivor lists and church services. The crisis brought calls for protection of the Internet from terrorists, including the systems used by local, state, and national governments and utility companies. There was no specific mention of trying to screen the Internet for disinformation, which could be another weapon that terrorists might use.

The American Web sites fell short, however, in providing foreign coverage of the attacks and their repercussions, a reflection of the decisions of managers and editors who had closed foreign bureaus and reassigned foreign correspondents, not of the Internet. As a result, foreign Web sites got a surge of business after the attacks, but participation was less than might have been expected, given the situation of an American public trying to fill what had been a virtual void of information about Afghanistan and al-Qaeda. If Internet users clicking through American sites for information chose mostly the familiar ones, they were even more cautious in checking distant sites whose politics and accuracy may not have been immediately verifiable. Some are simply propaganda for a cause; some, conduits for government handouts.

One filtering device for American users are the online services that collect information from a variety of foreign Web sites, evaluate it, and post it. An example is the Foreign Policy Association of New York. Its online service, Global Views, provides excerpts from and links to reputable foreign sites. *World Press Review*'s Web site also has a broad selection of foreign press reporting and opinion, including international wire service reports of breaking news.

THE INTERNET'S FUTURE

Newspapers lost more than $300 million on their Web sites in 2000. The *Washington Post* has expanded its Web staff to include related activities such as a political newsletter sent out by e-mail and a system to deliver information to handheld devices, and most other major news sites are trying similar measures. If not profitable, newspaper Web sites are, at least, popular. For local information, newspaper sites outrank television and radio sites. *Washingtonpost.com* had the highest percentage of local users, perhaps reflecting the large numbers of government employees with computer access, with 32 percent of the local adult population, followed by the newspaper sites in Austin, Charlotte, Raleigh, and Minneapolis, all of which attracted more than 20 percent of the population.

The sites' popularity is the result of considerable effort on the part of newspaper management. Major newspapers, wary of the competition of the other Internet sites and portals, have worked for years to provide a full basket of information, from current temperatures to movies and restaurant listings.

Internet sites for foreign news range from the clear and abundant to the inadequate. The *Tampa Tribune* has received great media attention for its system of combining newspaper, Web site, and television station newsroom and reporting duties but has made no innovations in the way it presents foreign news. Rather, the *Tampa Tribune* offers lists of hypertext headlines with as little explanation or differentiation as a government news agency in some one-party state would offer. Busy with reporting and editing for all three media, the *Tribune* staff apparently wants every user to be his or her own wire editor. MSNBC is complete and encyclopedic, with screens divided up by region and an abundance of news and analysis. *CNN.com* and the BBC are in the same league. It's not a question of large organizations versus small ones, as the intelligent presentation of New Hampshire's *Keene Sentinel* site's foreign section shows.

More and more people are turning to the Web, but whether they are in search of foreign news or other information or entertainment isn't clear. Sixty-two percent of U.S. consumers, more than 176 million people, use the Web from home or work, according to Nielsen/Net ratings. Most of them access the Internet from home and spend an average of half an hour a day roaming the Internet. Some specialists note that Web user measurements are suspect, since many people use the Internet exclusively to exchange e-mail—sort of like lumping your telephone calls with your television viewing to produce a combined rating.

The number of residential users of the Internet increased, sometimes by huge amounts, from 1990 to 2001, when the first dip was measured as some free Internet gateways folded during the economic slowdown. But the percentage of American adults connected to the Net still stood at more than 63, which means that nearly two-thirds of the nation spend an average of fifteen hours a month on the Internet, nineteen if they have connections at both home and work. People who have broadband connections spend more time, but the growth of such services has been slower than anticipated. The collapse of many dot.com enterprises reduced the demand for and development of the two kinds of broadband, cable and phone line. As demand slows, prices have been rising, the opposite of what usually happens in the technology sphere. Large cable and telephone companies have elbowed out some of the start-up entrepreneurs who were caught in the dot.com retrenchment. The result, according to FCC figures, was that only about ten million Internet users are connected by means of the speedy digital subscriber line (DSL) technology by their telephone companies or cable-modem arrangements with their cable companies, but the figure is increasing by about a half million a month. With fewer providers, prices rose by as much as 20 percent, to $50 a month. DSL is also limited technologically. That is, customers must be within a radius of about three miles of the network's center, which is fine for urban areas but impossible or difficult for those more sparsely populated.

All these drawbacks may be temporary, but they have slowed the growth of broadband and put off the day when ordinary consumers will be willing to pay a great deal more to watch television on their computers. Only when broadband growth and the widespread adoption of high-definition television screens to computers converge, industry experts say, will the Internet really take off as a medium with the good-quality video and immediate accessibility that will make it a real competitor for TV and cable.

Broadband users, called "speedies," spend as much time on the Internet as they do on television and other media, an Arbitron study shows. But even with a broadband connection, those surveyed said they weren't happy with the quality of streaming video, and those trying to sell more broadband connections concede that until quality improves on computer screens, most people won't go out of their way to get it in their homes.[26]

The profusion of technical terms that didn't exist a few years ago should not obscure the fact that some form of electronic delivery of information from all over the world is going to be a routine part of Americans' lives. But what kind of information? It is up to the nation's journalists, editors, producers, and media managers to make sure its accuracy, incisiveness, ideas, and analysis are up to the standards set by the best of the Internet's predecessors: newspapers, television, and radio. This can best be done by keeping those old media engaged in the new media.

"The central word is *journalism*," *Nightline*'s Tom Bettag explains.

We need to know how dangerous this form is and how it's going to be exploited. The nature of the Web, with many hundreds of sites claiming to be news sources, and as many entry points as there are computers with modems, makes all of the sins of traditional journalism easier to commit.

Journalism schools have a responsibility to try to make sure every student has a chance to report from Asia, Africa, Latin America, and other parts of the world.
— Loren Ghiglione, dean of the Medill School of Journalism, Northwestern University

We need better delivery systems for these journalistic efforts, especially given the collapse of foreign bureaus at so many media outlets.
—Orville Schell, dean of the Graduate School of Journalism, University of California at Berkeley

9

CONCLUSION: THE JOURNALISTIC GUERRILLAS

The demand for foreign news that followed the attacks on the United States put the word *world* back in the banner headlines and lead stories on television news. It transformed the gossip-driven network newsmagazines into thoughtful programs that sought to explain the how and why of the crisis. Provincial newspapers, no longer arguing that providing local news was their only duty, added the wire services of the big papers and expanded news holes to explain the challenges the nation faced. Local television stations used far more footage from abroad, and even some of the radio stations that had eliminated news of all kinds as bad for ratings began to interrupt their music and commercials with crisis news, which they found was good for ratings.

But as the war on terrorism became a routine part of America's life, these surges in foreign news coverage began to level off once again. Media managers looked at the high costs of reporting the crisis at home and abroad and worried about the decline in advertising revenue caused by a weak economy. The same return to routine meant that more and more Americans resumed their old news-consuming patterns of the stars and entertainment, the tax rate, and the mayor.

Slipping back to America's normal neglect of international affairs is dangerous in an age when conflict anywhere in the world can move swiftly and lethally to the United States. Keeping the level of foreign coverage high is as important as deploying troops and intelligence forces.

An extra effort must now be made to keep a corps of correspondents out in the world, providing information and analysis not only of the immediate threats to the United States but also of the long-term trends that could lead to such threats: religious and racial extremism, weak and corrupt governments, and poverty. Such reporting requires skills, persistence, and the patience to understand that not every months-long effort will win prizes or even be the top story in the paper or newscast. It is the kind of professionalism that characterized the American correspondents' corps through the cold war and produced reporting on the abuses of apartheid, the death squads in Central America, the human rights violations of the Soviet bloc, and the outbreak of ethnic violence in the Balkans. A strong overseas press presence kept the American people informed and helped them make decide when to support U.S. intervention and when not to, whom to aid, and which opposition cause to support. Often the explanations and warnings changed little, but one example alone makes the case for the power of on-the-ground reporting: the Vietnam War. Peter Arnett and Malcolm Browne of the AP, Neil Sheehan of UPI, David Halberstam of the *New York Times*, and many other newspaper and television journalists provided a skeptical counterpoint to the constant government assurances that the war, so costly in American casualties, was leading to victory over the Communists.

After September 11, as networks and newspapers rushed in journalists to cover the war on terror, an army of young freelancers also went into the field. Some were equipped only with notebooks, but many others had video cameras, radio-reporting and -editing equipment, and laptops that could be linked in seconds via the Internet to editorial rooms thousands of miles away. Many had language skills and background in foreign societies through study or service abroad, knowledge that leads to sharper reporting and more nuanced presentation. Some were skilled in the storytelling that goes beyond the headlines of the day and attracts audiences who identify with the stories' subjects.

Some of the elements are in place for maintaining this worldwide corps after the war on terror winds down, but there is no certainty that such an effort will succeed, even though the journalists are there with the technology to serve them, and many editors and producers are working to keep foreign news holes large and prominent.

One missing ingredient is funding. Media outlets are caught between the extraordinary expenses of foreign coverage and the decrease in revenues brought by recession and crisis. Another is organization. Freelancers working by themselves have an uphill fight for publication or broadcast. Freelancers organized in a news service would do much better.

These journalistic guerrillas, as Tom Bettag calls them, have already accomplished the hard part. They are working abroad or can quickly return there. They know their territories, and they know how to report and file their stories. All they need is more assurance that their work will reach audiences at home.

The audiences are there if the gatekeepers at newspapers, Web sites, and broadcast stations can resist a return to complacency. In some newsrooms around the country, editors are committing themselves to keeping their focus on foreign news, not at the high level of coverage that the drama of the terrorist attacks and the Afghan war generated, but not at the level of neglect or dismissal, either.

The technological means to carry out a sustained level of foreign reporting is readily available. Even correspondents who may be equipped only with laptops find that the Internet has simplified contacts and links to editors in the United States and other countries that might be interested in their stories. Miniature video cameras and software that allow field editing has expanded opportunities for journalists filing to Web sites or television. A digital camera and software capable of broadcast-quality footage costs less than $5,000 and can be operated by the correspondent without a crew. "Video journalists can spend more time doing in-depth reporting overseas at a fraction of the cost of conventional television," according to Louise Lief, a former foreign correspondent now with the Pew International Journalism Program.[1]

The growth of cable outlets and the increased use of video on news Web sites provides new opportunities for this kind of video reporting. Regional cable news networks, proliferating around the country, have a twenty-four-hour space to fill and would welcome well-told stories from abroad. Journalists who could find some regional connections in their stories would improve their chances.

Stories can't be covered and brought before audiences by enthusiasm and electronic gadgets alone. What the guerrillas need is financial support to reach the scenes of important stories and organizational support to deliver their material to the public.

The commercial networks aren't going to do it. They've got their own teams and their own problems of cost containment. Newspapers already are overstretched, although many of the better ones have Web sites open to freelance contributions. Government help is anathema, particularly in light of the denial of journalists' access to troops in the Afghan war and the disclosure of Pentagon plans to plant disinformation in the media.

Foundations and universities are the logical institutions to meet this need to sustain foreign coverage after the shooting dies down. For decades foundations have been a bedrock of support for public service journalism, enabling freelancers like Seymour Hersh to expose the My Lai massacre during the Vietnam War or keeping NPR and PBS viable and comprehensive monitors of the world. Three of the United States' leading universities—the University of California at Berkeley, Columbia, and Northwestern—have news services, magazines, or Web sites run by their journalism faculties that could serve as links between young journalists working abroad and the public. Northwestern and Berkeley already have graduate students in the field serving as foreign correspondents.

Foundations responded quickly with support for media in the aftermath of September 11. Funding from foundations helped launch two PBS programs that are providing insights into America's role in the world. *NOW with Bill Moyers* went on the air as an ad hoc response to the attacks and then became a regular weekly forum, taking up topics like the detention of terrorism suspects and providing extensive coverage of the conflicting viewpoints in the Middle East. *Frontline*, the PBS documentary program, expanded into a new format called *Frontline/World*, providing shorter segments on the pattern of 60 *Minutes*. The Knight Foundation established World Affairs Fellowships to give ten to twelve editors of small- and medium-size daily newspapers two to three weeks abroad for study and background. The aim is to show the editors that international issues have local relevance. Brandt Ayres, publisher of the *Anniston Star* in Alabama, proposed the fellowship to the foundation and said he thought editors were better candidates than reporters to receive it because they are the ones who determine what news their papers print.

Foundations have long had a role in the reporting and dissemination of foreign news in the American media. Over the years, they have sponsored individual journalists on investigative or other foreign-reporting assignments, supported the news and public affairs programs of public broadcasting, and trained young professionals who want to become international reporters.

Foundation help may enable more of these stories to be covered, printed, and broadcast, but it is not without controversy in the journalism profession. There is general agreement that help for the education and training of journalists, in universities or mid-career programs, has done much to raise standards. But when that support is directed to the work that journalists actually do, opinions diverge.

Some absolutists argue that since all foundations have an agenda, using their money to support reporting projects of any kind advances that agenda, whether or not the journalist is aware of it.

Others contend that general support is perfectly acceptable but draw the line at supporting specific projects or areas of interest. In this view, the Hewlett Foundation's role in funding *The News Hour with Jim Lehrer* or the Ford Foundation's continued support for the Corporation for Public Broadcasting is fine, but the Kaiser Foundation's backing of the *San Diego Union-Tribune* for its 1997 series on health care problems on the U.S.-Mexican border is not. Defenders of such grants say that the projects are well insulated from any foundation pressures on what to cover and how to write about it.

The foundation role is easily recognizable when a public radio or television program gives credit to its sponsors, but there are many other ways that nonprofits have helped make up for the shortcomings of the commercial networks and newspapers in covering the world.

George Soros's Open Society Institute operates directly in the media field with its EurasiaNet, providing a variety of Internet services that have their own editors and journalists to report on Central Asia. Soros, a billionaire financier born in Hungary, first used his money to establish objective reporting from eastern Europe after the fall of Communism and then, as the problems diminished there, moved on to the trouble spots of Central Asia. EurasiaNet is a source for both journalists and those interested in the area. It is headed by Justin Burke, who used to report from the region for the *Christian Science Monitor*, and uses the reporting of an international staff, including many from the countries it covers. Its stories got more use from scholars than from journalists until the terrorist attacks, when it became a hot source for reporters, specialists, and those in the general public trying to understand the new situation in Central Asia. Its dispatches on the war in Afghanistan by Ahmid Rashid, a respected Pakistani journalist and author, were consistently ahead of those of most Western media. "This was a place no one paid any attention to after the breakup of the Soviet Union," Burke said. "We've tried to cover issues like oil and trade, nationalism and conflict, to make people aware of its importance."[2]

The International Consortium of Investigative Journalists, funded by Carnegie, Ford, Soros, and other smaller foundations, focuses on the international aspects of what has become known as "public-interest journalism." The consortium identifies investigative reporters in many countries and links them via the Internet, conferences, and an institutional support structure that gives out annual awards for the best stories. It was founded to extend the programs of its partner organization, the Center for Public Integrity, beyond the borders of the United States, carrying out investigative work abroad for the benefit of citizens there as well as of Americans, whose concerns are more and more international.

Charles Lewis, who heads the Center for Public Integrity, says borders are irrelevant to international wrongdoers and should not stop journalists from trying to investigate the drug cartels, corruption, and underworld networks that cross them. "For some international corporations, the world is their candy store—cheap labor, low taxes, weak environmental standards—just pick a country," he explained. "Conventional journalism can't investigate and explain these and other complex subjects adequately. The typical one-country perspective is too narrow and misleading."[3]

The consortium supplies an international networking mechanism for reporters, providing contacts for Americans abroad and editing for foreign contributors. Investigative reports by its members include Ray Bonner's exposé of Russian money laundering by the Bank of New York for the *New York Times* and Rick Tulsky's examination of abuses in the U.S. asylum system for the *San Jose Mercury News*.

Many individual journalists who received the financial push they needed to go abroad have remained there or are frequent visitors who write and broadcast about foreign affairs. The syndicated columnist Georgie Ann Geyer got a Fulbright to Austria at the start of her career. Guy Raz won an Arthur Burns fellowship for an internship in Germany and stayed on as the Berlin correspondent for National Public Radio. Peggy Simpson spent the first decade after the fall of Communism in eastern Europe as a freelancer, helped along the way with an Alicia Patterson Fellowship that enabled her to do longer pieces and work on a book.

Without foundation support, San Francisco's New California Media initiative might not be functioning at its present strength, nor might university-connected organizations like the *Online Journalism Review* and the *Columbia* and *American Journalism Reviews*.

A number of programs permit working journalists to take time off for further training or support them for reporting abroad. Learn-and-go programs require a year or semester of academic work on the region and editorial guidance for the field trip that follows. The pioneer in this field was the Latin American program of the University of Southern California. The current model is the Pew International Journalism Fellowships, a small group advised by John Schidlovsky, a former China correspondent for the *Baltimore Sun*. Pew fellows spend a semester of study at the Johns Hopkins School of International and Strategic Studies, where they take regular academic courses and participate in seminars linking journalism and international affairs. At the end of these studies, they're supported for travel abroad to work on their projects for print, photography, or video. In addition to the two groups of about seven each fall and spring, Pew selects two or three journalists returning from foreign assignments and offers them support to work on books.

Pew fellows produce a wealth of stories on foreign issues rarely covered or not covered in as much depth. Meredith Davenport, a freelance photojournalist, wrote about the cycle of war in Sudan that has kept croplands from being cultivated for fifteen years and cost more lives than the wars in Somalia, Bosnia, Kosovo, and Rwanda combined. In a photo essay for the *San Francisco Chronicle*, she focused on a Nubian mountain community, where some families have both Muslim and Christian members, to explain the conflicts between their moderation and African identity and the Muslim extremists who have kept the country in turmoil. "For almost a decade, three provinces in northern Iraq have been the de facto state of Kurdistan," David Aquila Lawrence wrote after his field trip to the region in a story for the *Christian Science Monitor*. "They use their own currency, patrol their own borders," and benefit from the UN embargo against the Iraqi regime.[4]

Raney Aronson, an ABC news associate producer and Pew fellow, reported on activists in India working for the sexual rights of women, both prostitutes and ordinary wives, whose lives are being devastated by the AIDS epidemic. Her small handheld camera, she said, enabled her to focus on ordinary people telling their stories without the intrusion of a crew and lots of equipment."We focused on the street level," she said."We got very intense street-level shots."[5]

In Calcutta, the hour-long documentary features the leader in a union of sex workers numbering forty thousand, fighting for equal rights and blanketing their community with information about how to prevent AIDS. Aronson shows that married women as well as prostitutes have been devastated by AIDS, since traditional societies give women little power to protect themselves from being infected by husbands who have had extramarital affairs."AIDS is often referred to as mother in law's disease," she says."Pressure on the women to bear children—regardless of her husband's HIV status—often results in the mother-in-law assuming child-care responsibility after the woman contracts HIV from her husband and either dies or is driven out of the home."[6]

Karen Brown of the public radio station WFCR in Amherst, Massachusetts, used a Kaiser Foundation grant to interview refugees from wars in Southeast Asia and Bosnia about their mental health problems and what the authorities were doing to alleviate them. In other radio interviews after the terrorist attacks, Brown described how some refugees are using their own experiences with trauma to counsel their American neighbors in learning to live with the fears and uncertainties of the new situation.

Ford Environmental Reporting Fellowships send journalists to report on environmental issues abroad and organize seminars to help local journalists cover such stories. Bill Allen of the *St.Louis Post-Dispatch* spent three months in Nicaragua, where he wrote about the Bosawas Biosphere Reserve, retraced the trip that Mark Twain made across the isthmus in 1866, and taught a workshop for nineteen local journalists on pollution in Lake Managua. His stories ran as series in the *Post-Dispatch* and its Web site, along with audio and links to related subjects. Julie Titone of Spokane's *Spokesman Review* wrote about a dam project that threatens Ghana's last hippopotamus habitat. She also coached journalists at the Ghana News Agency and students at the Institute of Journalism on how to tackle difficult environmental problems in a country where many people are afraid to speak out because of past repression. Other fellows have reported about polluting coal-fired power generation in the Balkans, a chemical spill in Mozambique, and uncontrolled development on the tip of South America."No issue will be more important in the coming century than environmental degradation," says David Anable, president of the International Center for Foreign Journalism, which administers the fellowships.[7]

There are no terrorists in these kinds of stories and not even any major crises. But all provide information on vital issues in parts of the world with huge populations, issues that also affect American concerns, directly or indirectly, such as when voters decide on foreign aid policies, issues that in the past were routinely ignored in foreign news coverage.

The two existing university news services, which regularly file domestic news stories to newspapers and broadcast stations, and Berkeley's Web site and magazine dedicated to foreign issues could play an important role as clearinghouses for the work of the hundreds of American freelancers now abroad.

With the news services, the infrastructure for assigning, reporting, editing, and distributing this news is already in place. The Columbia News Service of that university's Graduate School of Journalism distributes its stories on the *New York Times* syndicate and the school's own Web site. Its graduate student reporters regularly cover the foreign ethnic communities of New York City, but none file for it from abroad.

Northwestern's Medill School of Journalism is expanding its Medill News Service offerings to include the work of foreign-based graduate students. Dean Loren Ghiglione has arranged to have the students file from countries they have selected themselves for eleven-week reporting tours. The students get professional equipment and training, with laptops, digital cameras, and digital editing equipment, all linked by electronic or satellite feeds. A second program uses student reporters to link ethnic communities in the United States with their home countries. The school's news service in Washington, D.C., covers local-angled stories on politics and the economy for media across the country. Its clients include twenty-two newspapers and magazines, nine television stations, and eight radio stations. In the weeks after the terrorist attacks, the twenty-five students (sixteen print and nine broadcast) got so close to the story in covering the Senate that six of them had to be tested for anthrax.

Ghiglione says those attacks made it more important than ever that Medill extend its scope to cover international affairs. "Only a minority of our journalism students have the opportunity to report from abroad. Journalism schools have a responsibility to try to make sure that every student has a chance to report from Asia, Africa, Latin America, and other parts of the world," Ghiglione wrote soon after September 11. "The country needs less reality-TV-style reporting and more calm, tough-minded coverage of the reality beyond our borders."[8]

Soon afterward, Ghiglione started working with graduate students on their foreign assignments and set up Gateway to Global News, a program that sends undergraduates to local ethnic neighborhoods for stories and then follows up with reporting from their nations abroad. "My mission is to make Medill a truly international place, to send students abroad in a systematic fashion to report and write," he says.[9]

Berkeley's Asia-Pacific Project posts students' Asia-related works on its Web site and also serves as a resource for the Bay Area community and beyond to learn about Asia-related events. Orville Schell, an author and China specialist who is dean of Berkeley's Graduate School of Journalism, says that however laudable the first days of television coverage of the terror attacks were, "the retreat to file footage when it came to covering such places as Afghanistan, Pakistan, Iran and Central Asia was a reminder of how the commercial networks have largely amputated their international news operations."[10] Schell says that like Medill and Columbia, "we too have a strong emphasis on international reporting," with current projects in Ghana, Hungary, and Japan, and earlier ones in Cuba, Hong Kong, and the Middle East. "The object is always to work on a series of articles, with a photographer, do a Web site or put together a magazine. We need better delivery systems for these journalistic efforts, especially given the collapse of foreign bureaus at so many media outlets."[11]

Ghiglione says the new foreign-reporting program will initially be limited to graduate students but thinks there may be room later for recent graduates already working abroad. Foreign and wire editors agree that this is a good idea. Reporters on the scene, able to work and move independently without time limits, they believe, are in a much better position to provide this coverage than are students, even graduate students, on relatively short trips abroad. They also are more experienced in knowing sources, issues, and dangers to avoid.

Only Berkeley's service is presently focused on foreign news and issues, but the others have reported extensively on the impact of immigration on the United States and other foreign-related themes. Many other resources are available for establishing a foreign news service at universities without regular news services. One example is the work of Louisiana State University's John Maxwell Hamilton, who has held workshops to help reporters and editors find the links between foreign stories and local connections and concerns.

Leading schools of international affairs, including those at Harvard, Stanford, Johns Hopkins, Georgetown, and Tufts, could also supply foreign correspondents in training to the news service. These connections might work best with international affairs schools on the same campus as journalism schools participating in the program, such as those at Columbia, Northwestern, and Berkeley.

Professor Donald Johnston, who directs a joint journalism–international affairs program at Columbia, thinks that a news service that would use graduates of such programs already working in the field might work better than relying solely on student participation. Johnston estimates that about three hundred graduates of his program may be working abroad, the majority for AP, Reuters, and Bloomberg, but that many others are freelancing, including some employed by nongovernmental organizations in the field who also file freelance stories. "Most try to line up somebody like Reuters or AP who will at least look at the stuff they send them," he said. They would welcome a university-based service or any other new outlet, since "the more exposure they get on any kind of wire the better they like it."[12]

The editors and producers that I interviewed about the news service idea stressed that strong editing is the sine qua non of such an operation but that there are many ways of attracting good professionals for these positions. Fellowships like the Knight program for aiding journalists in eastern Europe and the Third World might be extended to support international editing assignments at home. News media downsizing and early retirement offers have made available many journalists with foreign experience, some of them men and women reluctant to acquire academic credentials or lecture on communications theory but quite happy to be occupying editors' or producers' chairs to work with students and recent graduates. Others could be enticed with half-time workweeks in pleasant campus surroundings. It is important that this editor and producer corps be large and flexible enough to keep the foreign news service running year round. A frequent criticism of domestic university news services by the professionals who want to use their copy is that they dry up in summers and over school holidays.

If the benefits of this suggestion were only that the nation would have more foreign news, setting up the new service would not be worth the effort. The quantity of wholesale foreign news reaching the retail stage—which is to say wire service and correspondents' reports transmitted to newspapers and broadcast outlets—is immense. Rather, it is the quality of foreign news that would be affected. Not that the Associated Press and Reuters are providing foreign news of anything but high quality, but much of it has to be the bread-and-butter stuff of cabinet changes, trade treaties, and defense budgets. The foreign-reporting guerrillas would produce stories and videos that the journalists working for the established services would like to find the time to do.

The news service should contain a strong international investigative component, again supported by foundation money, to permit some of the best or most interested reporters to detach themselves from daily coverage, form teams with reporters from other nations, and sniff out the future corruption scandals, economic mismanagement, or supporters of terrorist groups that affect not only those who live in the country of their origin but people around the world.

The money could smooth the way for an often neglected facet of such projects, which is to provide access to the public. Public television and radio stations could set aside program time—and not at 6 A.M. on Sundays—for regular viewing and listening of a "New World" program. College newspapers and broadcast stations would provide ideal audiences. The service might produce a tabloid insert for college and other newspapers on the pattern of *Monitor Week*, the *Christian Science Monitor's* experiment in packaging foreign news.

Would all this compete with the efforts of other journalists working for the commercial broadcasters and newspapers? It certainly would. But after an era when foreign news was all but ignored, after the worst attack the nation experienced for more than half a century, such competition should be welcomed. It would have the double benefit of providing a larger and more diverse offering of foreign news and analysis and of alerting the papers and stations to new ways of presenting news from abroad. It would help return the nation to the relative abundance of foreign news that characterized most of its modern history and provide safeguards against the attitudes of ignorance and unconcern toward the rest of the world that aided the terrorists in carrying out their attacks.

NOTES

1. INTRODUCTION: THE TEST OF WAR

1. Marvin Kalb, "How to Cover a War," *New York Times*, October 18, 2001.
2. Chris Peck, speech to APME convention, Milwaukee, October 11, 2001; *www.poynter.org*.
3. Telephone conversation with network news producer, October 9, 2001.
4. Project for Excellence in Journalism, "Before and After: How the War on Terrorism Has Changed the News Agenda," November 19, 2001; *www.journalism.org*.
5. Interviews with CBS news producer and executive, July 1999 and May 2001.
6. Panel discussion, Pew Fellowships in International Journalism conference, May 4, 2001; and conversations with Tom Bettag, Columbia Graduate School of Journalism.
7. Survey results quoted by Edward Seaton in "The Diminishing Use of Foreign News Reporting," International Press Institute World Congress, Moscow, May 26, 1998; *www.freemedia.at*; and George Krimsky in *Bringing the World Home* (Washington, D.C.: Freedom Forum / ASNE, 1999).
8. Interview with network news producer, July 1999.
9. Kofi Annan, remarks to a United Nations conference on television, Associated Press, November 18, 1999.
10. T. Christian Miller, "Arab Satellite TV Station a Prime Battle in Information War," *Los Angeles Times*, October 12, 2001.
11. Daniel Williams, "Bin Laden Tape Brings Notice to Arab Station," *Washington Post*, October 13, 2001.
12. PBS Online NewsHour: "Administration Cautions Networks," October 10, 2001.
13. Mike Allen and Lisa de Moraes, "TV Networks to Limit Use of Tapes from Bin Laden," *Washington Post*, October 11, 2001.

14. Condoleezza Rice, al-Jazeera interview text, U.S. Newswire, October 12, 2001.

15. "Leaders of Journalism Groups Challenge Information Clampdown," October 17, 2001, Society of Professional Journalists; *www.SPJ.org*.

16. Howard Kurtz, "CNN Chief Orders 'Balance' in War News," *Washington Post*, October 31, 2001.

17. Jeffrey A. Dvorkin, "Using Words for Effect," October 5, 2001; *NPR.org/your-turn/omb/11005.html*.

18. Panel discussion, Alfred I. duPont Forum, Columbia University Graduate School of Journalism, January 16, 2002.

19. Poynter Institute, "Web Tips," October 30, 2001; *www.poynter.org*.

20. Interview with network news producer, November 2000.

21. Neil Hickey, "Money Lust: How Pressure for Profit Is Perverting Journalism," *Columbia Journalism Review*, July/August 1998, cover story.

22. Senator James Inhofe, *Daily Oklahoman*, January 19, 1999.

23. Television News Archive, Vanderbilt University, Evening News Abstracts, January and February 1999.

24. The newspapers surveyed for January and February 1999 and their circulations: *Allentown* (Pennsylvania) *Morning Call*, 136,000; *Deseret News* (Salt Lake City), 176,000; *Fargo* (North Dakota) *Forum*, 55,000; *Manchester* (New Hampshire) *Union Leader*, 72,000; *Nashville Tennessean*,135,000; *Omaha World-Herald*, 212,000; *New Orleans Times-Picayune*, 265,000; *Newark* (New Jersey) *Star-Ledger*, 470,000; Oklahoma City *Daily Oklahoman*, 217,000; and *Richmond* (Virginia) *Times-Dispatch*, 239,000.

25. David D. Newsom, *The Public Dimension of Foreign Policy* (Bloomington: Indiana University Press, 1996); and correspondence with David D. Newsom.

26. George Gallup, foreword to *The Public and American Foreign Policy*, by Ralph B. Levering (New York: Morrow, 1978), 10.

27. Ibid., 152.

28. Remarks on World Press Freedom Day, Associated Press, May 4, 1998.

2. GATEKEEPERS AND BOOKKEEPERS

1. Pew Research Center on the People and the Press, "Striking the Balance, Audience Interests, Business Pressures and Journalists' Values," March 30, 1999.

2. ASNE/ Freedom Forum Roundtable: "How to Improve Newspapers' International News Coverage," Vanderbilt University, Nashville, Tennessee, December 9, 1998.

3. Committee of Concerned Journalists, "Changing Definitions of News," March 6, 1998; *www.journalism.org/ccj*.

4. Interview with wire service executive, July 2001.

5. Interview with newspaper publisher, March 2001.

6. Jay Harris, "Statements Relating to Harris Resignation," Poynter Institute, April 11, 2001; *www.poynter.org*.

7. E-mail exchanges with former *Miami Herald* editor, January 2002.

8. Interview with CBS news executive, May 2001.

9. Ibid.

10. Panel discussion, Pew Fellowships in International Journalism conference, May 4, 2001; and conversations with Tom Bettag, Columbia Graduate School of Journalism, New York.

11. Ibid.

12. Interview with network news producer, November 2000.

13. Alex S. Jones and Susan E. Tifft, *The Trust* (Boston: Little, Brown, 1999), 589.

14. Ibid., 755.

15. John Lavine, *The Power to Grow Readership* (Evanston, Ill.: Media Management Institute, Northwestern University, 2001); *www.readership.org*.

16. Commencement speech to Columbia University Graduate School of Journalism students, May 2001.

3. GETTING THE NEWS FROM ABROAD

1. Interview with American network producer, November 2000.

2. Jonathan Fenby, *The International News Services* (New York: Schocken Books, 1986); and correspondence with Jonathan Fenby.

3. Ibid.

4. Ian Stewart, "Life Ends and Begins During a Barely Noticed War," Associated Press dispatch, July 10, 1998; conversations and correspondence with Ian Stewart; and Ian Stewart, *Freetown Ambush* (Toronto: Penguin Books, 2002), 106.

5. Stewart, *Freetown Ambush*, 63.

6. Ian Stewart, panel discussion, Stanford University, *Stanford Report*, March 5, 2002.

7. E-mail interview with Sandra Dibble, February 2002.

8. Panel discussion, Pew International Journalism conference at Columbia University Graduate School of Journalism; and conversations with Tom Bettag, May 4, 2001.

9. Interview with *Newsweek* correspondent, May 1999.

10. Interview with bureau chief, February 2001.

11. Panel discussion, Cabot Prize winners, Columbia University, October 3, 2001.

12. Sebastian Rotella, "Jungle Hub for World's Outlaws," *Los Angeles Times*, August 24, 1998.

13. Larry Rohter, "Brazil's Prize Exports Rely on Slaves and Scorched Land," *New York Times*, March 25, 2002.

14. Daniel Pearl and Robert Block, "Underground Trade: Much-Smuggled Gem Called Tanzanite Helps Bin Laden Supporters," *Wall Street Journal*, November 16, 2001.

15. Ian Stewart, remarks at Associated Press Managing Editors convention, San Antonio, Texas, October 23, 2000.

16. Interview with wire editor, July 1999.

17. Interview with foreign editor, October 2000.

18. Interview with editor, August 1998.

19. John Russial, "Tips for Managing Pagination," Poynter Institute, 1997; *www.poynter.org*.

20. George Krimsky, ASNE/Freedom Forum Roundtable, "How to Improve Newspapers' International News Coverage," Arlington, Virginia, May 5, 1998; and conversations with George Krimsky.

21. Tom Kent, "How to Improve Newspapers' International News Coverage," Arlington.

22. Ibid.

23. Krimsky, "How to Improve Newspapers' International News Coverage."

24. Interview with newspaper editor, July 2000.

25. Interview with wire editor, June 2000.

26. Interview with Chris Peck, June 2001.

27. Correspondence and telephone interviews with small-town newspaper editor, 2000 and 2001.

28. Telephone interview with James B. Johnson, March 2001.

4. BROADCASTING

1. "Sixty-first Annual George Foster Peabody Awards for Broadcast Excellence Announced," March 27, 2002; University of Georgia, *www.peabody.uga.edu*.

2. Associated Press, March 19, 2001.

3. Interview with senior producer, April 2002.

4. Testimony of Gene Kimmelman, Consumers Union, July 17, 2001; *www.commerce.senate.govhearings/071701/Kimmelman*.

5. Walter Cronkite, *CBS Evening News*, February 27, 1967.

6. Sally Bedell Smith, *In All His Glory* (New York: Simon & Schuster, 1990), 16.

7. Ted Koppel, *Off Camera* (New York: Knopf, 2000), 63–64.

8. Mark S. Fowler, remarks, May 14, 1982, in "What the Chairman Said," *Hastings Journal of Communications and Entertainment Law* (University of California), winter 1988, 411.

9. Fowler, remarks, February 19, 1982, in "What the Chairman Said," *Hastings Journal of Communications and Entertainment Law* (University of California), winter 1988, 435.

10. Richard Wald, remarks in panel discussion, Alfred I. duPont-Columbia Forum, Columbia University Graduate School of Journalism, January 17, 2001.

11. Lawrence Tisch, remarks, Gannett Center for Media Studies conference, New York, April 28, 1987.

12. Richard S. Salant, *CBS and the Battle for the Soul of Broadcast Journalism* (Boulder, Colo.: Westview Press, 1999), 147, note.

13. Dan Rather, "From Murrow to Mediocrity?" *New York Times*, March 10, 1987.

14. Tisch, remarks, Gannett Center conference.

15. Lawrence K. Grossman, *The Electronic Republic* (New York: Viking, 1995), 177.

16. As television took hold in the nation after World War II, CBS and the other networks promoted entertainment and pushed news out of the best places in the schedules. Murrow objected to this in a speech to the Radio-Television News Directors Association in Chicago in 1958. TV, he said, was dominated by "decadence, escapism, and insulation from the realities of the world." Instead of simply pursuing profits, the networks should levy a tax or tithe to increase news and public affairs. "This instrument can teach, it can illuminate; yes, it can even inspire. But it can do so only to the extent that humans are determined to use it to those ends. Otherwise it is merely wires and lights in a box."

17. Ken Auletta, *Three Blind Mice* (New York: Random House, 1991), 17.

18. Grossman, *The Electronic Republic*, 188.

19. Joe Foote, ed., *Live from the Trenches: The Changing Role of the Television News Correspondent* (Carbondale: Southern Illinois University Press, 1998), 108.

20. Panel discussion, Alfred I. duPont-Columbia Forum, Columbia University Graduate School of Journalism, January 17, 2001.

21. Reuters, "Roone Arledge Steps Down As ABC News Chief," May 29, 1998.

22. Stephen Battaglio, "Dan Rather: I'm Not Leaving CBS Anchor Chair Anytime Soon," *Inside*, November 1, 2000; *www.inside.com*.

23. Interview with Andrew Tyndall, April 2001.

24. duPont-Columbia Forum, January 14, 1998.

25. duPont-Columbia Forum, January 17, 2001.

26. *www.journalism.org*.

27. Koppel, *Off Camera*, 64.

28. Interview with Andrew Tyndall, April 2001.

29. Walter Cronkite, remarks at "Fifty Years, Fifty Moments" tribute, December 8, 2000, *www.freedomforum.org/news/2000*.

30. Interview with network producer, December 1999.

31. Interview with network producer, November 2000.

32. Ibid.

33. Ibid.

34. Steve Kroft, and Leslie Cockburn, remarks in "The Winners' Circle," panel discussion by duPont-Columbia award winners, January 17, 2002; and conversation with Steve Kroft, Graduate School of Journalism, Columbia University.

35. Interview with Charles Kravetz, January 2002.

36. WNDU, South Bend, Indiana, *www.WNDU.com*.

37. Carl Gottlieb, Online NewsHour, February 7, 2001.

38. Telephone interviews and correspondence with Edward Seaton, 1999–2002.

39. *www.rtnda.org*.

40. James McChesney, Alfred I. duPont-Columbia Forum, Columbia University Graduate School of Journalism, January 17, 2001.

41. Anthony Violanti, remarks in panel discussion, Alfred I. duPont-Columbia Forum, Columbia University Graduate School of Journalism, January 17, 2001; Robert Bartlett, *www.rtnda.org*.

42. Randy Michaels, "Reaching over 110 Million Listeners," Clear Channel Communications news release, February 6, 2002; *www.clearchannel.com/news*.

43. Michael Montgomery and Stephen Smith, "Massacre at Cuska," radio documentary, American RadioWorks and National Public Radio, February 2000.

44. Interview with Jonathan Dyer, March 2001.

45. Interview with Tony Kahn, March 2001.

46. Interview with Jonathan Dyer, March 2001.

47. Interview with Bob Ferrante, March 2001.

48. Telephone interview with Bob Ferrante, October 2001.

49. Interview with *The World* producer, March 2001.

50. Smith, *In All His Glory*, 235.

51. William S. Paley, *As It Happened, a Memoir* (Garden City, N.Y.: Doubleday, 1979), 173.

52. Karen Everhart Bedford, "PBS in Talks to Create Crisis Series for Friday Nights," *Current*, October 21, 2001, *www.current.org*.

53. Interview with Lester Crystal, July 2001.

54. Elizabeth Farnsworth, "AIDS in Africa," *The NewsHour*, May 14, 2001.

55. Fred de Sam Lazaro, "Favoring Boys in India," *The NewsHour*, October 29, 2001.

56. Interview with Lester Crystal, July 2001.

57. Ibid.

58. Interview with *NewsHour* producer, July 2001.

59. Interview with Lester Crystal, July 2001.

60. *Frontline*, "Hunting bin Laden," *www.PBS.org/WGBH/pages/frontline/shows/ binladen*.

61. Interview with *Frontline* staff producer, January 2002.

5. EVOLUTION, NOT REVOLUTION

1. Edward Seaton, American Society of Newspaper Editors Convention, July 9, 1999; *www.org/kiosk*; and telephone interviews and correspondence with Edward Seaton.

2. George Krimsky, *Bringing the World Home* (Washington, D.C.: Freedom Forum / ASNE, 1999), 10.

3. Interview with Aly Colon, March 2001.

4. Conversation with Stephen Gray, November 2001.

5. Danna Harman, "Yemen's Real Counterterrorism Campaign: Democracy," *Christian Science Monitor*, February 21, 2002.

6. Shai Oster, "Behind the Label 'Made in China,'" *Christian Science Monitor*, July 2, 2001.

7. Cameron Barr, "A Pattern of Violence," *Christian Science Monitor*, March 14, 2000.

8. Interview with David Clark Scott, February 2002.

9. Interview with *Christian Science Monitor* editor, February 1999.

10. Interview with Tom Regan, March 2002.

11. Ibid.

12. Conversation with Stephen Gray, November 2001.

13. Interview with Elisa Tingley, July 2001.

14. Andrea Stone, "Gore Scrambles to Gain Arab Vote," *USA Today*, October 31, 2000; and Andrea Stone, "In Cairo, Atmosphere Is Festive Despite War News," *USA Today*, November 19, 2001.

15. Jack Kelley, "Palestinian Radio: All the News That Fits the Case," *USA Today*, October 26, 2000.

16. Allen Neuharth, *Confessions of an S.O.B.* (New York: Doubleday, 1989), 167–68.

17. Reese Schonfeld, *Me and Ted Against the World* (New York: Cliff Street, 2001), 135–37.

18. Ibid., 161–65.

19. Steve Redisch, CNN In Depth, "CNN at 20," *www.cnn.com/specials/2000/ cnn20*.

20. Ibid.

21. Ibid.

22. Redisch, CNN InDepth; conversation with Charles Bierbauer.

23. Interview with Iris Adler, January 2002.

24. Interview with R. D. Sahl, January 2002.

25. R. D. Sahl, "Cover Story: Shintaro Ishihara," NECN 9 P.M. news, June 22, 1999, *www.necn.com*.

26. R. D. Sahl, "Cover Story: Tokyo Homeless," NECN 9 P.M. news, June 21, 1999, *www.necn.com*.

27. R. D. Sahl, "Cuban Dissidents," Half-hour special, NECN, January 28, 1998, www.necn.com.

28. Interview with Charles Kravetz, January 2002.

6. ABROAD AT HOME

1.   George Krimsky, *Bringing the World Home* (Washington, D.C.: Freedom Forum / ASNE, 1999), 30; interviews and correspondence with John Maxwell Hamilton, 1985–2002.

2.   John Lavine, *The Power to Grow Readership* (Evanston, Ill.: Media Management Institute, Northwestern University, 2001), *www.readership.org*.

3.   John Maxwell Hamilton, *Main Street America and the Third World* (Cabin John, Md.: Seven Locks Press, 1988), 1–12, 39–44, 54–59, 68–73, 77–87, 92–100, 103–7, 111–16, 120–24, and 143–46; interviews and correspondence with John Maxwell Hamilton.

4.   Interview with WGN producer, June 2001.

5.   Interview with *San Jose Mercury News* editor, May 1998.

6.   Interview with stringer, May 1998.

7.   David Hawpe, ASNE / Freedom Forum Roundtable: "How to Improve Newspapers' International News Coverage," Arlington, May 5, 1998.

8.   Interview with Associated Press editor, May 2001.

9.   Associated Press, May 25, 2001.

10. Interview with Stacy Lynch, June 2001.

11. Bennie Ivory, panel discussion at American Society of Newspaper Editors Convention, July 9, 1999; *www.asne.org/kiosk*.

12. George Gedda, Associated Press, "In the News: Convictions in China," *St. Louis Post-Dispatch*, July 25, 2001.

13. Richard Foristel, "Letter from Shanghai," *St. Louis Post-Dispatch*, July 20, 2001.

14. Interview with Harry Levins, April 2002.

15. Richard Read, "South Korean Recalls Ordeal with Portland INS," *Portland Oregonian*, April 25, 2000.

16. Richard Read, "The French Fry Connection," *Portland Oregonian*, October 18, 1998.

17. Ibid.

18.   Interview with Richard Read, June 2001.

19.   Ibid.

20.   Jim Camden, "Northwest Owes Braceros Debt of Gratitude," *Connections, Spokane Spokesman-Review*, September 5, 1999.

21.   Interview with Chris Peck, June 2001.

22.   Jan Schaffer, Pew Center for Civic Journalism, "Journalism Interactive Survey Pinpoints a Sea Change in Attitudes and Practices," July 26, 2001; *www.pewcenter.org*.

23.   Tom Kent, ASNE / Freedom Forum Roundtable, Arlington, Virginia, May 5, 1998.

24.   Telephone interviews and correspondence with Edward Seaton, 1999–2002.

25.   George Krimsky, panelist, "Covering the World," ASNE Convention, April 14, 1999.

26.   Krimsky, *Bringing the World Home*, 72–73.

27.   Telephone interview with Chris Waddle, November 1999.

28.   Ibid.

29.   Jonathan Lifland, "Chemwar's Global Garbage," *Anniston Star*, October 24, 1999.

30.   Stephen Buttry, "An Unhappy Marriage: Sudanese Custom, U.S. Law," *Omaha World Herald*, March 11, 2001.

31.   Diane McFarlin, *Sarasota Herald-Tribune*, panel discussion, American Society of Newspaper Editors convention, April 14, 1999.

32.   Matthew Storin, *Boston Globe*, panel discussion, American Society of Newspaper Editors convention, April 14, 1999.

33.   Timothy Gallagher, *Ventura* (California) *County Star*, panel discussion, American Society of Newspaper Editors convention, April 14, 1999.

34.   Jane Gargas, "Family Ties, Search for Better Life Keep Pipeline Open Between Michoácan, Yakima Valley," *Yakima Herald-Republic*, February 26, 1995.

35.   Interview with Bob Crider, June 2001.

36.   Ibid.

37.   Jessica Luce, "Poverty Propels Politics of Sister City," *Yakima Herald-Republic*, May 22, 2001.

38.   Interview with Jessica Luce, June 2001.

39.   Correspondence with Edward Seaton, 1999.

7. NEWS FROM ABROAD
FOR THOSE FROM ABROAD

1.   Theodore Andrica, *Cleveland Press*, August 25, 1968.

2.   Theodore Andrica, *Cleveland Press*, November 3, 1972.

3.   Conversations with Theodore Andrica, 1968.

4. Ruben Salazar, *Border Correspondent* (Berkeley and Los Angeles: University of California Press, 1995), 179.

5. Ibid., 185.

6. Ibid., 251.

7. Ibid., 253.

8. Jacob C. Rich, *Eighty Years of the Jewish Daily Forward* (New York: Forward Association, 1957),30–31.

9. David Shub, *New York Times Magazine*, March 23, 1930, 1.

10. Interviews with Carlos Castaneda, March 2001.

11. Interviews with Yves Colon and Haitian artist, March 2001.

12. Manning Pynn, "*El Sentinel* Contains Some Articles in Spanish and Some in English," *Orlando Sentinel*, August 12, 2001.

13. Correspondence and telephone interview with Maria Padilla, November 2001.

14. Lisa Broadwater, "The Melting Pot Revisited," *Arkansas Times*, May 4, 2001.

15. E-mail and telephone interviews with Alan Leveritt, March and May 2001.

16. Melita Marie Garza, "Growth Market," *Quill*, April 1994.

17. Telephone interviews with Odie Arambula, February and March 2002.

18. Ibid.

19. Telephone interview with Miguel Ramirez, March 2002.

20. Interview with Jorge Ramos, October 2001.

21. Ibid.

22. Associated Press, "NBC to Purchase Spanish-Language Telemundo," October 12, 2001.

23. Ibid.

24. Interview with Michael Devlin, March 2002.

25. Ibid.

26. Ibid.

27. Ibid.

28. Angela Kocherga, "Migrant Farm Workers Staying South of the Border," October 4, 2001; "The Promise of Prosperity Eludes Many in Mexico," March 22, 2002; and "Afro-Mexicans Begin to Explore Their Roots," March 25, 2002, all at *www.khou.com*.

29. Interview with Michael Devlin, March 2002.

30. Jorge Ramos, *The Other Face of America* (New York: HarperCollins, 2002), 208.

31. Ibid.

32. Ibid., xxii.

33. Telephone interview with Steven Klineberg, April 2002.

34. Ibid.
35. Tomás Rivera Policy Institute, "Hispanics and TV," March 23, 1999; *www.trpi.org*.
36. Interview with Telemundo executive producer, March 2001.
37. Interview with Telemundo news producer, March 2001.
38. María Elena Salinas, "The Evening News en Español," *Nieman Reports*, summer 2001, 34–35.
39. Interview with Franz Schurmann, June 2001.
40. Interview with Sandy Close, June 2001.
41. Franz Schurmann, "Bush Administration Avoids Surprises for China," *www.NCMonline.com*, January 31, 2001.
42. Ibid., June 27, 2000.
43. Andrew Lam, " My Father's War," *San Francisco Chronicle*, April 29, 2001.
44. Mary Jo McConahay, "The New Face of Farm Labor," August 27, 2001, *www.NCMonline.com*.
45. Franz Schurmann, "Asian Press Reveals U.S.-Chinese Tension Overblown," *www.NCMonline.com*, May 23, 2001.
46. Franz Schurmann, "What the Arab Press Is Saying about the Israel-Palestine Crisis, *www.NCMonline.com*, May 23, 2001.
47. Correspondence with Jon Funabiki, February and March 2001.
48. Interviews with Sandy Close and Franz Schurmann, June 2001.
49. Interview with NCMonline Web editor, June 2001.
50. Interviews with Sandy Close and Franz Schurmann, June 2001.
51. Interview with NCM editor, June 2001.
52. Kenji G. Taguma, "A Time to Take a Stand," *Nichi Bei Times*, September 27, 2001, *www.NCMonline.com*.
53. Donal Brown, "Leading Iranian American Writer on Terrorism," *Iran Today*, September 26, 2001, *www.NCMonline.com*.
54. "African Leaders Decry Bully Tactics, Urge Fairness," September 26, 2001, *www.NCMonline.com*.
55. Andrew Reding, "Marxists Unlikely Ally to U.S.," *Confidencial*, September 27, 2001, *www.NCMonline.com*.
56. Franz Schurmann, "The Chinese Press on the Mideast," *World Journal*, September 25, 2001, *www.NCMonline.com*.
57. *Sing Tao Daily* and *Al-Sharq al-Ausat*, November 5, 2001; *www.NCMonline.com*.
58. "Can Britain Save the Electoral Process?" May 22, 2001; "Will Nicaragua's Aleman Be the Next Estrada?" May 21, 2001; "Civil War Among Colombia's Militias," May 21, 2001; and "Indian-Americans Top Census Chart Among Asian-Americans," May 18, 2001; all at *www.NCMonline.com*.

8. THE ELECTRONIC NEWSPAPER

1. Interview with Doug Feaver, July 2001.

2. ASNE / Freedom Forum Roundtable, Vanderbilt University, Nashville, Tennessee, December 9, 1998.

3. Conversation with Randall Palmer, April 2001.

4. Pew International Journalism conference at Columbia University Graduate School of Journalism, May 4, 2001; conversation with David Fanning.

5. Remarks in "The Winners' Circle," panel discussion by duPont-Columbia award winners, January 14, 2001; and conversation with Stephen Smith, Graduate School of Journalism, Columbia University.

6. Interview with Tom Kennedy, July 2001.

7. Conversation with *New York Times* political reporter, April 2001.

8. Interview with network news producer, November 2000.

9. Pew International Journalism conference, May 4, 2001.

10. Video screened at Pew International Journalism conference , May 4, 2001.

11. *www.poynter.org/tips*.

12. Correspondence with Jim Anderson, March 1999.

13. Interview with Vince Winkel, February 2002.

14. Ibid.

15. Radio-Television News Directors Foundation, "RTNDF Study Examines Development of Local Web News," March 14, 2001; *www.rtnda.org/news/2001/study.shtml/*.

16. M. David Arant and Janna Quitney Anderson, "Online Media Ethics," survey presented to the Association for Education in Journalism and Mass Communication convention, August 2000; *www.andersj.elon.edu*.

17. The *Wall Street Journal* has a clearly marked corrections tab on its Web page: *www.online.wsj.com/public/corrections*.

18. Arant and Anderson, "Online Media Ethics."

19. Rich Jaroslavsky, remarks at Online News Association Conference, Berkeley, California, October 26, 2001, Online News Association, *www.ona.org*.

20. Rich Jaroslavsky, statement to U.S. Senate Special Committee on the Year 2000 Technology Problem, 106th Cong., 1st sess., May 25, 1999.

21. Mike Wendland, "Evaluating Online Info," Poynter Institute, "Doing Journalism," January 19, 2000, *www.poynter.org/dj/011900/htm/*.

22. Daniel P. O'Brien, "eBooks Will Flop . . . ," press release, Forrester Research, Cambridge, Mass, December 22, 2000; *www.forrester.com*.

23. Pew Internet and American Life Project, "How Americans Used the Internet After the Terror Attack," September 15, 2001, *www.pewinternet.org*.

24. Rich Jaroslavsky, remarks at Online News Association Conference, Berkeley, California, October 26, 2001; Online News Association, *www.ona.org*.

25. Pew Internet and American Life Project, "How Americans Used the Internet."

26. Reuters, August 27, 2001.

9. CONCLUSION:
THE JOURNALISTIC GUERRILLAS

1. Remarks to Pew International Journalism conference at Columbia University Graduate School of Journalism, May 4, 2001.

2. Interview with Justin Burke, April 2001.

3. Remarks at International Investigative Reporting Panel, Columbia University Graduate School of Journalism, September 9, 2001.

4. Meredith Davenport,"Sudan's Cycle of War," *San Francisco Chronicle*, January 7, 2001; David Aquila Lawrence, "Iraqi Kurds Enjoy a De Facto State," *Christian Science Monitor*, May 3, 2000.

5. Remarks to Pew International Journalism conference at Columbia University Graduate School of Journalism, May 4, 2001.

6. Raney Aronson, *Asha*, a digital documentary film, 2001; *www.pewfellowships.org*.

7. David Anable, *The International Journalist*, summer 2001, 1; and conversations with David Anable, July 2002.

8. Loren Ghiglione, "Afghan War Puts the Press on the Defensive," *Newsday*, October 31, 2001.

9. Conversation with Loren Ghiglione, November 2001.

10. Orville Schell, "TV News, Our Town Commons During Crisis," *Los Angeles Times*, September 23, 2001.

11. Correspondence with Orville Schell, April 2002.

12. Conversations with Donald Johnston, February 2002.

INDEX